RECOMMENDATIONS.

THE undersigned having examined the general plan and some of the parts of a new work, termed *Christ and Antichrist,* believe that the publication of said work would much tend to promote the cause of our common Christianity.

The arguments both for the Messiahship of Jesus, and the Antichristian character of the Papacy, are strong and convincing. Much advantage, too, is derived from the fact, that these arguments are placed in a sort of *parallelism* with each other. No real Christian will be prepared to deny the Messiahship of Jesus. But the author shows, that the very same mode of proof will also establish the Antichristian character of the Papacy. In this way the argument against Popery is presented with great advantage.

The individual and peculiar views of the author we do not pretend to endorse; nor can we express an opinion as to those parts of the volume which we have not examined. So far, however, as our examination has gone, we take great pleasure in giving

RECOMMENDATIONS.

our approval to the publication of this new and apparently interesting work.

MOSES D. HOGE,
Pastor of the Second Presbyterian Church, Richmond, Va.

S. J. P. ANDERSON,
Pastor of the Presbyterian Church, Danville, Va.

ROBERT BOYTÉ C. HOWELL,
Pastor of the First Baptist Church, Nashville, Tenn.

EDWARD WADSWORTH,
Pastor of the Methodist Episcopal Church, Norfolk, Va.

JAMES R. GILLAND,
Pastor of Fishing Creek Presbyterian Church, Chester District, South Carolina.

DAVID CALDWELL,
Rector of St. Paul's Church, Norfolk, Virginia.

UPTON BEALL,
Rector of Christ Church, Norfolk, Virginia.

JAMES B. TAYLOR,
Corresponding Secretary of Foreign Mission Board, Southern Baptist Convention, Richmond, Va.

STEPHEN TAYLOR,
Pastor of the High Street Presbyterian Church, Petersburg, Virginia.

E. D. SANDERS,
Pastor of the Lebanon Presbyterian Church, Prince George county, Virginia.

JOHN LEYBURN,
Pastor of the Presbyterian Church, Petersburg, Va.

JOSEPH C. STILES,
Pastor of the United Presbyterian Church, Richmond, Va.

SAMUEL L. GRAHAM, D.D.
Professor of Oriental Literature, Union Theological Seminary, Virginia.

RECOMMENDATIONS.

From an exhibit made to me of the outline of this work by the author, I am exceedingly interested in his plan, as novel and advantageous; and hope he will be able speedily to put it to press, and that it will have wide circulation.

      JAMES G. HAMNER,
   Pastor of the Fifth Presbyterian Church, Baltimore.

It will give me great pleasure to see this work in print, and judging from the brief hearing I have had of its plan, as given me by its estimable author, I am prepared to hear that it will be well received by the Christian public, and extensively useful.

      HENRY V. D. JOHNS,
     Rector of Christ Church, Baltimore.

      G. W. MUSGRAVE,
   Pastor of the Third Presbyterian Church, Baltimore.

Circumstances have not permitted me to examine the work Mr. C. proposes to publish, but the plan, as explained by himself, strikes me very favourably; and his general reputation affords a sufficient guarantee that it is executed with ability. I hope the work will be published and widely circulated.

      H. A. BOARDMAN,
   Pastor of the Tenth Presbyterian Church, Philadelphia.
July 1, 1846.

I take much pleasure in saying, that I have great respect for the person and understanding of the author of the fore-mentioned work. I know that he has read and thought much on the subject of which he has written, and I regret very much that I cannot have an hour's leisure to examine the work. I can only say I shall look for the work with much interest, and hope the author may find a liberal publisher.

WILLIAM S. PLUMER.

Richmond, Virginia, *June* 24, 1846.

I regret that the stay of the author of the above work in Richmond is so brief, that I cannot have time to examine more fully than I have done his manuscript. But from my impresssion of the plan and execution, I am inclined to think that the chief excellency of the work consists in the distinctness with which it exhibits the evidence that Jesus is the Christ, and that the Papal Church is Antichrist—in its adaptedness to the capacities of ordinary readers, in its simplicity, and in its freedom from language and expressions calculated to give offence. The author has gone "to the Law and the Testimony," more fully than is common with writers on the Papacy; and this, after all, is the greatest recommendation of the work—for the word of God is that sword of the Spirit which must effect the conquest.

I could wish to see it not only published, but very extensively circulated, and such I am inclined to think will be the fact, when its merits become known.

B. GILDERSLEEVE,
Editor of the Watchman and Observer, Richmond, Va.

CHRIST AND ANTICHRIST

OR

JESUS OF NAZARETH

PROVED TO BE

THE MESSIAH

AND

THE PAPACY

PROVED TO BE

THE ANTICHRIST

PREDICTED IN THE HOLY SCRIPTURES.

BY THE
Rev. SAMUEL J. CASSELS
Late of Norfolk, Virginia.

המשכילים יבינו:—The wise shall understand.

PHILADELPHIA:

PRESBYTERIAN BOARD OF PUBLICATION.

Entered according to the Act of Congress in the year 1846, by A. W. MITCHELL, M. D., in the office of the Clerk of the District Court for the Eastern District of Pennsylvania.

CONTENTS.

PART I.

JESUS PROVED TO BE THE MESSIAH.

INTRODUCTORY REMARKS 19

CHAPTER I.
The Genealogy of Jesus.................................. 21

CHAPTER II.
The Birth of Jesus...................................... 28

CHAPTER III.
The Birth-place of Jesus................................ 36

CHAPTER IV.
The Time when Jesus made his Appearance................. 44

CHAPTER V.
The Testimony of Inspired Witnesses..................... 50

CHAPTER VI.

Direct Testimony from Heaven.............................. 55

CHAPTER VII.

The Personal Testimony of Jesus............................ 60

CHAPTER VIII.

The Miracles of Jesus...................................... 63

CHAPTER IX.

The Character of Jesus..................................... 71

CHAPTER X.

Jesus a Teacher.. 83

CHAPTER XI.

Jesus a Sacrifice and Priest................................ 95

CHAPTER XII.

Jesus a King.. 107

CHAPTER XIII.

The Resurrection of Jesus................................. 130

CHAPTER XIV.

The Blessings conferred on the Gentiles by Jesus............. 138

PART II.

THE PAPACY PROVED TO BE ANTICHRIST.

INTRODUCTORY REMARKS.................................. 151

CHAPTER I.
The Seat of Antichrist..................................... 155

CHAPTER II.
The Time of Antichrist..................................... 165

CHAPTER III.
Antichrist a peculiar Power................................ 181

CHAPTER IV.
Antichrist an Apostate from the Christian Faith............. 191

CHAPTER V.
Antichrist an Idolater..................................... 201

CHAPTER VI.
Antichrist a Blasphemer.................................... 209

CHAPTER VII.
Antichrist an Innovator 216

CHAPTER VIII.
Antichrist a Persecutor.................................... 231

CHAPTER IX.
Antichrist the Possessor of great Riches..................... 260

CHAPTER X.
Antichrist the Possessor of great Power..................... 273

CHAPTER XI.
Antichrist distinguished for Craft and pretended Miracles...... 304

CHAPTER XII.
Antichrist a Reprobate.. 320

CHAPTER XIII.
The Downfall of Antichrist................................... 330

Notes... 342

PREFACE.

As many judicious and excellent ministers of various Christian denominations have recommended the publication of the following work, the author sincerely hopes, that the mere circumstance that it is issued by a particular Board, will not hinder its general circulation. It is not a sectarian, but a Christian and Protestant work. Both the subjects, too, of which it treats are not only of general interest to all Christians, but of special interest to the whole church at the present time. More, probably, than at any past period, is the Church seeking the universal establishment of the kingdom of Christ on earth. Two special obstacles in the accomplishment of that result are Judaism and Antichristianity. Remove these, and how rapid and glorious would be the spread of the gospel over the whole earth! This fact is beginning to be well appreciated by Christians both in Europe and America. Hence, the recent missions to the Jews, and also, to several Papal countries. The author hopes, therefore, that he has taken his stand, not simply in the great controversy, but also in the great spirit of the age. Let then the following pages be perused, not with the belligerent feeling of religious controversy, but with the prayer of our Lord—"Thy kingdom come, thy will be done on earth, as it is in heaven."

INTRODUCTION.

The history of the human race has wonderfully exhibited the craft and malignity of Satan, as contrasted with the power and grace of God.

When the destiny of that race was suspended upon the observance of a particular precept, the great enemy, through his subtilty, effected the violation of that precept, and the consequent condemnation of the human species. But good arose out of evil. Divine grace had provided a Deliverer, and the assurance was given, that "the seed of the woman should bruise the serpent's head."

Soon after this, the malignity of Satan is seen, in promoting bloodshed and slaughter among mankind. Cain kills his brother, and "the earth is filled with violence." Here again Jehovah interposes. Noah is commanded to build an ark, in which, not only himself and family were for a time to be deposited; but, in which, through this one family, all future generations were to be preserved. A flood of waters then desolates the earth, the ungodly are destroyed; but the chosen family outride the storm, and are safely landed on the sunny top of Ararat.

A few centuries after this awful warning, the great deceiver introduces idolatry into the world. Those created things, which God had ordained to minister to the wants of men, are themselves converted into deities. The settlers of new colonies, the inventors of useful arts, venerated ancestors, are all considered as so many gods. Nor did the evil stop here. These distant objects and revered names, must be brought nigh to the worshipper; they must approach his senses. To effect this, pictures, images, and statues were introduced; and even these received divine worship! God interposes again. Abraham is called from Ur of Chaldea, and he and his posterity are made the depositaries of the truth and promises of Jehovah.

The enemy, however, pursues this chosen race. He raises up among them false prophets; he leads even Israel into idolatry! For these breaches of his covenant, God punished his people in various ways; and ultimately caused them to endure a long and afflictive captivity in a foreign land.

Rescued from their visible idolatry, the next device of the great apostate was to obscure and corrupt those living oracles of God, by which Israel was to be governed. The synagogue has now taken the place of the grove, and the Rabbi that of the prophet of Baal. The word of God is now the professed object of study. Learned men are raised up, and schools of biblical literature are established. But inquiries are pursued beyond the testimony of God, and tradition is made the interpreter of Scripture. Soon, this tradition is exalted into an authority equal, or even superior to that of the written word; while the strange spectacle is exhibited, of a people, with the law of God in their hands, yet following "the doctrines and commandments of men." It was at this period, the great Deliverer appeared.

The doctrines of Jesus were designed to bring men back from human testimony to that which is divine. Tradition, philosophy, human teaching, all he subjected to revelation. By his death too, and priestly intercession in heaven, he abolished the pre-existing priesthood and ritual, and introduced a simple and spiritual mode of worship, adapted to all nations, and designed for universal prevalence. He abolished, in short, the slavery of men, and introduced the freedom of God.

This new system met with special opposition from Satan. He stimulated first the Jews, and afterwards the Romans, to persecute and destroy it. Favoured however by God it ultimately triumphs. Embraced at first by the people, it afterwards enters the palaces of the great, and even ascends the throne of the Cæsars.

This new aspect of affairs, led Satan to a different mode of attack. Unable to crush the new system, he undertakes its corruption. This was effected chiefly by the Papacy, a scheme more subtle in its conception, more extensive in its operations, and more destructive in its effects, than any ever devised for the overthrow of the truth and church of God.

Already have God's people been, in a great measure, delivered from this tyrannical power. The yoke of iron has been broken, the walls of brass have fallen down. The light of the Reformation now happily shines upon a large portion of Christendom: and millions there are, who rejoice in the truths which Popery for centuries had eclipsed, and hidden from the world. Nor is this all; we have the promise of Jehovah himself, that the very last fragment of this oppressive system, shall ere long be banished from the earth. "Whom," says an Apostle, "the Lord shall consume with the spirit of his mouth, and shall destroy with the brightness of his coming."

In applying the term Antichrist ($Αντιχριστος$) to the usurping power here alluded to, the writer has not only followed great and ancient names, but the true etymology and meaning of the word. Macknight defines its meaning thus—"One who puts himself in the place of Christ, or who opposeth Christ." Schleusner says—"In Novi Testamenti libris, semper adversarium Christi ejusque religionis, significat"*—" in the books of the New Testament it always signifies an enemy of Christ and of his religion." How appropriately the history and character of the Papacy have fulfilled these descriptions, need not here be affirmed.

This term, too, has been applied both by the ancient fathers, and by modern writers, by Protestants and Romanists, to some great enemy to the church, not

---

* In verbo.

existing so early as the days of the Apostles. Speaking of the Roman empire, Tertullian says — "Cujus abscessio in decem reges dispersa Antichristum superducet *—"Whose separation into ten kingdoms will bring on Antichrist." Cyril, of Jerusalem, expresses himself thus on the same subject—"Decem simul reges Romanorum excitabuntur in diversis quidem locis, eodem tamen tempore regnantes. Post istos autem undecimus Antichristus, per magicum maleficium Romanorum potestatem rapiens."† "There will arise at the same time ten kings of the Romans in different places indeed, but reigning all of them at the same time. But after them the eleventh will be Antichrist, who, through magical wickedness, will seize the power of the Romans." Commenting on the passage in 2 Thessalonians, Jerome says—"Nisi, inquit, fuerit Romanum Imperium ante desolatum, et Antichristus præcessit, Christus non veniet." ‡ " Says the apostle, unless the Roman empire shall first be desolated, and Antichrist precede, Christ will not come." Augustine also employs the word in the same sense. "Nulli dubium est, eum de Antichristo ista dixisse; diemque judicii non esse venturum nisi ille prior venerit."§ "It can be doubted by none, but that he (Paul) speaks these things concerning Antichrist, and that the day of judgment will not come, unless he first appear." Gregory the Great, bishop of Rome, also employs the word in the same way. Reprimanding John, bishop of Constantinople, who was seeking to be made head of the whole church, he says—"Ergo fidenter dico, quod quisquis se universalem sacerdotem vocat, vel vocari desiderabit in elatione sua, Antichristum præcurrit."‖ "I say confidently, therefore, that whosoever calls himself universal bishop, or even desires in his pride to be called such, is the forerunner of Antichrist."

The Reformers generally, and since them, the great body of Protestants, have uniformly employed this

---

* De Resurrectione Carnis, ch. 24.   † Cat. xv. 5.
‡ Algasiæ, Ques. ii.   § De Civitate Dei. i., 20, 19.   ‖ i. 6 Epis. 30.

INTRODUCTION.   13

term to designate "the man of sin" of the apostle Paul, the "little horn" of Daniel, and the "beast" predicted by John.

The very same use is made of this term by Romanists themselves. "But Antichrist," says Calmet, "the real Antichrist, who is to come before the universal judgment, will, in himself include all the marks of wickedness, which have been separately extant in different persons, who were his types or forerunners."† The commentator on the Doway Bible, in his remarks upon the "man of sin," says, "It agrees with the wicked and great Antichrist, who will come before the end of the world."

There is also exegetical evidence, that the term *Antichrist*, in the epistles of John, is legitimately used in its application to the head of some great apostasy from the Christian faith. There is strong probability, that these epistles were written after the destruction of Jerusalem. If so, "the last time" of John, cannot refer to a period just preceding the subversion of that city. It seems rather to be synonymous with "the latter times," spoken of by Paul. Nor is there any objection to this in the fact, that John says, "Even now are there many Antichrists." The apostle Paul makes the same statement concerning "the man of sin"—"The mystery of iniquity doth already work." Each of these apostles too, represents the person, or persons of whom they speak, as those who had departed from the Christian faith. "Now the Spirit speaketh expressly, says Paul, that in the latter times, some shall depart from the faith." John also describes his Antichrist, or Antichrists, as those who "deny the Father and the Son," and as persons who "went out" from the church.

The true interpretation of these passages seems to be the following: The Spirit of God had revealed to the apostles, that at some future period there would be a great corruption of the Christian faith. Even in their own day there were some, who had begun al-

* In verbo

ready to depart from that faith and to corrupt it. These the apostles considered as the forerunners of those later apostates, who would more generally and dreadfully pervert the gospel of Christ. In a more general way therefore, they classify them all together, but give a more particular description of the later and more notable apostates.

The preceding observations and authorities will justify, it is hoped, the use of the term *Antichrist* as employed in this volume. As the writer firmly believes that the "little horn" of Daniel, the "man of sin" of Paul, and "the beast" of John, all symbolize the papal power, he has felt no hesitation, in applying the word *Antichrist* directly to that power.

The author has also to state, that the motive which has led him to unite the two subjects, Christ and Antichrist, into one volume, is that the two sets of testimonies may act with reciprocal force upon each other. The first argument is with the Jew, "beloved for the fathers' sake;" the second is with the Romanist, pitied for the Saviour's sake. The same mode of proof is employed in both cases. And it is sincerely hoped, that if the Jew shall see any reason from these pages, why the Romanist should be convinced, he may also find something to lead him to his own Messiah; and that if the Romanist shall here find any thing which he supposes ought to satisfy the Israelite, he may also discover reasons to renounce his own system of error.

It is not, however, for either Jews or Romanists that these pages are chiefly written. The specific object is, to convince men in general, that the Papacy is the Antichrist predicted in the word of God. Most who will read these pages, are Christians, at least in name. They have no doubt, but that Jesus is the Christ. The author, therefore, proceeds, upon the same ground on which the Messiahship of Jesus is established, to prove the Antichristian character of the Papal power. To his own mind, the one set of arguments is as strong as the other; so, that if it be

INTRODUCTION. 15

admitted, that Jesus is the Christ, he sees not how it can well be denied, that the Papacy is the Antichrist.

There is a strange similarity on this subject, between the infatuations of the child of Abraham and the disciple of the Pope. Both are looking for the proper subjects of these prophecies as yet future. To the Jew, Messiah is yet to come. Jesus to him is an impostor, a malefactor; his death was merited, his name is to be execrated. To the Romanist, Antichrist is yet to come; he is to arise but a little this side the last day. To him the Papal is the only true church, nor is there salvation in any other. Here is agreement, a strange agreement in infatuation and delusion! Surely God hath "blinded their eyes" and given them up to their own understandings.

Possibly some may think, that in a few of the chapters, sufficient regard has not been had to the unity of the argument. These apparent digressions have been indulged in, to exhibit more fully by contrast, the Christian and Antichristian systems. Popery never looks more deformed than when brought into comparison with true Christianity.

That God may bless this volume for the promotion of the truth, and the advancement of his own glory, is the sincere desire of the author.

PART I.

CHRIST;

OR

JESUS OF NAZARETH

PROVED TO BE

THE MESSIAH.

INTRODUCTORY REMARKS.

If it be admitted, that, as a transgressor, man needs a Saviour, and that one has been provided for him; then, all the evidence which establishes the personal identity of such a Saviour, must be considered as invested with fearful interest. Who is he? When did he appear? What is his character? What has he done? How is an interest in him to be secured? These, and similar questions, a serious and reflecting mind will not only propose, but desire to them all satisfactory answers.

The mere knowledge of the fact, that we need a Saviour, however deeply felt, cannot save us: nor can any reliance, however strong, we repose in a pretended deliverer, secure our everlasting peace. In the former state of mind, we only perceive the ruin in which sin has involved us, without being rescued from such ruin. In the latter, our reliance being placed upon a false foundation, must, of course, disappoint us, when the time of trial comes.

Besides, one who undertakes to rescue us from sin and death, must demand our confidence, and ought to receive both our homage and our obedience. But how can that confidence be demanded by one unknown? And how can such homage and obedience be rendered to one, whose merits and character are concealed?

The very existence therefore, of spiritual character, and of a well founded hope for eternity, must depend upon a proper knowledge of Him, whom God hath sent "to destroy the works of the devil," and "to bring in everlasting righteousness."

What then, is the nature and strength of the evidence, upon which Christians have so uniformly regarded *Jesus of Nazareth, and none other*, as their great Deliverer and Hope? It is known, that the Jews as a race, do not agree with Christians in this faith. It is known, that the larger portion of the world are altogether ignorant of such a person as Jesus. It is also lamentably true, that many, who are familiar with his name and history, yet reject him as a Saviour. Why is it, that in distinction from all these, Christians repose their trust in Jesus, and make him, and him only, the foundation of their hope for eternity?

The ground upon which such confidence is reposed in Jesus, can of course be none other, than the firm conviction, that he is in truth the great Deliverer, promised to mankind from even the earliest ages. If deceived on this point, all Christians are in a dreadful delusion; and, notwithstanding their most sanguine hopes, must still be under the power of sin and the displeasure of God. On the contrary, if Christians be not deceived in their faith, and if indeed, Jesus of Nazareth be the promised Messiah, and "the only name given under heaven whereby men must be saved;" then are the rest of mankind in a most perilous and dreadful condition. Whether therefore the one or the other be in error, the evidence, which substantiates the claims of Jesus of Nazareth to Messiahship, can be considered only with the deepest interest. It is that evidence which we now proceed to exhibit.

CHRIST PROVED TO BE THE MESSIAH.

CHAPTER I.

THE GENEALOGY OF JESUS.

One sign, which was to designate the person of the promised Messiah, was, his regular descent from Abraham, through the tribe of Judah, and family of David. If the will of God had so determined, the Messiah might have descended from any other nation than the Israelites, or from any other tribe than Judah, or from any other family than that of David. But since the purpose of God has marked out successively, Abraham, Judah, and David, as the lineal ancestors of the promised Saviour, it is in that line, and that only, that we must expect his birth. And should every other part of the evidence be complete, and yet this be wanting, it could not be proved, that Jesus of Nazareth is really the Christ. He might have been an illustrious prophet; he might have been a great "teacher sent from God;" his life might have been the most blameless and pure, and his doctrine the most exalted and heavenly; he might too, have effected a great moral change among the Jews, and also in the state of the world generally; still his claims to Messiahship could not be established, unless he were born in the predicted line of ancestry.

When God called Abraham from Ur of Chaldea, among other promises, he gave him the following, "And in thee shall all families of the earth be blessed." Gen. xii. This promise was afterwards repeated when Abraham was called to offer up his son Isaac. Gen. xxii. Now, whatever blessings mankind may in general have derived from the Israelites, it is evident, that this promise refers to the Messiah. The Apostle Paul has given us its true exegesis—"He saith not, and to *seeds*, as of many, but as of *one*, and to thy seed, which is Christ." Gal. iii. The Messiah then was to be a lineal descendant of Abraham.

He was also to descend from the tribe of Judah. When the patriarch Jacob was blessing his sons, he pronounced, by divine inspiration, the following remarkable prediction concerning Judah: "The sceptre shall not depart from Judah, nor a lawgiver from between his feet, until Shiloh come, and unto him shall the gathering of the people be." Gen. xlix. Whatever criticisms the learned may have made upon this passage, the opinion has almost universally obtained, both among Jews and Christians, that its reference is to the Messiah as descended from the tribe of Judah. "The Jews," says Hengstenberg, "regard verse 10th, as predicting the Messiah. Thus it was interpreted by the Chaldaic paraphrases; the Targum of Onkelos, of Jerusalem, and of Jonathan; the Talmud, the Zohar, and the old book Bereshith Rabba; and even by several of the more modern commentators, as Jarchi. The Samaritans also explain this passage of the Messiah. In the Christian church, the Messianic interpretation has, from the earliest times been generally approved."* Gesenius renders the passage thus—"Judah shall not lay aside the sceptre of a leader, until he shall have subdued his enemies and obtained dominion over many nations; referring to the expected Kingdom of the Messiah, who was to spring from the tribe of Judah."†

The same reference to the Messiah, as descended from the tribe of Judah, is to be found in Psalm cviii, where it is said of that tribe, "Judah is my lawgiver." This passage may have primary reference to the establishment of the throne in that tribe; but its allusion evidently extends farther, and designates that future and illustrious Lawgiver, whom not only the

* Chris. in loco.   † Lex. in loco.

Jews, but all the nations of the earth were to obey. "Perfectissime hoc completum in Christo,"*—says Poole—*This is most perfectly fulfilled in Christ.*

The prophet Isaiah is even more explicit. "And I will bring forth a *seed* out of Jacob, and out of Judah an *inheritor* of my mountains, and mine elect shall inherit it, and my servants shall dwell there." The allusion here is so obvious as to need no explanation. The Messiah, therefore, was also to be a descendant from the tribe of Judah.

He was also to be of the house or family of David. "And thy house and thy kingdom," said God to David, " shall be established forever before thee: thy throne shall be established forever." 2 Sam. vii. The Psalmist in alluding to this promise, represents Jehovah as saying—"Once have I sworn by my holiness, that I will not lie unto David. His seed shall endure; and his throne as the sun before me. It shall be established forever as the moon, and as a faithful witness in heaven." Psalm lxxxix. These promises include *specifically* and with great emphasis, the *perpetuity* of the throne in the house of David. Now, from Solomon to Zedekiah, there was included but a period of about four hundred and thirty years. And from Zedekiah to the dispersion of the Jews by the Romans, only a period of about six hundred more: unless, therefore, the throne of David be set up in the person of Messiah, these promises can have no real fulfilment.

But the prophets are more specific—"And there shall come forth a rod out of the stem of Jesse, and a branch shall grow out of his roots. And the Spirit of the Lord shall rest upon him. And he shall not judge after the sight of his eyes; neither reprove after the hearing of his ears: but with righteousness shall he judge the poor, and reprove with equity for the meek of the earth. And righteousness shall be the girdle of his loins, and faithfulness the girdle of his reins." Isa. xi. The reference of this passage to the Messiah

---

* In loco.

is not only proved by the context, but also by a similar one in Jeremiah. "Behold the days come, saith the Lord, that I will raise unto David a righteous Branch; and a King shall reign and prosper, and shall execute judgment and justice in the earth; and this is his name whereby he shall be called—The Lord our Righteousness." Jer. xxiii. But, even if there were any obscurity in these passages, there can be none in the following. Speaking of the Messiah, Isaiah says—" Of the increase of his government and peace, there shall be no end, upon the throne of David, and upon his kingdom, to order it, and to establish it with judgment and with justice from henceforth even forever." Isaiah ix.

These prophetic passages sufficiently explain the promise originally given to David, and so delightfully dwelt upon by the ancient Israelites in their inspired songs. The *perpetuity* of David's throne and kingdom, was to exist in the person of the Messiah; who according to the flesh was to be made of the seed of David. David himself died soon after the promise was given. The line of earthly kings descending from him, terminated in the period of a few centuries. Even the dependent and afflicted dominion of the family of David and of the tribe of Judah which succeeded, was terminated under Titus and the Roman legions. All these were to pass away. But the kingdom of *Messiah* was to be strictly "*everlasting*," and his dominion without end. In him, the throne of David was to be re-established, and was destined to continue "*forever*."

The descent then of the Messiah was to be through Abraham, Judah, David. Any other descent therefore must destroy the title and defeat the claims of him, who pretends to be the subject of these remarkable predictions. *Was Jesus of Nazareth, of such descent?*

This question is both fully and satisfactorily answered in the New Testament. The evangelists, Matthew and Luke, have each given genealogies of Jesus, the express object of which was to exhibit these facts.

These tables are in many respects different; but in that which is essential, they perfectly agree. Luke traces the genealogy of Jesus to Adam; Matthew only to Abraham. Luke follows either the line of Mary's ancestry, or of Joseph's *legal* ancestry; Matthew that of Joseph's *natural* ancestry. From Jesus to David, Luke mentions forty-two names; Matthew but twenty-seven. Matthew has also omitted three names found in First Chronicles, chapter iii.

Now, notwithstanding these discrepancies, and the various methods adopted by the learned to reconcile them, *the facts,* about which we are inquiring, are obvious in both tables. Each evangelist traces the genealogy of Jesus to David. They take different routes, but arrive here at the same point. Nor is there the least variation between them from David, through Judah to Abraham. Here the tables perfectly agree, and the testimony of each is, that Jesus of Nazareth was lineally descended from David, Judah, Abraham.

In explanation of the differences between these tables, the following observations of Bloomfield will be found appropriate. " As to the reconciling this (Matthew's) genealogy with that of St. Luke, it is best done, by supposing that St. Matthew gives the genealogy of Joseph, and St. Luke that of Mary. And therefore the former, who wrote principally for the Jews, traces the pedigree from Abraham to David, and so through Solomon's line to Joseph the *legal* father of Jesus. And it must be remembered, that among the Jews, *legal* descent was always reckoned in the *male* line. St. Luke, on the contrary, who wrote for the Gentiles, traces the pedigree upwards from Heli, the father of Mary, to David and Abraham, and thence to Adam, the common father of all mankind. Finally, whatever difficulties, even after all the diligence of learned inquirers, shall exist on certain matters connected with these genealogies, we may rest assured, that if these genealogies of Christ, which must be understood to have been derived from *the public records in the Temple,* had not been agreeable thereto, the deception would have been instantly detected. And thus, whether Christ's pedigree be traced through the line of Joseph or of Mary, it is undeniable, that Jesus was descended from David and Abraham, agreeably to the ancient promises and prophesies that the Messiah should be of their seed."*

The following statements from the learned Dr. Clarke are also valuable. "Mary therefore appears to have been the daughter of Heli. Joseph and Mary were of the same family; both came from Zerubbabel; Joseph from Abiud, his eldest son; Mary by Rhesa his youngest. Thus it appears, that Jesus, son of Mary, re-united in himself all the blood, privileges, and rights, of the whole family of David; in consequence of which he is emphatically called, *the son of David.*"†

There is another remarkable fact recorded in the New Testament, which casts light upon the ancestral descent of Jesus. Luke records it in the following manner—"And it came to pass in those days, that there went out a decree from Cæsar Augustus, that all the world should be taxed. And all went to be taxed every one to his own city. And Joseph also went up from Galilee, out of the city of Nazareth, into Judea, unto the city of David, which is called Bethlehem (because he was of the house and lineage of David) to be taxed, with Mary his espoused wife." Luke ii. Here is an event in which we see most clearly the hand of Divine Providence. The emperor Augustus makes a decree, which in its operation, requires every Jew to be enrolled in his own family and tribe. The names of Joseph and Mary are entered at Bethlehem, as belonging to the house of David. What a remarkable occurrence! What a public and authentic attestation of the real ancestry of Jesus! The humble circumstances of Joseph and Mary; their remoteness especially from the ordinary dwelling-place of the illustrious family of David, might have obscured the ancestry of their extraordinary Son. But a circumstance occurs forever to dispel all doubt on that

---

* Notes on Mat. † Notes on Luke.

subject. By an imperial mandate, they are enrolled at Bethlehem, as the descendants of the royal house of the son of Jesse!

But there are a great many different passages in the New Testament, which distinctly state, that the genealogy of Jesus was such as the Old Testament Scriptures had assigned to the Messiah. Thus the Apostle Paul declares, that Christ "took not on him the nature of angels, but the seed of Abraham." Heb. ii. Again he affirms, that "it is evident, that our Lord (that is Jesus) sprang out of Juda." Heb. vii. Zachariah also speaks of Jesus as "a horn of salvation raised up in the house of David." Luke i. Peter affirms, that Jesus was "the fruit of the loins" of David, Acts ii; and Paul, that Christ, "was made of the seed of David according to the flesh." In truth, so numerous are the statements of this sort to be found in the writings of the Apostles, that it is impossible to deny, that their plain, uniform, and invariable testimony is, that Jesus was descended from David, Judah, Abraham.

The evidence then, in behalf of the Messiahship of Jesus of Nazareth, so far as *ancestral descent* is concerned, is perfect. The purpose of God and prophecy require, that the Messiah should be descended through certain persons, specially designated, in the Old Testament Scriptures. The Evangelists and Apostles furnish indisputable testimony, that Jesus of Nazareth was thus descended. His genealogy, both *legal* and *natural*, passes through these very persons. The most authentic records are employed to show, that these were his ancestors. And those who knew him best, never considered him as belonging to any other *family*, *tribe* or *nation*.

CHAPTER II.

THE BIRTH OF JESUS.

Besides the evidence arising from the previously defined ancestors of the Messiah, there was to be one circumstance connected with his birth, so peculiar and extraordinary, as to point him out in distinction from all others—*He was to be born of a virgin.* True, a fact of this kind might be of more difficult proof than many others, in the life of the promised Saviour. Delicacy too, would naturally cast a veil over it for a time. Still however, it might be proved; and when proved, it would powerfully tend, not only to identify the person of the Messiah, but to demonstrate also, the extraordinary character of his mission.

In Genesis iii. 15, are these words, "And I will put enmity between thee and the woman, and between thy seed and her seed; it shall bruise thy head, and thou shalt bruise his heel." The reference in this passage is evidently to the Messiah. We have already seen that the term *seed*, employed in the promise given to Abraham, refers to the predicted Saviour. The same allusion is intended by the word in the present instance. The Messiah was to be, not only a son of Abraham by natural descent, but a son of *the woman*, by miraculous conception and birth.

That which is here affirmed of this seed is applicable only to the Messiah. He was to bruise the head, that is, to overthrow the kingdom of the serpent, or Satan. But who is competent to a work of this kind, save the chosen of God, the Saviour of men? Nor was Eve the *specific* woman alluded to in this promise. The Messiah was not born of *her;* for, he was afterwards promised to Abraham and David. Eve, therefore, could not be the woman here meant. The prophecy must therefore refer to some other woman, who should exist in after ages. "He, (Christ) says Scott, is called *the seed of the woman*, and not the seed *of Adam,* though descended from both; not only because Satan had prevailed first against the woman, but likewise with an evident prophetic intimation of his miraculous conception and birth of a pure virgin."* "Christ is called the seed of the woman, says Lowth, by way of distinction, as not to be born in the ordinary way of generation."† Bloomfield also speaks of Mary, as "that particular virgin who was prophesied of from the beginning, and whose seed was to bruise the serpent's head."‡

The prophet Isaiah, is still more explicit, in predicting the miraculous birth of the promised Deliverer. "And he said, Hear ye now, O house of David! Is it a small thing for you to weary men; but will ye weary my God also? Therefore, the Lord himself shall give you a sign. Behold, a virgin shall conceive and bear a son, and shall call his name Immanuel." Isa. vii. 13, 14. Attempts have been made to explain away the meaning of this passage, by asserting that the Hebrew word עלמה here translated *a virgin*, denotes also *a young married woman*, and by applying the language either to the son of the prophet himself, or to some other child, born about that time. This mode of interpretation seems almost inexcusable in *Christian* commentators, from the fact that the Evangelist Matthew applies the passage directly to Mary and to Jesus. A *safer* expositor, no plain and honest believer could desire. Gesenius, although he asserts the meaning of the word in this place to be, "a youthful spouse," yet defines it as generally meaning, "*a girl, maiden, or virgin, of marriageble age.*"§ "The primary meaning of the word, says Lowth, is *hid*, or *concealed;* from whence it is taken to signify *a virgin*, because of the custom in eastern countries, to keep their virgins *concealed* from the view of men."‖ The He-

* In loco.   † On Isaiah.   ‡ Com. on Mat.
§ Heb. Lex. in verbo.   ‖ On Isaiah.

brew word, says Scott, most properly signifies *a virgin;* and so it is translated here, by all the ancient interpreters, and it is never once used in the Scriptures in any other sense."*

There is, however, another and very obvious objection to the application of this language in the manner above alluded to. The birth of the predicted child was to be a *sign*, a *miracle*. Now, what sign or miracle could it be, that a young *married* woman should bear a son? Evidently, the force and propriety of the language, are entirely destroyed by such an interpretation. Nor is it any objection to the Messianic character of the passage, that in the context, the prophet alludes so much to the existing state of things among the Jews. It is the usual practice of the ancient prophets, not only to make rapid transitions in their subjects, but also to mingle their predictions of the Messiah, and his kingdom, with the state of the Jewish commonwealth around them. The latter was a sort of *prophetic observatory*, from which these holy men contemplated and described the more distant objects under the Messiah's reign, a sort of *national prism*, casting its various hues upon the glories of the latter day.

The *name* also of the predicted child, forbids the application of this passage to any ordinary Jewish family—"And shall call his name *Immanuel.*" This name which is made up of three Hebrew words combined, means literally, *God-with-us.* Now, it is certain, that such a name was really given to no child born at the time, of which we have any account. It is also certain, that such a name could be *appropriately* given to no ordinary Jewish child whatever. Of whom, but of the promised Son of David, the *Messiah*, could such a name be descriptive? He and he only, could be, "*God-with-us.*"

If then we associate these passages together, we have two distinct and positive declarations, the one made immediately by God himself, the other by a

* In loco.

prophet in his name, that the promised Saviour was to be *virgin-born;* that he was to be peculiarly and independently *the woman's son.* How do these prophecies apply to *Jesus of Nazareth?*

The circumstances and manner of his birth are thus given by Luke: "And in the sixth month, the angel Gabriel was sent from God unto a city of Galilee, named Nazareth, to a virgin espoused to a man whose name was Joseph, of the house of David; and the virgin's name was Mary. And the angel came in unto her and said, Hail, thou that art highly favoured; the Lord is with thee. Blessed art thou among women. And when she saw him, she was troubled at his saying, and cast in her mind, what manner of salutation this should be. And the angel said unto her. Fear not Mary, for thou hast found favour with God. And behold thou shalt conceive in thy womb, and bring forth a son, and shalt call his name Jesus. He shall be great, and shall be called the Son of the Highest: and the Lord God shall give unto him the throne of his father David; and he shall reign over the house of Jacob forever; and of his kingdom there shall be no end. Then said Mary unto the angel, How shall this be, seeing I know not a man? And the angel aswered and said unto her; The Holy Ghost shall come upon thee, and the power of the Highest shall overshadow thee; therefore also, that holy thing which shall be born of thee, shall be called the Son of God." Luke i. 26-35.

The narrative as furnished by Matthew is the following: "Now the birth of Jesus Christ was on this wise: when as his mother Mary was espoused to Joseph, before they came together, she was found with child of the Holy Ghost. Then Joseph her husband, being a just man, and not willing to make her a public example, was minded to put her away privily. But while he thought on these things, behold, the angel of the Lord appeared unto him in a dream, saying, Joseph, thou son of David, fear not to take unto thee Mary thy wife; for that which is conceived in her is of the Holy Ghost. And she shall bring forth a son, and thou shalt call his name Jesus; for he shall save his people from their sins. Then Joseph being raised from sleep, did as the angel of the Lord had bidden him, and took unto him his wife; and knew her not till she had brought forth her first-born son: and he called his name Jesus." Matt. i. 18–25.

Jehovah, to execute his purposes of grace to man, and to fulfil the prophecies previously delivered, sends an angel to Nazareth in Galilee, to make known to a virgin there, that *she* had been selected as the mother of the long expected Saviour. With conscious innocence, but deep interest in the tidings brought, the virgin states, what seemed to her an insuperable barrier to the accomplishment of the event announced. Her doubts however, are removed by the angel, who informs her, that the birth of her son was to be *miraculous*, and not ordinary. Mary was at the time espoused to a man, also living at Nazareth, whose name was Joseph. Joseph, in the course of time discovers the condition of his intended wife. He loves, he esteems her; but being "a just man," and not willing by a public act of marriage, to cover a crime he considered so heinous and offensive, he resolved to give her a bill of divorce, and thus, according to the Jewish usages, to destroy the contract of marriage existing between them. He determined, however, from the regard he felt for his intended bride, to do this *privately*. While meditating upon these things, an angel appears to him also, and informs him, not only that Mary had not offended, but that the child she was about to bring forth, was the promised Deliverer of men. So satisfied was this just and good man with the information given him by the angel, that all his fears were dissipated, and he hesitated not *publicly* to receive Mary as his wife, and thus to become not only her guardian and protector, but the guardian and protector also, during his infancy and childhood, of her illustrious Son.

There is in these simple and undisguised narratives, every possible appearance of *truth*. There is nothing improbable, that the birth of *a Saviour* should

THE MESSIAH.

be attended with miracle. And if such a birth be miraculous, there is nothing improbable in the visitation of angels on the occasion, and especially, of their visitation to the parties most deeply concerned. The reserve too and modesty of the virgin, the fears and anxieties of Joseph, the native simplicity which pervades the narratives, all tend to give great probability to the facts here stated.

Besides the testimony of Mary and Joseph to the miraculous conception and birth of Jesus, another witness is introduced by the Evangelists. This witness is Elizabeth. Being informed by the angel that Elizabeth was also about to become the mother of an extraordinary personage, Mary pays her a visit. Upon her entrance into the presence of Elizabeth, the latter is filled with divine and extraordinary influences. Under these supernatural impulses, she announces to her visitor the very facts communicated by the angel to Mary, and with which she supposed none acquainted but herself. Luke i. 39–45. Elizabeth, herself a woman of great piety, was the wife of a very reputable priest, by the name of Zacharias. Her testimony, therefore, was well calculated to confirm the extraordinary statements made by Mary and Joseph, concerning the supernatural conception and birth of Jesus.

Nor would facts like these be apt to be withheld from Zacharias, or from the other relatives of both families, indeed, of the *three* families. Mary would be likely to narrate them to some at least of her immediate and most trust-worthy friends. Joseph would no doubt, make them known to some of his; and Elizabeth and Zacharias, to some of theirs. By this means, a number of persons would soon be informed of these wonderful events. The near approach too of the long expected and earnestly desired Messiah, would be too good news to be kept altogether a secret. Modesty, it is true, together with the extreme sacredness of the matter, might prevent clamour or commotion. There might be no *general* fame, no *widespread* report. Still, however, there would be found

4*

a sufficient number of faithful hearts, to which, like Mary's, these wonders might be confided. And that this was *really* the case, there can be no doubt. Matthew and Luke both speak of them as of events *well known.*

Nor can we suppose, that the statements of the Evangelists are themselves but *inventions*, to embellish their history and to exalt their hero. All the evidence which proves the truthfulness in general of the Gospels written by these two Evangelists, will also go to establish the accuracy of these particular parts of those Gospels. The facts here stated, therefore, must stand or fall with the New Testament itself. Besides, had these statements of the Evangelists been false, that fact might easily have been detected. So that instead of adding to the interest of their composition, or to the dignity of Jesus, the imposture would have produced just the contrary effect. The Evangelists, however, speak of these things, as of *facts* worthy of the utmost credit; of facts too, which the subsequent and illustrious life of Jesus, served but to confirm and establish in the minds of men. We cannot, therefore, without minds capable of resisting the strongest evidence, capable of denying the positive statements of the most authentic history, disbelieve the miraculous conception and birth of Jesus of Nazareth. His mother, Joseph, Elizabeth, two of his disciples, and many of his most intimate acquaintances, all agree in their testimony on this point.

But if the birth of Jesus was *miraculous*, then have we another, and a most powerful proof of his being the Messiah. According to two express prophecies concerning the Messiah in the Old Testament, he was to be "the woman's seed," "a virgin's son." He was to be born, not in the ordinary method of human generation, but by the exercise of Divine and supernatural power. A body was to be prepared, for the manifestation of the Godhead in human flesh. *These prophecies have been fulfilled in the birth of Jesus.* Nor have they been fulfilled in the birth of any other person whatever. Abel, Noah, Abraham,

David, John and Peter, were all born in the ordinary way. Even the mythological stories about the birth of Alexander, Romulus, Æneas, and others, were not believed by the very historians, among the Greeks and Romans, who narrated them. Nor can the history of the world, save the New Testament, produce *one probable case*, of a miraculous conception and birth. This has been peculiar to *one* only, of all the multitudes that have lived upon our globe. That one is *Jesus*. He, and he only, was *miraculously* conceived; he, and he only, was born of a *pure virgin*. So far then as *these prophecies* are concerned, Jesus must be the Christ, must be the promised Saviour of men.

CHAPTER III.

THE BIRTH-PLACE OF JESUS.

ANOTHER indication of the person of the Messiah, as presented in prophecy, is to be found in the place of his nativity. He must not only be descended from certain specified ancestors, and born of a virgin, but his birth must occur in *a particular town.* A birth, therefore, any where else, even should it be miraculous, would destroy the claims of him who might pretend to be the Messiah.

The designation of the birth-place of the Messiah is thus given by the prophet Micah: "But thou, Bethlehem Ephratah, though thou be little among the thousands of Judah, yet out of thee shall he come forth unto me that is to be Ruler in Israel; whose goings forth have been from of old, from everlasting." Mic. v. 2. As in most of the ancient prophecies, the Messiah is not named in this passage; he is, however, so significantly referred to, as to render the name altogether unnecessary. Long before the days of Micah, this remarkable personage had been revealed to the Israelites as some great king, whom God would set over them. He was to be more righteous and wise than other sovereigns, and in his day there was to be great peace and prosperity. Such prophecies fixed, of course, the eyes of all Israel on this predicted and pre-eminent Prince. They turned to him as a bright star in a cheerless night, and even when oppressed and enslaved, looked forward to his day, as to one of deliverance and triumph. When, therefore, one of Israel's own prophets, as he looks far down the future, speaks of Him, "*who is to be Ruler in Israel,*" certainly he can be understood to refer to none else,

THE MESSIAH.

but to that distinguished Sovereign, the *Messiah,* whom the Lord God was to raise up in the latter day.

The reference in this passage evidently cannot be to *David.* Micah, as both the title and the contents of the book prove, prophesied in the days of Jotham, Ahaz, and Hezekiah; that is, about two hundred and sixty years *after* the reign of David. Nor can the reference in this passage be to any of the royal descendants and successors of David. Josiah was the only one of any note among them, who filled the throne after the days of Micah. It is evident, however, that he is not meant; the description does not suit him, nor was he born in Bethlehem, but in Jerusalem. There is no one then to whom this prophecy can be legitimately applied, but to that Great King, the *Messiah,* whom God, in later times, was to set upon the throne of Israel.

The description here given of the *character* of this extraordinary Sovereign, also limits the application of the passage to the Messiah: " His goings forth have been from of old, from everlasting." Such language, which can in no case be applied to mere mortals, is precisely such as is applied in many other passages of Scripture to the Messiah. There is a sublimity, a greatness, a sort of prophetic obscurity in language of this kind, which at once indicates the person to whom it is to be referred, and marks out, as with the light of sunbeams, the extraordinary character both of his nature and office.

The ancient Jews also uniformly applied this passage to the Messiah. When a number of them were almost persuaded that Jesus was the Christ, others said, "Shall Christ come out of Galilee? Hath not the Scripture said, that Christ cometh of the seed of David, and out of the town of *Bethlehem,* where David was?" John vii. 47. The objection here raised, was to the supposed fact that Jesus was born at Nazareth in Galilee. The very objection however proves that Bethlehem was to be the birth-place of the Messiah.

We have, however, not simply the opinion of the multitude on this subject. The Sanhedrim, the highest court formerly of the Jewish nation, expressed the same sentiment. Herod, alarmed at the visit of certain Eastern Magi, who had come to Jerusalem to inquire after him "who was born king of the Jews," instituted the inquiry before this celebrated council, "where Christ was to be born?" The answer given was, "In *Bethlehem* of Judea; for thus it is written by the prophet: "And thou, Bethlehem in the land of Judah, art not the least among the princes of Judah; for out of thee shall come a Governor, that shall rule my people Israel." Matt. ii. 5, 6. This is decisive. The very text itself is used by the Jewish Rulers and Rabbins, to prove the birth-place of the Messiah.

If then this passage have reference to the Messiah, it is perfectly clear, where that Messiah must be born; not at Jerusalem—not at Nazareth—not at Hebron or Capernaum—but in *Bethlehem*. Nor would any place by the name of Bethlehem answer the purpose. It must be Bethlehem *Ephratah;* that is, Bethlehem in the land of *Judah*, as distinguished from another Bethlehem in the tribe of Zebulun. Any other birth-place, therefore, than that of *Bethlehem of Judah*, would destroy all other evidence of one's being the Messiah. *Where then was Jesus of Nazareth born?*

And here, we cannot but admire that overruling providence of God, which employs, not only various, but often apparently contradictory means, to effect its purposes. Joseph and Mary had been living at Nazareth, a town in Galilee. It was in this town they had seen their extraordinary visions. It was in this town they had loved, had wedded. Nor had the visiting angel informed them, that *Bethlehem* must be the birth-place of the predicted child. Nor did Joseph and Mary seem at all to suppose that the birth of their son, occurring at Nazareth, would vitiate his claims to Messiahship. Probably the passage in Micah had escaped their notice, or they had forgotten it. Of themselves, there is not the least probability, that they would have visited Bethlehem. The distance was considerable, and the condition of Mary unsuited to the fatigues of travel. But He who has ordained the *end*, has also

THE MESSIAH. 39

ordained the *means*. God never forgets a promise, or overlooks a word he has spoken. Cæsar Augustus, ignorant alike of prophecy and of the Messiah, having no knowledge of the Divine decrees, nor any intention to fulfil them—holding, it may be, the whole nation of the Jews in contempt, and believing not a word of all their sacred writings—this distant, and proud Emperor is made to fulfil a prophecy, of whose very existence he was entirely ignorant. Either to gratify his vanity, or to fix a regular rate of taxation, the Emperor issues a decree, "that all the world should be taxed;" that is, *enrolled*. To accomplish this, it was necessary for each Jew to report himself in his own tribe and town. This edict, so unexpectedly issued, brings Joseph and Mary from Nazareth to Bethlehem, just at the time when Mary was about to be delivered of her extraordinary son! Thus the birth of Jesus, which, under ordinary circumstances, would have occurred at Nazareth, was made to happen at *Bethlehem*, according to the prediction of the prophet Micah, many centuries previously.

But what evidence have we that Jesus was really born at Bethlehem? To satisfy ourselves on this point, we must consult the testimony given us by the two evangelists, Matthew and Luke. The statement of the latter is the following: "And it came to pass in those days, that there went out a decree from Cæsar Augustus that all the world should be taxed. And all went to be taxed, every one to his own city. And Joseph also went up from Galilee, out of the city of Nazareth, into Judea, unto the city of David, which is called Bethlehem; (because he was of the house and lineage of David) to be taxed, with Mary his espoused wife, being great with child. And so it was, that while they were there, the days were accomplished that she should be delivered. And she brought forth her first-born son, and wrapped him in swaddling clothes, and laid him in a manger; because there was no room for them in the inn. And there were in the same country, shepherds abiding in the field, keeping watch over their flock by night. And lo, the angel of the Lord came upon them, and the glory of the Lord shone about them; and they were sore afraid. And the angel said unto them, Fear not; for behold, I bring you good tidings of great joy, which shall be to all people. For unto you is born this day, in the city of David, a Saviour, which is Christ the Lord. And this shall be a sign unto you; ye shall find the babe wrapped in swaddling clothes, lying in a manger. And suddenly there was with the angel a multitude of the heavenly host, praising God and saying, Glory to God in the highest, and on earth peace, good-will toward men. And it came to pass as the angels were gone away from them into heaven, the shepherds said one to another, Let us now go even unto Bethlehem, and see this thing which is come to pass, which the Lord has made known unto us. And they came with haste, and found Mary and Joseph, and the babe lying in a manger. And when they had seen it, they made known abroad the saying which was told them concerning this child. And all they that heard it, wondered at those things which were told them by the shepherds." Luke ii. 1–18.

The narrative of Matthew is the following: "Now when Jesus was born in Bethlehem of Judea, in the days of Herod the king, behold, there came wise men from the East to Jerusalem, saying, Where is he that is born King of the Jews? For we have seen his star in the East and are come to worship him. When Herod the King had heard these things, he was troubled, and all Jerusalem with him. And when he had gathered all the chief priests and scribes of the people together, he demanded of them, where Christ should be born. And they said unto him, In Bethlehem of Judea. Then Herod, when he had privily called the wise men, inquired of them diligently what time the star appeared. And he sent them to Bethlehem, and said, Go and search diligently for the young child, and when ye have found him, bring me word again, that I may come and worship him also. When they had heard the king they departed; and lo, the star which they saw in the east, went before them, till it came and stood over where the young child was. When they saw the star, they rejoiced with exceeding great joy. And when they were come into the house, they saw the young child with Mary his mother, and fell down and worshipped him. And when they had opened their treasures, they presented unto him gifts; gold and frankincense and myrrh. And being warned of God in a dream, that they should not return to Herod, they departed unto their own country another way." Matt. ii. 1–12.

From these narratives, we infer the following facts concerning the birth of Jesus at Bethlehem. The decree of the Emperor Augustus, was the palpable reason of the visit of Joseph and Mary to that town. Owing probably to the situation of Mary, their arrival was late. The best accommodations, as is usual where great crowds collect, had already been engaged and occupied. Joseph and Mary are, therefore, compelled to take that part of the caravansary, or inn, which, according to Eastern custom, is occupied jointly by men and cattle. The birth occurs probably, the very night of their arrival; at any rate but a short time afterwards. It was the very night of the birth, and while Joseph and Mary were still occupying their humble lodgings, that the shepherds paid to the infant stranger their remarkable visit. Not long after this, Joseph and Mary are removed to a comfortable house. Either the dispersion of the crowd gave them more room, or the visit of the shepherds brought them into higher notice. Shortly after this removal, the visit of the eastern Magi occurred, who, "when they were come unto *the house*, saw the young child with Mary his mother, and fell down, and worshipped him." This again was soon followed by the descent into Egypt, and the bloody work of Herod, in slaughtering all the babes in Bethlehem and its coasts, in order to destroy in the mass, the infant King of the Jews.

In reference to the *evidence* which these narratives afford, that Jesus of Nazareth was born at *Bethlehem*, I offer the two following remarks. It is in the first place, not at all probable, that the birth of Jesus at Bethlehem is a mere invention of the Evangelists. True, these Evangelists must have known, that had Jesus been born at Nazareth, and not at Bethlehem, this one fact must have invalidated greatly, all their testimony to his Messiahship. Still, however, it was impossible for them to have transferred his birth from Nazareth to Bethlehem, had he not really been born in the latter town. It may be difficult in the earliest ages of society, to determine the birth-place of distinguished men. Thus, seven towns of ancient Greece, contended for the honour of having given birth to Homer. No such difficulty, however, exists in a more polished and literary age. How impossible would it be, for instance, for any historian of the present age, to establish the birth of Napoleon at Paris, or that of Washington at New York! The undertaking would be ridiculed; and the author who should attempt such an imposition upon the credulity of an enlightened age, would destroy the reputation of both himself and his work in the attempt. Similarly situated were the two biographers of Jesus. They lived in the Augustan age of Roman literature. Jesus too was a man so famed for his doctrines and mighty works, as to attract general attention. How absurd, then, must have been the attempt of these men, to prove that he was born at Bethlehem, had he really been born at Nazareth, or elsewhere! The undertaking would have been hazardous to themselves, and ruinous to their work.

Nor can we, in the second place, suppose the Evangelists to have been deceived, as to the true birth-place of Jesus. So did Providence order events, as to give great publicity to his birth at Bethlehem. The decree of Augustus, the visit of Joseph and Mary to Bethlehem to be taxed, the testimony of the shepherds, the unusual appearance at that time of the eastern Magi in the town, the subsequent slaughter of the infants—these were all facts of so very public a nature, as to leave no doubt whatever, concerning the true birth-blace of this remarkable personage. Indeed, if it be not proved by these things that Jesus was born in Bethlehem-Judah, then can we establish the birth-blace of no one whatever. We have the testimony of his own biographers, the testimony of his parents, the testimony of the shepherds, of the Magi, indeed the testimony of *the age* in which he lived; for no one in all that age has even started the doubt, that Jesus was *not* born in Bethlehem-Judah.

The testimony, therefore, given by the Evangelists to the true birth-place of Jesus is both reasonable and credible. It is such as if given by any other historians, in reference to the birth-place of any other distinguished individual, would not be questioned. We are, therefore, bound to receive it. In receiving it, however, we admit another proof, that Jesus of Nazareth is the Messiah. Micah had predicted, ages before, that "the Ruler of Israel," the Messiah, was to come forth of Bethlehem-Judah. The Evangelists show to a demonstration, that Jesus of Nazareth was actually born in that very town. In this particular, therefore, does the history of Jesus, accord with the ancient predictions concerning the Messiah. And if all other parts of his history shall agree as well with those predictions, then may Jew and Gentile, yea, angels and men, unite in the song, "Glory to God in the highest; on earth peace, good will towards men;" for "unto us *has been born* in the city of David, a Saviour, which is Christ, the Lord."

CHAPTER IV.

THE TIME WHEN JESUS MADE HIS APPEARANCE.

Another criterion for determining the person of the Messiah was, *the time of his appearance.* The prophecy, which most accurately fixes that time, is one delivered by Daniel. "Seventy weeks," says Gabriel, "are determined upon thy people, and upon thy holy city, to finish the transgression, and to make an end of sins, and to make reconciliation for iniquity, and to bring in everlasting righteousness, and to seal up the vision and prophecy, and to anoint the Most Holy. Know therefore and understand, that from the going forth of the commandment to build and to restore Jerusalem, unto the Messiah, the Prince, shall be seven weeks, and threescore and two weeks; the street shall be built again, and the wall even in troublous times. And after threescore and two weeks, shall Messiah be cut off, but not for himself. And the people of the prince that shall come, shall destroy the city and the sanctuary; and the end thereof shall be with a flood; and unto the end of the war desolations are determined. And he shall confirm the covenant with many for one week, and in the midst of the week, he shall cause the sacrifice and the oblation to cease, and for the overspreading of the abominations, he shall make it desolate, even until the consummation and that determined shall be poured upon the desolate." Dan. ix. 24–27.

This is one of the most remarkable prophecies in the Old Testament. In many parts of it there is obscurity, and critics have exhausted much time and patience in its elucidation. Still, however, the leading facts are remarkably clear. It evidently refers to

THE MESSIAH. 45

the Messiah. It both names and describes him. It also assigns a definite time for his appearance. This time was *sixty-nine weeks*, or *four hundred and eighty-three years*, after the issuing of the decree "to restore and to build Jerusalem;" or, it was *sixty-two weeks*, that is, *four hundred and thirty-four years*, after the complete re-establishment of Jerusalem and the Jewish polity.

To understand this better, it will be necessary to observe, that the Jews had two kinds of weeks, one of *days*, including seven days; and another of *years*, including *seven years*. Lev. xxv. 8. It is evident, that the former kind of weeks cannot be meant; for seventy weeks of *days*, which would be less than a year and a half, would be entirely too short a time, even to build Jerusalem, much less to complete what the prophet mentions, as occurring long after that event. The prophet must therefore speak of *weeks of years*. Seventy of such weeks would make *four hundred and ninety years*; which is the whole space of time specified in the prophecy.

This four hundred and ninety years was to begin, "from the going forth of the commandment to restore and to build Jerusalem." The chief difficulty in the application of the prophecy is, that there were no less than *four* decrees, overspreading a space of at least *eighty-four* years, which were issued by the Persian kings, in reference to the restoration of the Jews. The first of these was published by Cyrus, (Ezra i.) in the first year of his reign, and one year after Daniel was favoured with this revelation. Dan. ix. 1. The second was published by Darius Hystaspis. (Ezra vi.) about sixteen years later. A third was issued by Artaxerxes, son of Xerxes, in the seventh year of his reign, (Ezra vii. 1,) which was fifty-five years after the one issued by Darius, and seventy-one after that issued by Cyrus. Artaxerxes also delivered the fourth decree to Nehemiah, in the twentieth year of his reign. Neh. ii. 1.

Cyrus founded the Persian empire about the year 536 before Christ. Now, if this prophecy be applied

5*

to the edict published by him in the first year of his reign, it will fall short of the vulgar Christian era by *forty-six years.* So also, if it be applied to the edict of Darius, it will anticipate the period of the birth of Jesus, about *thirty years.* Prideaux, therefore, and many others have selected the *third* edict, or the one published in the seventh year of Artaxerxes, as the commencement of this prophetic period. According to the data above, this would bring the reckoning down to the year of our Lord 26, which was about the time that John the Baptist began his public ministry. There are some variations however, in the modes of computing dates. Prideaux, therefore, makes the termination of this prophecy, *precisely* coincident with the death of Jesus. "The beginning, therefore, says he, of the seventy weeks, or four hundred and ninety years of this prophecy, was in the month Nisan of the Jewish year, in the seventh year of Artaxerxes king of Persia, and in the 4256th of the Julian period, when Ezra had his commission; and the end of them fell in the very same month Nisan, in the 4746th of the Julian period, in which *very year* and *very month,* Christ our Lord suffered for us, and thereby completed the whole work of our salvation, there being just seventy weeks of years; or four hundred and ninety years from the one to the other." *

Usher, and many others, are best satisfied with the *last* edict, as the one with which to begin this prophecy. According to this mode of reckoning, the seventy weeks would end Anno Domini 38. Usher however, and they who think with him, employ *lunar* instead of *solar* months in computing these dates. They also make allowance for some few years during which Artaxerxes was associated with his father in the throne of Persia. Cruden remarks on this calculation as follows : " This hypothesis or system seems to be the most rational of any proposed by the ancients, and is adhered to, some small particulars ex-

---

* Connexions, Part I.

cepted, by the greatest part of interpreters and chronologers."*

It will be seen however that all of these interpretations terminate the prophecy within a period of 84 years of each other; that which takes its beginning from Cyrus, falling 46 years *before* Jesus was born, and that which places it in the 20th of Artaxerxes, terminating 38 years *after* that event. Now, if we make some allowances for the different methods of computing dates, and for some other inaccuracies in the calculations of critics and commentators, and especially if we keep it in mind, that some of these calculations, very nearly, if not precisely concur, with the epoch of Jesus; if, I say, we consider these facts, there certainly is a most remarkable coincidence between the *prophecy* and the *history* of the Evangelists. Indeed, we may affirm positively, that if this prophecy relate to the Messiah, of which there can be no doubt, then *must* the Messiah have appeared, *somewhere* between the 46th year before the Christian era, and the 38th after that era. Here is certainly a narrow, and considering the nature of the subject, a *very narrow* compass in which to look for the Saviour of the world. The date is no doubt, accurately given; and if we err, it is through our ignorance of some of the facts in the case. The error however, is so trifling, that no one need mistake the *person* to whom the prophet alludes.

But this prophecy was rendered more perspicuous, especially to the Jews, by being divided into three parts. During the first forty-nine years, the city of Jerusalem in particular and the Jewish commonwealth generally, were to be established. At the termination of the next four hundred and forty-one years, the Messiah was to appear. And sometime during the remaining *seven*, he was to die as a sacrifice for sin, and thus bring in "everlasting righteousness." Here are allusions to events so palpable, that one would think, the people among whom they occurred, could not possibly have misapplied the prophecy.

* Cruden on "weeks."

But in addition to the dates here given, there are other things mentioned, which unquestionably had their fulfilment in connexion with the personal history of Jesus. At or near the end of these seventy weeks, the Jewish nation was to be overwhelmed in a terrible war; their temple was to be profaned and burnt; their city and country laid in ruins, and the Jews themselves dispersed and scattered, until some remote period alluded to in the prophecy. Now, when did these events occur? Josephus, himself a Jew, fixes their date about forty years after the crucifixion of Jesus. His description of the events too, most wonderfully agrees with the prophecy. The Romans, after capturing every other important place in the land, laid siege to Jerusalem. The Jews held out an obstinate resistance. Subdued at length, however, by faction, by pestilence, and by famine, they surrendered to the conquerors. Their temple was destroyed, their city burnt and ploughed, and the nation, after suffering incalculable evils, was carried into a captivity, from which they have not even yet recovered!

If then, there be any thing in the dates of this prophecy to deceive us, the notorious facts which it contains would still strike conviction upon the mind. About the end of these seventy weeks, there did live an extraordinary personage, claiming to be the Messiah. He taught the most heavenly doctrines, he wrought the most illustrious miracles, he set the most perfect example, and he was eventually put to death by a public execution. The Jewish nation was soon afterwards conquered and scattered. Who was this extraordinary person? Who, if he was not the *Messiah*, the Saviour of the world?

The time then, according to prophecy, at which the Messiah was to appear, coinciding so accurately with that of Jesus of Nazareth, demonstrates, with almost positive certainty, that *he was the person* referred to by Daniel. Certain it is, that if this prophecy be not fulfilled in Jesus, it is difficult, if not impossible, to imagine another, in whom it either is to be or has been

THE MESSIAH.

fulfilled. Jerusalem has been already captured. The Jews have long ago been dispersed. The *seventy* weeks of Daniel therefore, have certainly *ended* many centuries ago. We are not then to look to the *future* for the fulfilment of these predictions. We must look to *the past*. And if to the past; where is there one, who can have any adequate claims to being the subject of these prophecies, but *Jesus?* He, and he *only* can claim them; and to him they most certainly refer.

CHAPTER V.

THE TESTIMONY OF INSPIRED WITNESSES.

That God may communicate supernatural knowledge to men, has been the uniform belief of all nations. Hence, the ancient Egyptians, Syrians, Chaldeans, Greeks, Romans, &c., had, not only temples, but *oracles*. They believed that certain consecrated persons had intercourse with the Deity, and could make known his will to others. Hence, even kings, often consulted such oracles about future events, especially in reference to the issues of battles, in which they were about to engage.

Among the Jews, belief in such divine inspiration, may be said to have been *universal*. It is true, many false prophets existed even among this people; their fabrications however, never destroyed the faith of the nation in the testimony of *well authenticated* prophecy. Hence, notwithstanding the number of the prophets of Baal who lived in' the days of Elijah, or of the impostors who lived in the days of Isaiah and Jeremiah, still, the national confidence was unshaken in the predictions of these faithful messengers of Jehovah. This confidence, too, in the truth of real prophecy, did not diminish among the Jews by the lapse of time; it rather increased. "We *know*," say they, in the days of Jesus, "that God spake unto Moses." John ix. 29. "For prophecy," says Peter, "came not in old time by the will of man, but holy men of God spake as they were moved by the Holy Ghost." 2 Peter i. 21.

Now, it happened, that when Jesus of Nazareth was on earth, no less than *five inspired persons*, of the very best reputation, bore witness to him as the Messiah. These were, Zacharias and Elizabeth, Simeon and Anna, and John the Baptist. Of the first two it is said, "they were both righteous before God, walking in all the commandments and ordinances of the Lord blameless." Luke i. 6. The testimony of Elizabeth is the following: "And she spake out with a loud voice, and said, Blessed art thou among women; and blessed is the fruit of thy womb. And whence is this to me, that the mother of *my Lord* should come to me?" Luke i. 42, 43. This testimony is not only explicit, but was spoken when Elizabeth "*was filled with the Holy Ghost.*"

The testimony of Zacharias is even more remarkable. For his unbelief, he had been made dumb for nearly a year. But upon writing the name of his son, *John*, his mouth was opened, he was filled with the Holy Ghost, and uttered the following prophetic language: "Blessed be the Lord God of Israel; for he hath visited and redeemed his people, and hath raised up for us *an horn of salvation* in the house of his servant David." "And thou, child, shalt be called the prophet of the highest; for thou shalt go before the face of the *Lord* to prepare his ways." Luke i. 68, 69, 76. In this prediction, Zacharias distinctly recognizes the son of Mary, as the Christ, that had been long promised.

Forty days after the birth of the infant Jesus, his parents, according to the law of Moses, presented him in the temple to the Lord. There was living at Jerusalem at the time, a very remarkable and pious Jew by the name of Simeon. To him it had been revealed, that he should not depart hence, until he had seen the Messiah. No doubt, this good man was filled with much anxiety, about the fulfilment of this revelation. He, probaby too, expected to behold in the person of the Messiah something remarkable, something unearthly. But while entering the temple along with Joseph and Mary, the Holy Ghost indicated to him, that the *babe* then brought in, was the Messiah he was to see. Taking the child at once in his arms, he exclaimed, "Lord, now lettest thou thy servant depart in peace, according to thy word; for mine eyes have seen thy salvation, which thou hast prepared before the face of all people; a light to lighten the Gentiles and the glory of thy people Israel." Luke ii. 29–32.

Scarcely had Simeon uttered these remarkable words, when a certain prophetess, by the name of Anna, drew nigh. She was a widow of more than fourscore years, and "departed not from the temple, but served God with fastings and prayers night and day." This woman also gave thanks to God at the sight of the babe; "and spake of him to all them that looked for redemption in Israel." Luke ii. 36–38.

The fullest and most remarkable inspired and contemporaneous testimony, however, is that of John, commonly called the Baptist. The mission of John, as the immediate precursor of the Messiah, had been predicted, both by Isaiah, (xl.,) and Malachi, (iv.) His birth, like that of Isaac, occurred when his parents were in extreme age. During the early part of his life, he seems to have lived in very great seclusion from society. And notwithstanding the remarkable occurrences attending his birth and that of Jesus, and the relationship between them, he seems to have had no personal knowledge of the latter, until the time of his baptism. John i. 33.

In the fifteenth year of Tiberius Cæsar, Pontius Pilate being governor of Judea, and Herod Antipas, Tetrarch of Galilee, John began his public ministry. His dress was remarkably simple, resembling that of the ancient prophets, and his mode of living very abstemious. The object of his ministry was, to reform the Jewish nation, and to designate to them the *person of the Messiah*. He enjoined the strictest morality, and condemned with an unsparing zeal, the vices of the times. He addressed all classes of men; and was equally faithful to scribes and pharisees, as to the humblest Jew; to the haughty Herod, as to the mercenary soldier. The influence of his ministry was powerful; and what made it more remarkable was, that it was accompanied with the solemn rite of baptism. Great multitudes flocked to hear him; and not only to hear him, but to receive his baptism. "Then went there out to him," says Matthew, "Jerusalem and all Judea, and all the region round about Jordan, and were baptized of him in Jordan, confessing their sins." Matt. iii. 5, 6. Even king Herod "feared him, knowing that he was a just man, and an holy, and observed him: and when he heard him, he did many things, and heard him gladly." Matt. vi. 20. He was for a time "a burning and shining light" among the Jews, being esteemed by all who knew him, not only a good man, but "a *prophet.*" Matt. xxi. 26. And, if it were proper here to employ the testimony of Jesus to his character, we would put upon him the climax of praise, by saying, "Among them that are born of women, there hath not arisen a greater, than John the Baptist." Matt. xi. 11. Such is the character of the witness; such the high estimation in which he was held at the time. What then is his testimony?

When the Jewish nation, from the peculiar life and preaching of John, began to agitate the question, whether he were not the Christ, his reply was, "I indeed baptize you with water: but one mightier than I cometh, the latchet of whose shoes I am not worthy to unloose: he shall baptize you with the Holy Ghost and with fire." Luke iii. 16. But a short time after this, John, while contemplating Jesus as he approached him said, " Behold the Lamb of God which taketh away the sin of the world. This is he, of whom I said, after me cometh a man which is preferred before me: for he was before me. And I knew him not, but He that sent me to baptize with water, the same said unto me, Upon whom thou shalt see the Spirit descending and remaining on him, the same is he which baptizeth with the Holy Ghost. And I saw and bare record that this is *the Son of God.*" Surely no testimony could be more explicit, as none at the time was more weighty, than this of John. Jesus is publicly designated *as the Messiah*, and the attention of the people, as it always ought to be, is turned away from the mere servant, to the contemplation of the great Master and Lord of all.

Now, if the express and well authenticated testimony of *one inspired witness*, is enough to establish any matter of fact whatever, the carefully recorded testimony of *five* such witnesses, all concurring in the same fact, ought much more to establish any point in which they thus agree. Here then are five such witnesses, all attesting, that Jesus of Nazareth is the Christ, the Son of the living God. Surely then, that incredulity must approximate even to madness, which deliberately rejects evidence of this sacred and weighty character.

CHAPTER VI.

DIRECT TESTIMONY FROM HEAVEN.

There are several instances recorded in the Old Testament Scriptures, in which Jehovah, by a *public acknowledgment*, recognized certain persons as his servants. Thus, when the Israelites were at mount Sinai, God made, in their view, a public and awful manifestation of his presence and glory on the top of that mountain, and thus recognized, in the strongest possible manner, the mission of Moses. Exod. xix. Thus also at mount Carmel, there was a visible and public recognition on the part of Jehovah, that Elijah was a true prophet, and that his ministry was directed by the will of heaven. 1 Kings xviii. There are also many other cases, in which God was pleased directly to interpose in the attestation of his truth.

It is not wonderful then, that testimony of this kind should be vouchsafed to Jesus, if he were indeed the Messiah. There are *three* instances of this sort recorded by the Evangelists. The first occurred at his baptism: "And Jesus, when he was baptized, went up straightway out of the water: and, lo, the heavens were opened unto him; and he saw the Spirit of God descending like a dove, and lighting upon him. And, lo, a voice from heaven, saying; *This is my beloved Son, in whom I am well pleased."* Matt. iii. 16, 17. This recognition of Jesus as the Messiah, was of the most public nature. Thousands of Jews were spectators of the baptism of Jesus; and this extraordinary manifestation was made in their presence. Bloomfield supposes that the opening of the heavens here spoken of, was "a preternatural light" which accompanied the descent of the Spirit upon Jesus; and that the allusion to the *dove*, does not suppose a *natural* dove, or the Spirit in *shape* of a dove; but refers to "the *gentle* and *hovering* manner," in which this extraordinary light rested upon Jesus.* The person spoken of as hearing the voice, is no doubt John. It was to assure his mind in the clearest manner possible, of the person of the Messiah, that this extraordinary manifestation was given. But, whether we suppose the voice to have been intelligible only to John, or to have been understood at once by the spectators, still the miracle remains unimpaired, and the actual and heavenly attestation to Jesus, as the Son of God, continues an authenticated and well established fact.

The second instance of this kind occurred when Jesus was spending a night in devotion, with three of his disciples, on one of the mountains of Galilee, by many supposed to be Tabor, by others, one of the peaks of Hermon. Sometime during the night, probably near morning, when the disciples were sleeping, a cloud of extraordinary glory covered the top of the mountain. Such was its brightness, that the disciples seem to have been awaked by it. Luke ix. 32. When thus aroused, they beheld not only the glorious cloud, but three glorious forms before them. Their Master had in the meantime, entirely changed his appearance, becoming so luminous and bright, that they could scarcely gaze upon him. Besides him, there were Moses and Elias, whose countenances were also overcast with the brightest glory. The disciples, amazed at the extraordinary scene, and experiencing a peculiar delight at the unusual glory before them, desired to dwell upon the top of the mountain. But while they were thus ravished and captivated with the heavenly glory they were permitted to behold, a voice issued from the cloud, saying, "*This is my beloved Son in whom I am well pleased; hear ye him.*" Matt. xvii.

Such was the extraordinary splendour of this scene, and such its testimony to the Messiahship of Jesus, that

---

* In loco.

THE MESSIAH. 57

we find the apostle Peter, who was one of the spectators, alluding to it long afterwards, as proof of this very fact. " For, says he, we have not followed cunningly devised fables, when we made known to you the power and coming of our Lord Jesus Christ, but were eye-witnesses of his Majesty. For he received from God the Father honour and glory, when there came such a voice to him from the excellent glory, 'This is my beloved Son in whom I am well pleased.' And this voice which came from heaven, *we heard*, when we were with him in the holy mount." 2 Pet. i. 16–18.

Here then are *three* credible witnesses, Peter, James, and John, who were *eye-witnesses* of this glorious display, and who actually *heard* the voice from heaven, recognizing Jesus as the Christ. And so universally was the truth of this vision believed among the early Christians, that Matthew, Mark, and Luke, have each of them inserted it in his history of Jesus.

The last instance of such divine and heavenly attestation to the Messiahship of Jesus is recorded by John. Jesus had just uttered the prayer, " Father, glorify thy name. Then came there a voice from heaven, saying, *I have both glorified it; and will glorify it again.* The people therefore that stood by, said it thundered. Others said, an angel spake unto him." John vii. 28, 29. Doddridge paraphrases the passage thus, "Then at that very instant, while he was speaking, there came a voice from heaven which said, I have both already glorified it by the whole of thy ministry thus far; and I will glorify it again in a more signal manner, by what yet remains before thee. The multitude, therefore, who stood by and heard it, though not all in a manner equally distinct, were perfectly astonished at the awful sound; and some among them said it thundered, while others, who were nearer, said that an angel spake to him from heaven. But Jesus answered and said to his disciples, who stood near and distinctly heard it, This voice from heaven came not chiefly for my sake but for yours, that you may not be offended at the treatment I shall meet with, and quit

6*

your hope in me, on account of any of the sufferings that are coming upon me."*

Here, then, are three distinct and important instances in which the Lord, Jehovah, by an audible voice from heaven, bore witness to the peculiar character of Jesus. He acknowledged him on the banks of the Jordan before assembled multitudes; he acknowledged him in a yet more glorious manner on the top of Tabor, or of Hermon; and he acknowledged him, near the close of his ministry, in the neighbourhood of Jerusalem, and in the presence of many spectators and witnesses. If then the ancient Jew, who witnessed the Divine recognition of Moses and of Elijah, entertained no doubt that God spake by them, with what just pretence can the modern Jew, or the unbeliever, deny the testimony which proves even from heaven itself, that Jesus is the Christ, the Son of the living God?

Nor can the evidence above alluded to, be evaded, by supposing that either these voices from heaven were the inventions of the Evangelists, or the auricular illusions of the original witnesses. The Evangelists, if not inspired, were at least *honest* historians. No one can read their statements, especially in connexion with each other, and not perceive every possible mark of historical fidelity. But if honest, they have stated these facts only upon what they considered adequate testimony. That they were competent judges of such testimony, no one can doubt, who considers, either their relation to the original parties, or the general accuracy in their various narrations. They evidently state, therefore, what was generally *believed* in their day to have taken place.

Nor can we suppose the original witnesses to have been deceived. The words uttered were entirely intelligible; they were heard by several, if not by many persons; and these persons were men of the highest character, men who taught the purest doctrines, who lived the most exemplary lives, and some of whom

* In loco.

sealed their testimony with their blood. How is it possible for so many men, of such irreproachable character, on so many occasions, to have been deceived? Surely the hypothesis which admits such deception, must not only disprove all similar communications mentioned in the Old Testament, but must also deny that the ear is a safe guide in all matters of hearing and sound.

The evidence then cannot be set aside by either supposition. It must, therefore, be true. But if true, then has Jehovah announced from heaven, by an audible voice, and at three different times, that *Jesus is the Christ, the Son of the living God.*

CHAPTER VII.

THE PERSONAL TESTIMONY OF JESUS.

There is a general disposition among mankind, to receive as true, what is delivered upon personal testimony, especially if the person testifying is known to be honest, and the fact he relates be in itself credible. Hence, the degree of credit with which we receive the promises and statements of friends. Hence, the confidence reposed in the testimony given by the eye-witnesses of any fact whatever. It is too, upon this principle, that witnesses are allowed to give testimony upon the most important matters in law; and that men are often permitted, in their own behalf to affirm upon oath, certain matters of fact, which it is important for them to establish. Ignorance, fraud, the habit of prevarication, and the absurdity of the thing stated, are the most common causes of disbelief. Now none of these causes operate to invalidate the testimony of Jesus concerning himself. He certainly was not ignorant; for even his enemies were astonished at his wisdom and knowledge. Nor was he influenced by any selfish or base motives. Such was the benevolent and holy character of his life, that a motive like this cannot, with the least degree of probability, be imputed to him. Nor was he in the habit of prevarication; nor was the thing itself incredible. The Jews had long been expecting a Messiah. It was a part of their national faith, to look forward to his appearance. Certainly then, the actual manifestation of the Messiah among them, was not a thing in itself incredible. There is no reason, then, why the testimony of Jesus concerning himself should be rejected.

This testimony to his own Messiahship was given by Jesus during the whole of his life; and it was for bearing this testimony that he was condemned to suffer death.

In the first place, he never *denied* that he was the Messiah. There were numerous occasions when he might have done so. He was often placed in circumstances, when it would seem to be his interest, to have done so. But on no occasion whatever, does he at all intimate, that he is *not* the Messiah. Under the circumstances too, in which he was placed, this very *silence* of Jesus is testimony to the fact. Men regarded him as the Messiah. They worshipped him as the Son of God. They hailed him as the King of the Jews. All this he received as *his due*, never once intimating, as John the Baptist had done, that the people were mistaken in his character, and that they were heaping upon him honours which he did not deserve.

Jesus too, as we shall see more fully hereafter, *acted* the character of the Messiah. In his manners, in his doctrine, in his works, in the tone of authority with which he spake, in every thing, there is such an exercise of the Messianic prerogatives, such an exhibition of more than human pretensions, as to leave no doubt about his own impressions and convictions on this subject.

But there is, as recorded in the gospels, an abundance of *express personal testimony* given by Jesus, to his Messiahship. When the woman of Samaria had said, "I know that Messias cometh, and that when he is come, he will teach us all things;" the reply of Jesus was, "I that speak unto thee *am he*." John iv. 26. When John the Baptist sent two of his disciples to inquire of Jesus, whether he was the one about to come, or whether they should look for another; the answer given was, "Go, and show John again those things which ye do hear and see. The blind receive their sight, and the lame walk, the lepers are cleansed and the deaf hear; the dead are raised up, and the poor have the gospel preached unto them." Matt. xi. 5. The answer of Jesus is here given in the *affirmative;* and he appeals to his *works* as proofs of the fact.

When Peter, on another occasion, had expressed it as his belief, and as the belief of his fellow disciples, that his Master was the Christ, the Son of the living God, the reply of Jesus was, "Blessed art thou, Simon Barjona, for flesh and blood hath not revealed it unto thee, but my Father which is in heaven." Matt. xvi. 17. When too, Nathanael had said to Jesus, "Rabbi, thou art the Son of God, thou art the King of Israel;" the answer returned was, "Because I said I saw thee under the fig tree, believest thou? Thou shalt see greater things than these." John i. 50.

Such testimony to his Messiahship, Jesus uniformly gave to the Jews, and to the multitudes who thronged his ministry. He delivered it also to Pilate, at his examination, and it was his *solemn asseveration upon oath* before the Sanhedrim. "And the High Priest answered and said unto him, I adjure thee by the living God, that thou tell us, whether thou be the Christ, the Son of God. Jesus saith unto him, "*Thou hast said;*" Matt. xxvii. 64; that is, *I am the Christ.*

If, then, there be any case, in which a man may be allowed to speak for himself, and if there be any thing in moral virtue to create confidence in human testimony, in short, if there be any thing in the life and character of Jesus, upon which to base his high claims to Messiahship, then is *his own testimony* to those claims of the very highest character, and worthy of universal belief.

CHAPTER VIII.

THE MIRACLES OF JESUS.

A miracle is defined to be, "a supernatural operation performed alone by God." * The power, therefore, to perform miracles, is evidence, that a man is at least sent from God.

How far miracles may be *imitated* by the art and cunning of man, it is difficult to say : no *real* miracle however, can be performed in this way. The magicians of Egypt were enabled for a time to counterfeit the wonders wrought by Moses. But, they soon came to the end of their art, and were compelled to exclaim, " This is the finger of God." Exod. viii. 19.

The proof by which the reality of a miracle is established, is the *senses of the human body*. It is by these senses, that the regular operation of the laws of nature is known. It must therefore be, by the same means, that a *reversal* or *suspension* of those laws is ascertained. This however applies to the immediate or first witnesses of a miracle. Those who live at a distance, or who live in later ages, must depend upon *human testimony* for their belief in miracles. It is in this way that the whole nation of the Israelites credit the miracles of Moses; and it is in this way, that we must yield our assent to the miracles of Jesus. The Apostles and multitudes who witnessed these miracles, certainly had every possible opportunity for judging of their reality. These original witnesses, therefore, could not have been themselves deceived. Nor can we suppose, that they have *designed* to deceive us. The doctrines they taught, the lives they

* Cruden in verbo.

lived, and above all, the influence of Christianity upon the world, all convince us, that they were honest and credible witnesses. We receive therefore, as true, the miracles recorded in the Holy Scriptures, upon the same sort of evidence that we receive other similar truths.

The miracles performed by Jesus differed in several respects, from those wrought either by the Prophets or Apostles. They were in the first place *universally benevolent* in their design and character. This was not *always* the case with miracles wrought by others. Many of the miracles of Moses were of a *judicial* and *punitory* nature. His principal ones were wrought, in executing the *judgments* of God upon Pharaoh, and upon Egypt. Elijah also, called down fire from heaven, upon the companies sent by the King of Israel to arrest him. 2 Kings i. And even the miracle at Carmel resulted in the *slaughter* of all the prophets of Baal.

Several of the miracles too of the Apostles, were of a similar character. One performed by Peter was the smiting to death of two persons, Ananias and Sapphira. Acts v. Another wrought by Paul, was the infliction of *blindness* upon a certain false prophet. Acts xiii. On the contrary, the miracles of Jesus were universally *benevolent* in their character. He heals the sick; gives hearing to the deaf; sight to the blind; and causes the lame to leap for joy. The only instance, in which the least imputation of the want of benevolence can be alleged, is the miracle which resulted in the destruction of the swine at Gadara. Nor is this an exception. It was the transfer of demons from *a man* to swine. It was also, simply *allowed*, and that upon the earnest request of the evil spirits themselves. The swine-herds are also supposed to have been employed in an *illicit* trade at the time. The main object, however, of this permission, was to arouse the attention of the people of Gadara to his Gospel, and to himself, as the Messiah. He certainly exhibited nothing malignant in feeling toward the Gadarenes, when upon a simple *request* he left their borders.

Matt. viii. 34. No, there is no malignity in all the wonderful works wrought by Jesus. Do the Nazarenes attempt to cast him down headlong from the brow of the hill on which their city was built? He escapes from them miraculously, but injures none of them. Luke iv. 29. Do John and James petition that fire should be called down from heaven upon a city of the Samaritans, because they would not receive him? His reply is, "The son of man is not come to destroy men's lives, but to save them." Luke ix. 56. Does Judas come with a band of men to arrest him, while engaged at midnight in his devotions? Although the simple announcement, "*I am he,*" causes his enemies to fall to the ground, still he works no miracle either to extricate himself, or to punish them.

The miracles of Jesus were also more *numerous* than those wrought by others. His three years' ministry was but a constant succession of miracles. He performs them in Galilee, in Judea, in the temple, in the synagogue, in private houses, in the street, on the high-way, in the wilderness, on the sea. He often performed great numbers of them in a few hours on the same day. What a catalogue, for instance, is the following: "And they brought unto him all sick people that were taken with divers diseases and torments, and those which were possessed with devils, and those which were lunatic, and those that had the palsy; and *he healed them.*" Matt. iv. 24. Or the following: "And when the men of that place had knowledge of him, they sent out into all that country round about, and brought unto him all that were diseased, and besought him that they might only touch the hem of his garment, and *as many as touched were made perfectly whole.*" Matt. xiv. 35, 36. Or the following: "And great multitudes came unto him, having with them those that were lame, blind, dumb, maimed, and many others; and cast them down at Jesus' feet, and *he healed them!*" Matt. xv. 30. Or, still the following: "And the blind and the lame came to him in the temple, and *he healed them!*" Matt.

xxi. 14. What mighty works are here crowded together! What illustrious miracles here follow each other in rapid succession! No other ever performed so many, or so many together.

The miracles of Jesus were generally *superior* to those performed by others. He removed not only the ordinary bodily infirmities of men, but their most permanent and deep-rooted diseases and sufferings. Leprosies, palsies, lunacies, deafness, blindness, lameness, and similar afflictions, were among his ordinary cures. He delivered the bodies of men from satanic power, a power which seems to have been exerted at that time, with peculiar malignity. He raised the *dead;* and thus, not only arrested the power of corporeal corruption, but called back the spirit, from its invisible abode to its bodily home. He exercised also an absolute power over the *elements.* He walked upon the waters, and by a word he calmed their wildest commotions. He multiplied a few loaves and fishes, so that several thousands were fed by them! Such were some of the mighty works of Jesus of Nazareth. He stood upon the bosom of nature as its God and Author, controlling and directing all things simply by the energy of *his will.* " He spake and it was done, he commanded and it stood fast."

The miracles of Jesus differed also from those of the ancient prophets in what may be termed their *universality.* Most of the miracles of the Old Testament, were confined to the Israelites. Jesus seemed to take peculiar pleasure in overstepping this boundary of nationality, that he might exercise his miraculous power among Gentiles as well as Jews. He goes at the bidding of a *heathen* centurion, he yields at the call of a *Syrian* woman, and cures with delight a *Samaritan* leper. None are sent empty away; and to all, bond or free, Greek or Jew, his answer is, " Be it to thee, according to thy faith."

But that which distinguishes the miracles of Jesus more than any thing else is, the *God-like manner* in which they were performed. When Moses brings darkness upon Egypt; when he divides the sea, and when he furnishes water from the rock of Horeb, he is evidently but an *instrument*, a mere *servant*, in the whole matter. He is told what to do, and informed what will take place. *His own will* had nothing to do with the effect produced, save only so far as he obeyed the Being commanding him. Any other person or creature, would have answered just as well as Moses, in the history of the miracle. It was not his work but God's; it was not his will, but God's. He was a mere *mouth*, or a mere *hand* for another. The same is true of all the miracles performed, by both the prophets and Apostles. Does Elijah raise the son of the widow of Zarephath! He stretches himself three times upon the child, and calls upon the Lord to restore him to life. 1 Kings xvii. Does Isaiah bring the shadow ten degrees backward upon the dial of Ahaz! It is done only after he "had cried unto the Lord." 2 Kings xx. Does Peter heal the cripple at the beautiful gate of the temple? Acts iii. He acknowledges himself, that it was the *name of another* by which the miracle was wrought. And so of all the rest.

The miracles of Jesus, however, were differently performed. Does a leper petition for a cure? The reply is, " *Be clean;*" and immediately the leprosy departs. Does a centurion desire his servant to be healed? " *Be it unto thee according to thy faith,*" is the brief reply. Does a blind man seek for sight? The command is given to the sightless balls, " *Be opened;*" and vision is restored. Are devils to be cast out? " *Come out of him,*" is the command, and the evil spirits obey. Are the waves of the sea to be quieted? There is no prayer, no instrumentality used; but simply the command issued, " *Peace, be still.*" Is Lazarus to be raised from the dead? " *Lazarus, come forth*" is the fiat, and the dead is raised. And so of all the miracles of Jesus. There is a directness in them, an energy, a *power*, such as we behold no where else. Indeed, to find the like, we must go back to the history of the creation, and place the first and second chapters of Genesis, beside the gospels of the Evangelists, as affording the only *actual resemblance* in all the book of God. In the former, it is said, "Let there be light"—"Let there be a firmament"—"Let the dry land appear"—and the results follow immediately upon the issuing of the command. There is no delay, no hesitation. The simple *will* of the Creator produces the effect intended. Just so in the history of Jesus. The bare exercise of *his will*, without the intervention of any means whatever, effects the end contemplated. His word is power, his volition accomplishment. There is no resistance, no hinderance, no delay. Diseases, death, the elements, men, and devils, all yield to his *absolute authority*.

What should be remarked too, in this matter is, that Jesus was regarded by those around him, as the *independent dispenser* of such miraculous powers. He is so addressed by the sick who come to him, or by their friends who petition for them. "Lord, if *thou wilt* thou canst make me clean," is the manner in which the leper addresses him. "*Speak the word only*, and my servant shall be whole," is the language of the Centurion. "*Have mercy on us*," is the cry of the blind men. And, if at any time, there be a reserve, or the least hesitancy of faith, it is considered as derogatory to the character of Jesus. Such doubt must be abandoned, such reserve must be dissipated, before the miracle is wrought. The *absolute power* of Jesus, and the *entire independence of his will*, must first be recognized and trusted in, or else the intimation is given that the cure will not be effected. Matt. ix. 28; xiii. 58. Mark ix. 22, 23.

Nor is this all; not only did Jesus work miracles in this absolute manner, and not only was he considered by those around him, as the sole and independent *dispenser* of such influences, he also *communicated* miraculous powers to others. To the twelve, it is said, "he gave power against unclean spirits, to cast them out, and to heal all manner of sickness and all manner of diseases." Matt. x. 1. The same powers were also given to the seventy; for,

THE MESSIAH. 69

upon their return, they reported, "Lord, even the devils are subject to us *through thy word.*" Luke x. 17. It is true, that the Apostles and the seventy did not pretend to work any miracles, but in *subserviency to Jesus.* They spake in *the name* of their Master; they commanded through *his power.* They were but instruments; and in this respect, the miracles wrought by them, resembled all others performed by mere human instrumentality. The point to be observed here however, is, that Jesus, with the same *absolute independence* with which he himself wrought miracles, communicated also these supernatural endowments to others. Not that he could give, or men receive, either the *offices* or the *absolute powers* which he himself possessed. But in the same manner, in which Jehovah endued Moses, or Elijah, or any of the ancients, with power to work miracles in the same manner, did Jesus empower his disciples. He not only wielded an absolute control himself over natural causes and effects, but he permitted others in his name, and by his authority, to do the same thing. He not only exercised in his own person a *governing will* over all things around him, but he exercised such will also by means of others.

Such were the miracles of Jesus of Nazareth. More benevolent than all others, they were also greater; more numerous, they were also performed in a more God-like manner. The only conclusion to to which reason can come concerning them is, either that Divinity dwelt in humanity, in the person of Jesus, or that the Godhead gave to human nature *discretionary powers* in the use of its sole and absolute prerogatives. Whether the mystery be greater in the one case than in the other, or whether the one be more credible than the other, is left for each to decide for himself. But of this we are certain, that if there be a Christ yet to come, he cannot do *greater* miracles, or miracles in a manner *more divine,* than Jesus of Nazareth hath already done. John vii. 31. If miracles then, or the manner of performing them,

7*

can furnish evidence to the truth of Messiahship, then is the Messiahship of Jesus attested in the strongest and fullest manner possible. What greater works can any future Messiah perform? What higher prerogatives can he exert? What other laws of nature can he control? Surely the works of Jesus proclaim, as with the voice of thunder, that he is "the Son of God, the King of Israel."

CHAPTER IX.

THE CHARACTER OF JESUS.

We naturally expect that character should be adapted to office. In a parent we expect providence, in a friend fidelity, in a labourer industry, in a soldier bravery, in a judge justice, in a scholar learning, and in a king or governor wisdom and integrity. And whenever this expectation is disappointed, the mind experiences a sense of pain, resulting from the consideration of the unadaptedness of the office-holder to the office, of the agent to the end designed.

With men, and in all human things, incongruities of this kind often happen. How frequent is it, that judges are unjust, professed scholars unlearned, rulers weak, and friends treacherous! But, when God himself designates an officer to an office, or creates an agent for an end, we may calculate upon a wonderful adaptedness, between the character of the person chosen, and the sphere to be filled by him. Are Bezaleel and Aholiab appointed by Jehovah to build the tabernacle? God previously "fills them with wisdom, and understanding, and knowledge, in all manner of workmanship." Ex. xxxi. Is the youthful David chosen from the sheepfold, at Bethlehem, to be king over Israel? The Spirit of God accompanies the oil of consecration, and the inexperienced shepherd-boy is so endowed and trained, as to be fitted to occupy the throne in Israel. 1 Sam. xvi. Is Jehu designated as the instrument of executing the vengeance of God upon the impious house of Ahab? His natural vindictiveness of temper, his bold and fiery zeal, admirably qualify him for the bloody drama through which he was called to pass. 2 Kings ix. And so of all other instruments, directly chosen of God, to fulfil his pleasure in the history of human life.

These remarks must of course have a peculiar application to the personal character of the Messiah He was to rear a celestial tabernacle; to sway a divine sceptre. His office was to be the highest of all—his duties the most difficult of all. His character therefore must be proportionably exalted.

And what is here a deduction of reason, is matter of positive revelation. "Behold, saith the Lord, my servant whom I uphold; mine elect in whom my soul delighteth; I have put my Spirit upon him: he shall bring forth judgment to the Gentiles. He shall not cry, nor lift up, nor cause his voice to be heard in the street. A bruised reed shall he not break, and the smoking flax shall he not quench; he shall bring forth judgment unto truth. He shall not fail nor be discouraged, till he have set judgment in the earth, and the isles shall wait for his law." Isaiah xlii. Here it is expressly announced, that the character of the Messiah is to be peculiar, and wonderfully adapted to the exalted office he was appointed to fill.

It must be admitted that there is great difficulty in forming suitable conceptions of the appropriate character of a Saviour. We know not altogether what such an office requires. The office of a parent, of a judge, of a teacher, or ruler, is familiar to us. But when we consider an office, whose relations are chiefly spiritual, and which exercises its influence principally in eternity, we are at a loss rightly to conceive of its nature, and justly to estimate its magnitude.

Nor is this all. Even the *earthly* developments of this office are not as yet fully made known. How ill prepared was the ancient Jew to appreciate the events and histories of the new dispensation! And how disqualified are we to enter with minuteness and certainty into the hidden purposes of God, or to delineate with historical accuracy, the final results of unfulfilled prophecy! Even if Jesus be the Messiah, the whole of his character has not as yet been given; and there may be much in the future still to corrobo-

THE MESSIAH.

rate prophecy, and to furnish higher evidence than we now have, that the Son of Mary is the promised Christ, the Saviour of men.

But, abating these difficulties, what is the character which a Saviour for men might be expected to possess? This is best learned by considering the condition of the persons to be saved. If a man's condition were one of pecuniary embarrassment and bankruptcy, he would require in a helper, funds; if it were one of disease, he would require medical skill; if of sorrow, he would need a kind and sympathizing heart. Now, men are vicious and depraved; with them passion is predominant, and reason enslaved; inclination is law, and truth and duty trampled under foot. The character of a Saviour, therefore, for such, must tend to counteract this state of things. It must inspire a love for duty, a desire for holiness. It must awaken conscience and arouse all the high moral faculties of the soul. If a skilful general is commanding a cowardly army, he must show in himself contempt of danger, if he would inspire them with courage. And if Jesus would awaken in the breasts of sinners a love for moral virtue, they must find it first in his own example.

And, here, we rejoice to say it, the *only perfect model of moral virtue ever described or exemplified on earth*, is presented to us by the Evangelists in the *life of Jesus.* Here it exists in absolute solitariness, without a rival or another. Here, and here alone, we find a character with every fault absent, with every virtue present.

Cicero enters a complaint against ancient philosophers in the following language: "How rare is it, says he, to find a philosopher with a mind and life so regulated as reason requires, who deems his own doctrine, not a parade of science, but a rule of life; who yields obedience to himself, and deference to his own decrees. Whereas, how common to see some so full of vanity and ostentation, that it had been better for them not to have been taught; some the votaries of money; some of glory; many the slaves of their passions; so that their lives are strangely at war with their language."* An elegant writer too, of our own times, bears similar testimony to the practical results of ancient philosophy: "They promised what was impracticable; they despised what was practicable; they filled the world with long words and long beards, and they left it as ignorant and as wicked as they found it."†

Nor have modern times produced a solitary instance of absolutely perfect human character. Most of the best men lack many virtues; multitudes of them exhibit real faults and vices. How often in biographies do we find remarks like the following: "The characteristic peculiarity of his intellect was the union of great powers with *low prejudices.*‡ Or the following: "He had one fault, which of all human faults is most rarely found in company with true greatness— he was *extremely affected.*"§ So Cicero notes the vanity of Demosthenes, who confessed that he was delighted when a female water-carrier said, as he passed—" There goes that Demosthenes."‖

Similar complaints are alleged by inspiration against the worthies among the Israelites—against patriarchs, prophets, and apostles. Adam sinned when in innocence; Abraham prevaricated; Jacob was guilty of falsehood; Moses spake unadvisedly with his lips; David was guilty of even foul crimes; Peter was cowardly, and Paul and Barnabas quarrelled. There is, even on the page of revelation, but one perfect character, but one without a fault, but one possessing every virtue, and *that is the character of Jesus.*

It may very much be questioned, whether, if all human characters were put in common, and one had the privilege and the power to combine from the mass *one perfect man,* it could be done. Their virtues would be so defective, and their vices so subtle, that the effort would resemble that of a sculptor

---

* Tusculan Questions.   † Macaulay—Life of Lord Bacon.
‡ Macaulay—Johnson.   § Macaulay—Pitt.
‖ Tus. Questions.—Happiness.

attempting to produce a statue of marble from a forest of trees; or of a philosopher attempting to find one immortal in a world of mortals.

Indeed, we may go a step further and say, that even if men were allowed to draw from the world of absolute ideality—if they should forsake realities and proceed to conceptions of their own—it is doubtful whether a man could be found, who could either paint, chisel, or write the *perfect model of a perfect man.* Each inventor would be himself so much under the influence of human prejudices and infirmities, that he would be likely never to exhibit a specimen, which even the rest of his species would pronounce absolutely perfect. How can the blind construct a rainbow, or the deaf originate an anthem, or erring mortals, unless divinely inspired, portray one *unerring man?* But in the gospel we have both the *original* and the *description,* the faultless character, and its faultless delineation.

In all merely human biographies, we always discover, not only the faults of him whose life is given, but the faults of the writer by whom the character is drawn, either malignity, or partiality, or prejudice, or bigotry, or ignorance, is permitted to throw colourings upon the page, which the pen of independent truth could never sanction. Now virtues are magnified, now vices are concealed. Now facts are presented in a distorted condition, and now motives are ascribed to conduct which never existed. Now one character wears all the splendours of angelic perfection, now another is clothed in the vices of Apolyon.

Not like these are the narrations of inspired men. They speak as if they saw the throne of judgment, or as if they had been solemnly sworn in the court of Heaven. Their inspiration too, enables them to see all the facts, and to see them *as they are.* Hence they conceal nothing, invent nothing; but with the accuracy of a skilful surgeon's knife, following every muscle and nerve in the human body, they exhibit the character as it is, and not as they think it ought to be. Hence they speak as fearlessly of Lot's incest, as of his escape from Sodom; of Abraham's prevarication, as of his offering his son Isaac; of David's adultery as of his conquest over Goliath; of Peter's denial of his Master, as of his sermon on the day of Pentecost.

It was into the hands of writers like these that the character of Jesus was committed for portrayal. Nor have they failed to do it justice. Yet amid the glory of the most illustrious miracles—under the breath of a fame resembling the roarings of the whirlwind—in constant view of a character to which there had never been even an approximation, and while describing too the actions of their own Master, whom they devotedly loved, there are no exaggerations, no swellings of vanity, no attempt at ingenuity, no parade, no show! With the simplicity with which the sunbeam falls upon the flower in spring, or the drop of rain rests upon the unfolded leaf, do they tell and narrate all just as it happened. Their pens seem to have been steel, their arms iron, and their hearts stone. One never thinks of the writer, perhaps does not recognize his presence, but seems in his own person to be travelling in Galilee, or listening in the temple, or sitting by the sea-side, lost and amazed at the simple greatness, and the mighty works of *the illustrious Nazarene.* Surely Heaven must have held the hands which described its own model of virtue.

But what is that model? The character of Jesus exhibited, among others, the following excellences. It possessed the *most perfect and exalted piety.* Abraham was illustrious for his faith, Moses for his meekness, Daniel for his integrity, and David for being a man after God's own heart. But the piety of Jesus, not only concentrated all these, but far excelled them. Is prayer an act of piety? How often did Jesus rise before day, or spend the whole night in communion with his Father! Is obedience an act of piety? Hear him exclaim, "My meat is to do the will of Him that sent me, and to finish his work." John iv. 34. Is submission to the Divine will an evidence of piety? Hear him say, when crushed by the most over-powering sorrows—"Not my will, but thine be done." So shone the piety of Jesus. It was a full-orbed sun, without a cloud and without an eclipse.

The character of Jesus also exhibited the greatest *benevolence toward men.* He did not, like some eastern monarch, shut himself up in a palace, and communicate with his subjects only by means of others. He did not, like the more modern eremite, seek the wilderness, and there in a life of seclusion and abstinence, gratify an ambition, which could not find a suitable theatre for exercise among the abodes and miseries of living and active men. Nor did he, like the philosopher, spend his time amid dusty volumes, and learned demonstrations, to the neglect of the more practical duties of life. He mingles with society, he is surrounded by the multitude, he visits the market, the synagogue, the public festivals, the high-ways, and the haunts of misery and suffering. "He went about doing good." The ignorant, the wretched, the outcast, the afflicted, and the poor, are all the sharers in his divine munificence. Though without a place to lay his head, he invites to him the wearied and heavy laden that they may find rest. Though destitute of store-house and barn, he satisfies the hunger of the thousands around him. Though uneducated in the schools of the Rabbins, he instructs with the greatest kindness, the multitudes that attended his ministry, in a philosophy more elevated than that of Gamaliel, more heavenly than that of Moses. And though destitute of the protection of either Tiberius or Pilate, Herod or Caiaphas, he interposes the shield of his care around the persons of his followers to defend them from threatened danger. Indeed, his benevolence was boundless. He reasons with his enemies, comforts his friends, prays for his murderers, and dies for a world of sinners!

But see his unaffected humility! Does Nathanael affirm—"Rabbi, thou art the Son of God, thou art the King of Israel?" The simple reply of Jesus is— "Because I said, I saw thee, under the fig-tree, believest thou? Thou shalt see greater things than these." John i. 50. Does Nicodemus, a ruler of the Jews, and a member of their great council, approach him as "a teacher sent from God?" He is not the least flattered by the salutation, or by the approach of so illustrious a personage, but simply asserts—"Verily, verily, I say unto thee, except a man be born again, he cannot see the kingdom of God." John iii. Do the Apostles testify—"Thou art the Christ, the Son of the living God?" He does not deny but that they have asserted the truth; yet charges them to tell no man of that fact. Matt. xvi. Do the multitudes, from their admiration of his character and extraordinary powers, desire to make him their King? He retires from them and spends his time in the solitary retirement of some mountain top, far removed from both their admiration and their efforts. John vi. Do the crowds that follow him as he makes his last entrance into Jerusalem, shout as they proceed, "Blessed be the King that cometh in the name of the Lord; peace in heaven and glory in the highest?" He stops on the top of Olivet, and there pours out his tears in broken utterance at the approaching fate of the Metropolis of Judea. Luke xix. O wonderful humility! O lowliness of heart, beyond a parallel and without a rival!

But look at the *moral sublime* in the character of Jesus. This trait of character has always been admired by mankind. To be victorious over fortune, and composed when in the greatest danger, shows such self-respect, or such confidence in an overruling Providence, that all must consider it a rare excellence of human character. Hence, the reply of the vanquished Indian to Alexander, has always been admired. When the Macedonian asked, how he wished to be treated—"*Like a king*," responds the indomitable Porus! The reply of Cæsar, also, to his pilot has been celebrated: "Why are you afraid? *you carry Cæsar!*" There is also an instance recorded by Cicero, of the same kind. When the philosopher Theodorus was threatened by king Lysimachus with crucifixion, his reply was—" Reserve, may it please you, those threats of honour, for these thy minions, clothed in purple; for truly *it is nothing to Theodorus, whether he rots on the ground, or in the air!*"

There are, however, no instances of such elevation of character, to be found in the history of mankind, equal to those which every where crowd the life of Jesus. Do the disciples awaken him in a sea-storm, when in dreadful apparent peril? His reply is, " Why are ye fearful, O ye of little faith!" Matt. viii. Do the Pharisees inform him that Herod, (who had already put the Baptist to death,) was about to kill him; and do they urge him to use haste in his escape? "Go ye," says he, "and tell that fox, Behold, I cast out devils, and I do cures to-day and to-morrow, and the third day, I shall be perfected!" Luke xiii. Does an armed band seek to arrest him, at midnight, and do they come to him with " officers, lanterns, torches and weapons?" He goes to meet them, and asks "Whom seek ye?" and when they replied, " Jesus of Nazareth," his answer is—" *I am he!*" John xviii. Is he tried for his life before the Jewish senate? He is perfectly calm and unmoved; and when they fail in procuring testimony, he gives it himself; " *Thou sayest that I am!*" Is he brought before Pilate and accused of treason against Rome? See his self-possession, his unexcited manner! " Art thou a king, then?" asks the Procurator. " Thou sayest that I am;" says Jesus. " To this end was I born, and for this end came I into the world." John xviii. But look at him in the hour of crucifixion. Is he nailed to the cross? Is he mocked and hissed at? Is he elevated between thieves? Is he ridiculed by priests and people; by strangers and citizens? Not an angry word escapes his lips; not a frown contracts his brow; not a resentful feeling is enkindled in his heart!' No—nothing of this kind, but just the contrary. His look is still benevolent; his eye still friendly; his breast still affectionate; while the only utterance of his lips is, " Father, forgive them, they know not what they do!" Well might it be said, "if Socrates died like a philosopher, Jesus of Nazareth died like a God."

Such was the unyielding greatness of the soul of Jesus. No temptations could corrupt him, no dangers could alarm him, no subtlety could ensnare him, no sufferings could intimidate him. In all circumstances he was the same, in all places the same, to all men the same; condescending, but elevated; kind, but uncompromising; famed, but not exalted; obedient, but not self-righteous; he exhibited in himself a concentration of virtues, which must not only raise him for ever above the approximation of men, but render him worthy of the title given him by an Apostle, "*the brightness of the Father's glory, and the express image of his person.*" Heb. i. 3.

The Apostles who were most intimately acquainted with the character of their Master, who were with him in private and in public, who saw him in triumph and in sufferings, who heard his frequent instructions and were often under his plain reproof; they all testify that his life was the radiance of every virtue, and that he had not a *solitary fault*. Peter calls him "The Just;" 1 Peter iii. 18. And again, "The Holy One, and the Just." Acts iii. 14. Again, he says of him, "He did no sin, neither was guile found in his mouth; who, when he was reviled, reviled not again; when he suffered he threatened not; but committed himself to Him who judgeth righteously." 1 Peter ii. 22, 23. Paul says of him, "He was holy, harmless, undefiled, and separate from sinners." Heb. vii. 26. John says, "We beheld his glory, the glory as of the only begotten of the Father, full of grace and truth." Heb. i. 14. Again, he represents him as throwing out a challenge to his enemies, in the following words: "Which of you convinceth me of sin?" Heb. viii. 46. Nor is this all, but Jesus is made the pattern which Apostles were to imitate, and all believers were to follow. And when, too, human nature should arrive at its utmost perfection, that perfection was to consist in *resemblance to Jesus.* "Beloved," says John, "now are we the sons of God, and it doth not yet appear what we shall be; but we know, that when he shall appear, we shall be like him, for we shall see him as he is." 1 John iii. 2.

It was the consideration of the extraordinary virtues of Jesus, that extracted even from an enemy to the gospel, the following spirited eulogium. "Peruse the works of our philosophers, with all their pomp of diction, how mean, how contemptible are they compared with the Scripture. Is it possible, that a book at once so simple and sublime, should be merely the work of man? Is it possible that the *sacred personage* whose history it contains, should be himself a mere man? Do we find that he assumed the air of an enthusiast, or ambitious sectary? What sweetness, what purity in his manners! What an affecting gracefulness in his delivery! What sublimity in his [maxims! What profound wisdom in his discourses! What presence of mind! What subtlety! What truth in his replies! How great the command over his passions! Where is the man, where the philosopher, who could so live and die without weakness and without ostentation? Shall we suppose the evangelical history a mere fiction? Indeed, my friend, it bears not the marks of fiction; on the contrary, the history of Socrates, which no body presumes to doubt, is not so well attested, as that of Jesus Christ. The Jewish authors were incapable of the diction, and strangers to the morality contained in the gospel; the marks of whose truths are so striking and invincible, that the inventor would be a more astonishing character than the hero."*

Here then, if Jesus be not the Messiah, is one of the greatest wonders the world ever beheld. A man without depravity—a man without sin, or fault—a man, whose life exhibited every virtue, and who is the pattern to all others of absolute perfection! Why, such a character? Did Jehovah mean by such an exhibition to reproach the weaknesses and errors of mankind? Was it a mere freak in his government—

* Rousseau, Works, Vol. V. pp. 215-218.

the mere dropping down upon earth of the inhabitant of some other sphere? What does it mean? Why spotless holiness in a world of pollution? Why immaculate benevolence in a world of universal selfishness? Why the image God, where that of Satan is chiefly familiar? Surely, this was not contempt, and it could not be accident. The moral character of Jesus proves him to have been sent to us, on some high errand of mercy—proves, that he came as our moral and spiritual liberator—proves, that he was the Messiah—the Son of God—the Saviour of men.

CHAPTER X.

JESUS A TEACHER.

There are four things to be considered in estimating the character of a teacher; his preparation for the task, the sources whence he derives his information, the nature of the truths he teaches, and the manner of their delivery. A fifth might be added, viz: the moral character of the teacher himself. But, as we have in a previous chapter dwelt on this topic, it is omitted here, save only to remark, that the doctrines of Jesus were as fully illustrated in his life, as they were lucidly expressed by his lips; for, if it be true, that "never man *spake* like this man," equally true is it that never man *lived* like this man.

The preparation necessary to become an instructer of others in great and important truths, is usually laborious and protracted. Ancient philosophers not only read much, and took long journeys to distant countries for this purpose, but often subjected themselves to the most rigorous course of life for its accomplishment. They retired from the noise of politics, and the stir of business; they shut themselves up in cloisters and even in caves, that their habits of thought might acquire the greater perspicuity and elevation. Nor was this all; feeling the insufficiency of mere reason, both to discover and to sanction the truth, they even sought intercourse with the Deity, or with some invisible agent, from whom, as pretended at least, they received some of their best instructions.

The prophets of Israel seem also to have had a regular, and even a long probation, before entering on their office as public instructers. Hence Jeremiah complains of his youth, as a reason why he should not fill this office; and Hosea marks his case as a special exception to the ordinary course of things, inasmuch as he had been selected from "the herdsmen of Tekoa."

In reference to Moses, whose character and station as a public teacher, bore a stronger resemblance to Jesus than those of any other, his preparations were unusually thorough and extended. Providence placed him in the court of Pharaoh, where he was well instructed in "all the wisdom of the Egyptians." Nor was this all; he was allowed to spend *forty years* after this in such meditations and studies as might tend to qualify him for the important office to which he was to be called.

The training of Jesus was different from all these. Although, in obedience to the legal requirements of the Israelites, he entered not upon his public ministry until about thirty years of age, yet we have much more evidence, during this period, that he was a mechanic, than that he was a scholar. He no doubt received an education similar to that of Peter and of John; but that he was educated *in the schools*, is expressly denied by one of his own historians. John vii. 15. Jesus, then, may be said to have had *no adequate preparation*, in the ordinary acceptation of the term, for the great work of a moral and religious teacher. He had not been drilled in the metaphysics of Aristotle; he acquired no mental acumen from the disputations of the Stoics; he had not cultivated his taste with Plato or Homer; nor had he even been a regular pupil of the Scribes and Pharisees. In a high and peculiar sense he was both a self-made scholar and teacher.

But what were the sources from which Jesus drew his doctrines? He evidently did not derive them from his *education*. This was no better, nor even as good, as that of many of his hearers. Equally certain is it, that he did not borrow them from the Jewish doctors. His doctrine and theirs were generally diametrically opposite. Nor could he have gathered them from the learned men of other countries. He had no intercourse with such men; nor did either his theology or morality agree with theirs. Whence, then, did he deduce those truths of divinity, and those lessons of morality, which have been so lauded by all candid minds for the last eighteen centuries? To this we reply, from two sources—from revelations already given, and from Heaven.

No one can read the instructions of Jesus, and not be struck with his familiar and intimate acquaintance with the Scriptures of the Old Testament. He illustrates, enforces, and quotes them on all occasions. And although he often leveled to the dust the traditions of the elders, and the doctrines of men, yet he every where shows the greatest regard for the oracles of the living God. He put an infinite difference between tradition and Scripture; the writings of men, and the inspirations of Jehovah. The one he reverenced as the ancient Israelite did the temple, the altar, or the ark; the other, he regarded as the same Israelite did a common farm-house, a stable, or a barn. The one he re-affirms and inculcates, the other he often denies and subverts.

One source, then, of the doctrines of Jesus, was the Old Testament Scriptures. " He came not to destroy the law or the prophets, but to fulfil." In the language of another: " Although he proposed to erect a second temple of truth, the glory of which should eclipse the splendour of the first, yet he deigned to appropriate whatever of the ancient materials remained available."* As to the *moral truths,* however, he altered none.

The other source whence Jesus derived his doctrines was from *Heaven.* " My doctrine, says he, is not mine, but His that sent me." John vii. 16.

One of the most remarkable passages in the Old Testament is the following: " The Lord thy God, says Moses, will raise up unto thee a Prophet, from the midst of thee, of thy brethren, like unto me, unto him

* Great Teacher, by Harris, p. 81.

ye shall hearken." Deut. xviii. 15. The allusion here is evidently to the Messiah. Joshua was not a prophet, but a general; and of the other prophets, none of them exercised such authority over the Israelites as Moses had done. This remarkable prophet or Messiah was to resemble Moses in many things; he was to be like him, yet he was to be *superior* to him; for the Israelites are directed to submit themselves entirely to his instructions and teachings, as announcing in *all things* the will of Heaven.

The manner, however, in which Jesus received the will of Heaven, was totally different from that in which Moses received it. For this purpose Moses was called to the bush, called to the mount, or conversed with from the Shechinah—at most, he communed with the Holy One only "face to face." This, it is true, is great honour for a mere mortal; and it is distinctly stated, that Moses was the only one ever allowed to approach so near to Jehovah. But the manner in which Jesus held intercourse with the Deity, was wholly different. He had no dream or vision; he was called to no particular place; there was no visible oracle to which he resorted. He was *himself* the bush, the mount, the Shechinah, the image of God. True, he prays to his Father; and on several occasions, that Father called to him out of heaven. This, however, was done mainly to establish the faith of men in his mission. There is no instance recorded, where either by prayer he sought to know the Divine will, or where by a voice from heaven, that will was made known to him. No; the knowledge of that will was *internal* and *personal;* it was not from another, but from *himself.* In the language of an Apostle, "In him *dwelt* all the fulness of the Godhead bodily." Col. ii. 9.

It is owing to this mysterious and remarkable manner in which Jesus held communion with the Deity, that we often hear from him such language as the following: "No man knoweth the Son but the Father; neither knoweth any man the Father, save the Son, and he to whomsoever the Son will reveal him." Matt. xi. 27. "He that hath seen me, hath seen the

Father; and how sayest thou, then, Show us the Father? Believest thou not, that I am in the Father, and the Father in me? The words that I speak unto you, I speak not of myself: but the Father that dwelleth in me, he doeth the works. Believe me, that I am in the Father, and the Father in me; or else believe me for the very works' sake." John xiv. 9–11. And the following, more remarkable still: " And no man hath ascended up to heaven, but he that came down from heaven, even the Son of man which is in heaven." John iii. 13.

Such was the intimacy which Jesus had with the counsels of Jehovah. He is not caught up into heaven to learn them. No messenger is sent from heaven to communicate them. There is no trance or apparition. The holy oracle dwelt *in him*. The Divine mind emanated *from him*. His words were truth; they were attended with awful power; and his uttered will was unalterable and eternal. Surely such an one could not have been less than "God manifest in the flesh."

In reference to the truths, which this great Teacher delivered, they may be considered as the carrying out, or completion of a previously existing and partially developed system. He came not to " destroy the law or the prophets, but to fulfill."

The Old Testament Scriptures had left things in a half-finished state. A peculiar providence is there exhibited as cleaving to a certain people, amid all their infirmities and rebellions, without an adequate reason. A host of types are there displayed, all significant, all instructive, all useful, yet all referring to a future *something*, as yet undisclosed, and which was to constitute upon its manifestation, a key to all these religious symbols. Numerous prophecies are there recorded, all referring to *one* who had not as yet appeared ; and all speaking of a kingdom not as yet commenced. Revelation is there presented as half-made—religion as half-taught—the Church of God as half-built. It was left, therefore, for the Messiah, upon his appearance, to illustrate and complete a system, thus left in an unfinished state. This great work, *Jesus of Nazareth accomplished.* His history vindicated the providence of God towards the Jewish nation for preceding thousands of years. His teachings completed whatever was left obscure or unintelligible in previous revelations, and his death as an atonement for sin, unlocked the symbols of the past, and gave to ancient sacrifices and offerings their true and intended meaning.

Even then, if Jesus had never opened his mouth as a teacher, even if one unbroken silence had sealed his lips from the manger to the grave; still, his very life would have been instruction, and his every act an elucidation of some great doctrinal truth. But he did speak. Of him it is expressly said, that "He opened his mouth, and taught." And what teachings! In what is called his Sermon on the Mount, what a powerful elucidation and application of the moral law! In his parables, what beautiful and striking paintings of the new system he was about to set up! Who can read the one, without feeling the sword of the Spirit pierce the inmost recesses of his soul? Who can contemplate the other, without being inwardly drawn towards truths so inimitably depicted, and without being captivated by a teacher so simple yet so sublime, so faithful, yet so tender in all his instructions!

The doctrines of Jesus, so far as they may be considered as peculiar to a new system, or as constituting the *second part* of an old one, may be divided into three classes. They refer to the manifestation of the Godhead in man's redemption, to the duties obligatory upon those to whom the knowledge of such redemption should be communicated, and to the final results of his mission in the world to come.

The teachings of Jesus reveal God in the work of man's redemption. In the works of nature, God has always been revealed to the eye of reason; "for the invisible things of him from the creation of the world are clearly seen, being understood by the things that are made." Jehovah had also been revealed to Israel

THE MESSIAH. 89

as a lawgiver. Amid the darkness and smoke of Sinai, the lightnings of his inflexible justice were made fearfully to play; and the thunders of his indignation awfully to roll. In the incipiency too, of redemption, God was exhibited to the ancients, as a God of mercy. Every angelic visitant, every sweet promise, every burning lamb manifested the graciousness of the divine nature. It was left, however, for the Messiah, the Son of God, fully to make known the character of Jehovah, as a God of mercy. Hence it is said of Jesus, "no man hath seen God at any time: the Only Begotten which is in the bosom of the Father, he hath declared him."—And again, "the law was given by Moses, but grace and truth came by Jesus Christ." John i. 17, 18.

The paternal relation of the Deity to mankind, is clearly and strongly stated by Jesus. Does he teach his disciples to pray? he begins in the endearing manner—" Our *Father*, which art in heaven." Matt. vi. Does he teach them confidence in divine providence? It is by telling them, " your heavenly Father knoweth that ye have need of all these things." Matt. vi. Does he leave them in a world of trial and affliction? It is with the assurance—"I ascend to my Father and your Father, to my God and your God." John xx. 17.

The eternal Sonship of the Mediator is also clearly exhibited by Jesus. "I," says he, "and my Father are one." The Jews being about to stone him for this declaration, the reply of Jesus is, " Many good works have I shown you of my Father; for which of those good works do ye stone me?" The reply is, "For a good work we stone thee not, but for blasphemy; and because thou, being a man, makest thyself God." Jesus proceeds to vindicate himself from such a charge. " Is it not written in your law, I said ye are gods? If he called them gods, unto whom the word of God came—say ye of him whom the Father hath sanctified and sent into the world, Thou blasphemest, because I said, I am the Son of God? If I do not the works of my Father, believe me not; but, if I do, though ye believe

9

not me, believe the works, that ye may know, that the Father is in me, and I in him." John x.

The personality and work of the Spirit are also clearly taught by Jesus. "It is expedient for you that I go away; for if I go not away, the Comforter will not come; but if I depart, I will send him unto you. And when he is come, he will reprove the world of sin, of righteousness and of judgment." John xvi.

Thus did Jesus remove the thick darkness which surrounded the throne of the Eternal, and make known to a world of sinners, the character of God as a God of compassion and of grace. The Father pities the miseries and ruin of our world; the Son becomes incarnate and dies for its redemption; and the Spirit, by illuminating the hearts of men, and eradicating their moral pollutions, applies the grace of salvation, and constitutes them for ever the sons of the living God.

The duties inculcated upon those to whom the knowledge of redemption should come, are repentance, faith and holy obedience. The doctrine of the atonement effectually "condemned sin in the flesh," and not only rendered repentance obligatory, but acceptable. The price of the sinner's pardon also exhibited the evil of sin, and was well calculated to break and subdue any heart, not made of marble and stone. Nor was this all; the great Teacher demands an implicit faith, not only in his doctrines as divinely true, but also in his sacrifice as amply sufficient for the sins of men. Not a word he uttered is to be discredited, for he is himself "*the truth*" of God. Nor is another sacrifice to be mentioned, for he, and he only, is "the Lamb of God which taketh away the sin of the world."

These are the foundation duties, but others are also enjoined. Pride, anger, covetousness, worldly mindedness, every evil passion and act, are all condemned. Humility, meekness, purity, zeal, devotion, and brotherly love, are all enjoined. His disciples are to consider themselves as the citizens of heaven, as the sons and heirs of God, as the brethren of a common family;

and they are exhorted to make Jehovah himself their pattern and example. "Be ye therefore perfect, even as your Father which is in heaven is perfect." Matt. v. 48. If persecuted, they were not to resist, and if put to death, they were not to desert the faith taught them. External commotions were not to separate them from their Master; nor were internal agitations to alienate them from each other. United to Jesus by a common faith, they were to be united to each other by a common affection; and having renounced the world at the beginning of their discipleship, they were never more to allow it an ascendency over their hearts. They were to be "the light of the world," and "the salt of the earth;" and upon their full and patient exemplification of the doctrines of their Master, was to depend, not only the honour of their Christian character, but the esteem among men of Christianity itself.

But the teachings of Jesus were also prospective; they embraced another world. And here, one cannot but remark the vast superiority of his instructions above those of the ancient prophets. These prophets saw futurity at a great distance; and although they describe it, they describe it as one would a foreign country, and not as he would speak of his own. There is a veil thrown over it, and their images are cast indistinctly upon that veil. The actual geography of the future is not laid before us, nor do we seem to know and commune with its inhabitants. On the contrary, the doctrines of Jesus bring "life and immortality to light." Heaven and hell with him are places not far from Judea, and eternity presses upon the sun of to-morrow. There is no faintness or imperfection of description, but one has only to lift the eye, and he sees at once, as living realities at hand, all the glories or horrors of the invisible state. Here the soul of the rich man quails and cries in all the miseries and woes of the second death; there Lazarus reclines in the bosom of Abraham, with not an affliction felt, with not a want ungratified. Here the sudden cry, "the Bridegroom cometh," arouses the drowsy expectants of future glory; there the great white throne collects before it all the assembled sons of Adam. Here, on the one hand, we see the wicked, associated with devils, their former tempters and accomplices in crime, hastening to their final allotments in the world beneath; there, on the other, we contemplate the righteous, justified and vindicated, ascending to the realms of glory, to dwell for ever in the paradise of God. Here hell exhibits its lurid flames, its deathless worm, its ceaseless wailings and gnashings of teeth; there the loud song of heaven falls upon the ear, and the glorified worshippers are seen occupying their everlasting mansions. The veil is torn away, and the hearer of the great Teacher seems to see before him, in all the distinctness of actual vision, the realities of the future state.

The manner in which Jesus taught was adapted not only to the nature of his subjects, but also to the character of his hearers. What sublimity, and yet what simplicity, in his style! His thoughts are majestic enough for the contemplation of angels; and yet his language is plain enough for the comprehension of children. There is no pomp, no parade. The speaker never attempts to exalt himself or to astonish his hearers. All the ordinary accompaniments of scholastic oratory are unknown; yea, despised. There is no exact position of the feet, no regular and studied extension of the hand, no fore-taught intonations of the voice, no contortions of the countenance. On most occasions, he does not even stand to speak. He either sits upon the side of a mountain, or occupies a seat in a fisherman's boat. There is, too, no scaffold or pulpit built for him; no particular place assigned him, where the people are to expect an oration, or to anticipate a sermon: circumstances seem to have arranged all these. He is as ready on the road-side as in the temple; at the dinner-table as in the synagogue. He speaks to a few as readily as to a multitude; and to one class of persons as promptly as to another. His subjects were also selected in the same manner. There is no previous notice given to the people that he is to deliver a discourse on the law, or on the general judgment, against the errors of the Pharisees, or concerning the nature of his kingdom. His teachings seem generally to have resulted from some question asked him, or from some object brought incidentally before him. Do the birds of heaven fly over his head, or the lilies of the field bloom beneath his eye? He employs them in his discourse to inculcate confidence in the providence of God. Are the fishermen casting their net into the sea? He illustrates thereby the effects of his gospel in saving men. Does he attend a marriage-supper? He makes the customs of society, the midnight procession, the burning torches, and the cry of the porter, all to illustrate and enforce the great truths of futurity. Does he sit at the dinner-table among self-seeking guests? He inculcates humility in the selection of places in this world. Is the exclamation heard—"Blessed is he that shall eat bread in the kingdom of God?" He seizes at once upon the remark, and exhibits by it the exceeding reluctance of men, and especially of the Jews, to embrace the glad tidings of salvation. Do the disciples point to the magnificence of the temple? He takes occasion to predict its downfall, and even extends his remarks to the fading away of all earthly glory, and the final introduction of his eternal kingdom. With him, wells of water, dinner-tables, vines, the shepherd watching his flock, the sower casting his seed, the reaper cutting down his harvest, the eyes of the blind, the weakness of childhood, the rigour of creditors, the questions of enemies, and the mistakes of friends, all, all are texts from which he discourses; and with which he associates an elevation of imagery and a grandeur of thought, unsurpassed in the history of human instruction.

Nor are we left simply to the reported discourses of Jesus to ascertain the excellences of his mode of communicating truth. The effects of these discourses on the multitudes at the time, show their wonderful power. What vast audiences heard his sermon on the mount! What crowding companies pressed upon the sea-shore to listen to him as he sat in the fisherman's boat! What numbers crowd around the private houses where he teaches! What anxiety to hear him! What fixed attention! What bursting applause! Now the officers affirm, "Never man spake like this man." Now the people are said to be "astonished at his doctrine, for he taught them as one having authority, and not as the Scribes." And now the inmates of the synagogue are all "amazed at the gracious words which proceeded out of his mouth."

And yet, this great philosopher, this popular preacher, this more than a prophet, is but an *uneducated Galilean!* Well may we ask, as did his acquaintances of Nazareth, "From whence hath this man these things, and what wisdom is this which is given unto him?" Mark vi. 2. Why so superior to all other Galileans? Why so much exalted above philosophers and sages, above patriarchs and prophets? It cannot be ascribed to birth, or education. It cannot be ascribed to cunning and management. It cannot be attributed to either faction, or fanaticism, for the one was too weak even if it existed; and the other does not appear either in the life or doctrines of Jesus. Surely, if we had only the teachings of this remarkable personage as evidence before us, we should be compelled to admit, that if ever a Messiah was to come, *he* must be the person, and that if ever God dwelt in man, it was in Jesus of Nazareth.

CHAPTER XI.

JESUS A SACRIFICE AND PRIEST.

PROBABLY no part of the gospel is more offensive to carnal reason, than what may be termed its *glory-spot*—the vicarious death of its author. Too proud to acknowledge the need of atonement, too ungrateful to honour him who has made such atonement, haughty man passes scornfully by, nor turns a look to the cross, on which expires the Redeemer of the world. Thus has "Christ crucified" always been "to the Jews a stumbling-block, and to the Greeks foolishness." The hero who, at the expense of toils, and sufferings, and blood, has liberated his country, is loudly praised; the man who risks his own life to rescue from death his friend, is never forgotten. But Jesus, the author of salvation—Jesus, who has reconciled us to God by his own blood, is, alas! too often despised; and despised too, because of his wounds—because of his sufferings—because of his cross!

All know, that nothing in the history of Jesus was more obnoxious to the prejudices of the ancient Jew, than his death on Calvary. His birth in a stable was offensive; his origin at Nazareth was an objection; his humble and mean appearance caused many to reject him: but it was over his *crucifixion* that the whole nation stumbled. This offended them more than every thing else. "What!" they were ready proudly to ask, "What! can a *malefactor* save us? Can the *condemned* deliver us? Can one who has been *crucified* be the Christ, the chosen of God?" The same objection exists at present in the mind of the modern Israelite. Notwithstanding all the typical sacrifices which his forefathers offered, and the constant use they made of blood to cleanse the unclean, still he sees in the death of Jesus an insuperable objection to his being the Messiah. With such an objection it is our province to reason.

The first remark I here make is, that the doctrine of *sacrifice for sin* is neither contrary to reason, nor repugnant to the sentiments of mankind. Wherever wrong has been done, justice requires that satisfaction should be rendered. Hence, in all civil laws, such satisfaction is usually demanded by the civil code itself. When, too, the offender is made justly sensible of his crime, and is brought to a proper repentance for it, his own heart prompts him to some mode of restitution. He becomes willing either to apologize, to make payment, to serve, or to suffer, as the case may demand. The very same feeling is awakened in the human bosom, where God is the party offended. Not only is it admitted and felt in this case, that the offender should be punished, but so strong is this conviction, that wherever the hope of forgiveness is entertained, there is always a resort to some mode of penal satisfaction. Either the body is lacerated, or a fine is imposed for religious purposes, or a child is slain, or an animal is sacrificed.

No one at all acquainted with the history of mankind, can doubt the truth of these statements. This inward sense of the *need of sacrifice to take away sin*, is so much a component part of human nature, that it has not only existed in all nations, but may be said to have pervaded the principal institutions of every country. In proof of this, I offer the two following authorities. In the days of Tullus Hostilius, king of Rome, a celebrated rencontre took place between the Curiatii and Horatii—one of the Horatii alone survived. Provoked at the lamentations of his sister for the lover he had killed, he stabbed her to the heart. He was tried and condemned as a murderer. Through an appeal, however, made to the people by his father, his punishment was remitted. A sense of justice, however, produced the following mode of its remission: "Itaque, ut cædes manifesta aliquo tamen piaculo lueretur, imperatum patri, ut filium expiaret pecuniâ publicâ. Is, quibusdam piacularibus sacrificiis factis, transmisso per viam tigillo, capite adoperto, velut sub jugum misit juvenem."* "Wherefore, that so plain a case of murder might be expiated by some sort of atonement, it was required of the father, that he should expiate his son's crime at the expense of the state. He, certain propitiatory sacrifices having been offered, caused his son to pass under a beam suspended across a road, with his head covered, as if under a gallows." As murder was a crime against the state, the father of Horatius made the murderer pass under a beam, as a public recognition of his desert of death; but since it was also a crime against the gods, certain expiatory sacrifices were offered.

The next authority is that of a learned Jewish Rabbin. Abarbanel gives the following explanation of the import of ancient sacrifices: "They burned the fat and kidneys of the victims upon the altar, for their own inwards, being the seat of their intentions and purposes, and the legs of the victims for their own hands and feet; and they sprinkled their blood, instead of their own blood and life, confessing that in the sight of God, the Just Judge of things, the blood of the offerers should be shed, and their bodies burnt for their sins: but, that through the mercy of God, expiation was made for them by the victim being put in their place, by whose blood and life, the blood and life of the offerers were redeemed."†

I remark, again, that if the object of the mission of the Messiah be moral and not political; if it refer to deliverance from sin and misery, and not from national oppression, then was it necessary that he should bring with him some adequate sacrifice or satisfaction, in order to redeem men from the condemnation under which they were lying. The law of God had been violated; it must therefore be honoured.

* Livy, B. I. c. xxvi. † Magee, I. 200.

Divine wrath had been justly provoked; it must therefore be appeased. But how can this be done without a price—without a sacrifice? Had the Messiah, therefore, appeared as our great Deliverer, and yet brought with him no means of deliverance, no ransom for our souls, his mission would have been altogether abortive. Divine justice would still have held its captives, and Divine wrath would still have continued upon the offenders of a holy God.

Precisely what this sacrificial offering should be, on the part of the Messiah, human reason is not prepared to say. It might consist in the sacrifice of himself, or it might consist in some other mode of ransom. Mere human reason could never decide this question. But that a price should be brought, that satisfaction should be made, is the obvious dictate of the sentiments and consciousness of mankind on this subject.

I remark, thirdly, that the Jewish scriptures universally teach, that *the Messiah was to be a sacrifice for sin.* This is taught in the very first promise of a future Saviour. "He shall bruise thy head, and *thou shalt bruise his heel.*" The following exposition of this passage is given in Poole's Synopsis: "Christi caput est Divinitas; calcaneum Humanitas, quam dum offendit et occidit Dæmon, occisus est." "The *head* of Christ is his divinity, his *heel* his humanity; which while Satan persecuted and killed, he was himself destroyed.*" The same interpretation is given to this passage by Dr. Adam Clarke: "And Satan bruises *his heel.* God so ordered it, that the salvation of man could only be brought about *by the death of Christ.*"† Henry also says, "Christ's sufferings and death were pointed at in Satan's bruising his *heel,* which is his *human nature.*"‡ Thus is the very first ray of gospel light, tinged with a streak of sacrificial blood; thus does the first promise of deliverance for man, indicate a suffering Deliverer.

The same truth is also exhibited in all the human types of a coming Messiah. Is Adam a type of that

* In loco.   † In loco.   ‡ In loco.

Messiah? It was upon him that the sentence of death was pronounced. Was Abel a type of the Messiah? He was wickedly and unjustly slain by his brother. Was Noah a type of Messiah? He was for more than a year enclosed within an ark, and buried, as it were, in the bosom of a flood. Was Isaac a type of Messiah? His father's hand and knife were lifted up against him, and just ready to make him a burnt-offering, had not Jehovah prevented. Was Joseph such a type? He was hated of his brethren, cast into a deep pit, sold into Egypt, thrown into prison, and only by sufferings made his way to the throne. Was Moses such a type? He lay in infancy exposed to the crocodiles on the banks of the Nile, and was afterwards threatened with death by Pharaoh. Was David a type of Messiah? He was for years persecuted by Saul, and hid in the caves and dens of the earth. So of all the human symbols of the great Redeemer. Their lives were all characterized by suffering; and in this respect they prefigured Him who was "a man of sorrows," and "who gave his life a ransom for many."

It is, however, in the animal types of the ancients, that we more clearly learn the sufferings of a promised Messiah. The sacrifice of animals as a religious rite, had its origin at a very early period of the world. The first allusion to such a practice, was in the days of Adam. Gen. iii. 21. That Abel offered such sacrifices, is distinctly stated. Gen. iv. 4. The practice was also common in the days of Noah. Gen. vii. 20, 21. From these early patriarchs this custom extended itself among almost all the nations of the earth.

Now, whence the origin of this religious ceremony? It certainly was not a device of man. It must, therefore, have been from God. But if from God, what was its design? It certainly was not a vain ceremony; much less could it have been a mere act of cruelty. This practice was evidently introduced, as indicating *some method of removing sin*. Either the death of the animal excited compunction on the part of the offerer;

or, the animal itself was considered as his substitute; or, such sacrifice was typical of a nobler offering for sin. In the first of these methods alone, sin could not be removed. However deep one's sorrow for a crime, such sorrow can never make amends for the crime itself. The thief is not liberated because of his tears; nor is the murderer released when he repents. Nor can sin be removed by the second method. A mere animal can never be a legal satisfaction for sins committed against Jehovah. Even for crimes against a neighbour, the Jewish law required, not only sacrifice, but also restitution. Lev. vi. There were many crimes too, where sacrifice was inadmissible: but the criminal suffered *death* as the only adequate punishment. If, too, animal sacrifices were *real atonements* for sin, then ought they never to be abolished; for men would need them now as much as in past ages. It is evident, however, that such sacrifices were not considered by God as real atonements, nor were they so regarded, by the better informed of the Jewish nation.

What then was their design? They were evidently intended to prefigure the *vicarious death* of the Messiah, as the only adequate substitute for the guilt of man. They originated with the promise, " the seed of the woman shall bruise the serpent's head;" and they were abolished when Jesus exclaimed upon the cross, " *It is finished,*" and yielded up his spirit. It was then that " sacrifice and oblation were caused to cease," and that *real* " reconciliation was made for iniquity." Dan. ix. 24, 27.

Every sacrifice, therefore, that was offered under the Jewish economy—the dove, the lamb, the goat, the bullock—were all expressive of a suffering and dying Messiah. The sacrifices of Adam and of Noah, of Greeks and Romans, indeed of the whole world, were expressive of this truth.

But there are also many plain and express texts of Scripture, which assert, that the Messiah was to be a *sacrifice for sin*. In the 22d Psalm, the following language is put in the mouth of the Messiah

THE MESSIAH. 101

by the pen of inspiration—" I am poured out like water, and all my bones are out of joint: my heart is like wax: it is melted in the midst of my bowels. My strength is dried up like a potsherd ; and my tongue cleaveth to my jaws; and thou hast brought me to *the dust of death.* For dogs have compassed me : the assembly of the wicked have enclosed me: they pierced my hands and my feet. They part my garments among them, and cast lots upon my vesture." 14–18. That this Psalm refers to the Messiah is almost absolutely certain. " By far the greatest number of interpreters," says Hengstenberg, "acknowledge the Messiah as the *exclusive* subject of this Psalm. This interpretation was followed by a portion of the older Jews. It has also been the prevailing one in the Christian church."* If, however, this Psalm refer to the Messiah, then was that Messiah to be a *suffering and dying Messiah.* Indeed, the very manner of his death is predicted—that of *crucifixion,* " they pierced my hands and my feet."

Another passage even more explicit is found in the 53d chapter of Isaiah—" He is despised and rejected of men. He was wounded for our transgressions; he was bruised for our iniquities. The Lord hath laid on him the iniquity of us all. It pleased the Lord to bruise him; he hath put him to grief. When thou shalt make his soul *an offering for sin,* he shall see his seed, he shall prolong his days, and the pleasure of the Lord shall prosper in his hand." "The Jews," says Hengstenberg, " in more ancient times, unanimously referred this prophecy to the Messiah."† In this interpretation he also asserts "the best interpreters" to be agreed. "What impostor," asks Barnes, " ever would have attempted to fulfil a prophecy, by subjecting himself to a shameful death? What impostor could have brought it about in this manner, if he had attempted it? No. It was only the *true Messiah* that could or would have fulfilled this prophecy."‡ But, if these passages refer to the

* Chris. i. 132. † Chris. i. 541. ‡ Notes on Isaiah.

Messiah, then was that Messiah to die as *a sacrifice for sin.*

The prophet Zechariah employs on this subject the following language—" Awake, O sword, against my Shepherd, and against the man that is my fellow, saith the Lord of hosts. Smite the Shepherd, and the sheep shall be scattered." xiii. 7. Daniel is even more explicit. " And after threescore and two weeks shall Messiah be cut off, but not for himself." ix. 26.

All these, together with a great number of similar passages, plainly foretell that the Messiah was *to suffer death,* and that that death was to be a *sacrifice for sin.* Was the death then of *Jesus,* truly and properly such a sacrifice? That he died, neither Jews nor Christians will deny. It is the nature of that death about which we are concerned. On this subject I offer the following remarks.

The death of Jesus was evidently not for *crime.* We have already noticed that in all the relations and duties of life, " he was harmless and undefiled." Nor was he guilty of the specific crime alleged against him before the Governor. That crime was treason. His judge himself, however, declared, " I find in him no fault at all." John xviii. 38.

Nor was the death of Jesus a matter of coercion. True, he was bound by the soldiers, and afterwards violently condemned and crucified. Still he had all the power necessary for his deliverance. Even at this period of apparent weakness and desertion, " twelve legions of angels" stood ready at his call. He must then have suffered death voluntarily. But if he suffered death voluntarily, and was yet free from all crime, there is, to say the least, a strong probability that his death was of a *sacrificial* and not of an ordinary character.

But I remark thirdly, that Jesus uniformly taught, that *reconciliation* or *atonement* was to be effected by his death. " And he took the cup, and gave thanks, and gave it to them saying, Drink ye all of it; for this is my blood of the New Testament which is shed for many, for the remission of sins." Matt.

xxvi. 27, 28. The following testimony given after his resurrection is still more explicit: "And he said unto them, Thus it is written, and thus it behoved Christ to suffer and to rise from the dead the third day; and that repentance and remission of sins should be preached in his name, among all nations, beginning at Jerusalem." Luke xxiv. 46, 47.

The Apostles also put the same construction upon the death of their Master. They never for once considered him to have died as a martyr, much less as a criminal. They uniformly declare, that his death was *vicarious,* that by it forgiveness of sins was obtained, and that it was that alone which reconciled us to God. "For he hath made him to be sin for us who knew no sin, that we might be made the righteousness of God in him." 2 Cor. v. 21. In his Epistle to the Hebrews, the Apostle also declares, "Christ was once offered to bear the sins of many." Heb. ix. 28. And again, "Christ hath redeemed us from the curse of the law, being made a curse for us." Gal. iii. 13. This is their uniform testimony; and it was this fact—the *redemption that is in Christ Jesus*—which animated their hearts, and inspired them with a zeal, which no persecutions could allay, which no sufferings could extinguish. They gloried in the cross, as an expiatory offering for sin, and were willing to rest, not only their lives, but their souls, upon its sufficiency and validity.

Why then should the Jew, or the infidel stumble at the cross of Jesus? Have they no sin to be removed? or, do they imagine that sin can be pardoned without a sacrifice—without an atonement? Or if a sacrifice is necessary, why is it, that this one provided with so much cost, with so much preparation, should be despised? The death of Jesus as a sacrifice for sin, was predicted in the garden to Adam; it was even "fore-ordained before the foundation of the world." All the types and symbols of the pre-existing systems refer to it; and it was the burden of much of that Scripture which holy men of

God dictated, "as they were moved by the Holy Ghost."

Whatever use, however, Jew or Gentile shall make of the death of Jesus, still will it stand to the end of the world, as an irrefragable proof of his Messiahship. It was predicted of the Messiah, that he should be " bruised," that he should be "set at naught," that he should be "pierced," that "his soul should be made an offering for sin." All these things, even in the most minute manner, have been fulfilled in Jesus; and they have been fulfilled in *no other*. The very cross, then, its wood, its nails, its spear, its blood and death, all proclaim, that Jesus is the Christ, the Saviour of men.

But the Messiah was also to be *a priest*. "The term *Messiah*," says a Jewish writer, "is applicable to a king, to a prophet, and also to *a high priest*."* In proof of the last, he quotes from Ex. xxix. 7; " Thou shalt also take the anointing oil and pour it upon his (Aaron's) head and anoint him."

The passage of Scripture which more clearly exhibits the priestly character of the Messiah than any other, is Psalm cx. 4. " The Lord hath sworn and will not repent, Thou art a priest for ever after the order of Melchizedek." That the Messiah is the subject of this Psalm, has been almost universally believed. The Jews themselves in the days of Jesus, did not pretend to deny it. Matt. xxii. 41–46. And although their opposition to Christianity has induced many of them to consider Hezekiah, Zerubbabel, the Jewish nation itself, or even Abraham, as its subject, yet says Hengstenberg, "the weight of the internal evidence, and the authority of tradition induced many of the older Jews to adhere to the Messianic interpretation."† The Christian Church generally, and the early fathers in particular, considered this as the only true sense of the Psalm. Says Theodoret, " if David, who stood on the highest eminence of human greatness, called

* Rabbi Joseph Crooll.   Scott's Works, vol. ix.
† Chris. I. 108.

another his Lord, that person must of necessity possess more than human dignity"—(ουκ αρα μονον ανθρωπος, αλλα και θεος). If, however, the Messiah was the subject of this Psalm, he was to be not only a *king*, (מלך) but also a *priest* (כהן).

In the part of this Psalm, in which the priesthood of the Messiah is asserted, the following particulars are to be observed: His priesthood is introduced with an *oath*—" the Lord hath *sworn* and will not repent." This intimates not only the certainty of the event, but the vast importance of the priesthood itself. It is also asserted in this passage, that this peculiar priest was to arise, not after the order of Aaron, but after that of Melchizedek. He was to be a priest, not by human, but by express divine appointment. His priesthood, too, was to be perpetual; it was never to cease; "thou art a priest for ever." Nor was this perpetuity of the priesthood to result from a succession of different priests; it was to be confined to *one person*, THE MESSIAH.

Do the New Testament Scriptures then teach, that Jesus possessed any such priesthood? On this subject, we must refer particularly to the Epistle to the Hebrews. This Epistle was written by a Jew, was addressed to the Jews, and it discusses this very subject. In chapter iii, the Apostle says, " Wherefore, holy brethren, consider the Apostle and High Priest of our profession, Christ Jesus." Again, in chapter iv, he says, " We have a great High Priest, that is passed into the heavens, Jesus, the Son of God." Again, in chapter ix, he declares that, " Christ being come an High Priest of good things to come, by a greater and more perfect tabernacle, not made with hands, that is to say, not of this building; neither by the blood of goats and calves, but by his own blood he entered in once into the holy place, having obtained eternal redemption for us."

There is, then, a Christian as well as a Jewish priesthood. This Christian priesthood has been set up in the person of Jesus, our Lord and Saviour. It is not an earthly, but a heavenly office; nor is it temporary; it is to last to the end of the world. Being set up in one who rose from the dead, who is really immortal, it cannot be abrogated or changed by death.

Now there is no similar priesthood to this among the Jews; nor has there ever been. "*A priest for ever*," they have never known; nor have they had one set up "after the order of Melchizedek." But such a priesthood the New Testament makes known to us. It represents Jesus as the *very priest* predicted in the 110th Psalm. And what makes this more striking is, that this Christian priesthood is exercised at a time, when the Jews have neither temple nor altar, High Priest nor Holy of Holies; yea, when their capital is in the hands of strangers, and they themselves are scattered to the ends of the earth! What means all this? Surely, either Jesus must be both High Priest and King, or else royalty and priesthood have perished in Israel.

We consider, therefore, the present priestly character of Jesus, both as fulfilment of prophecy, and as proof of his Messiahship. The prediction of such a priesthood has been fulfilled in *no other;* it has, however, been fulfilled *in him.* He it is, who is now sitting "at the right hand of the Father," as a King and Sovereign; and who is also exercising a priestly office in heaven, not after the order of Aaron, but after that of Melchizedek.

CHAPTER XII.

JESUS A KING.

It is evident from the Old Testament Scriptures, that the Messiah was to be a sovereign. "The sceptre," says Jacob, "shall not depart from Judah, nor a lawgiver from between his feet until Shiloh come: and unto him shall the gathering of the people be." Gen. xlix. 10. In the second Psalm, Jehovah is represented as saying of the Messiah, "Yet have I set my King upon my holy hill of Zion." ver. 6. Jeremiah also employs the following language: "Behold, the days come, saith the Lord, that I will raise unto David a righteous Branch, and a *King* shall reign and prosper, and shall execute judgment and justice in the earth. In his days Judah shall be saved, and Israel shall dwell safely; and this is the name whereby he shall be called, The Lord our Righteousness." Jer. xxiii. 5, 6.

These are but a few of the many passages which predict the royalty of the great Deliverer. Indeed, the Jews themselves have never doubted but that their Messiah was to be a Prince. It was, too, chiefly for the unprincely appearance of Jesus, that they were led to reject and crucify him.

If, then, it be affirmed that Jesus of Nazareth was the promised Messiah, his pretensions to royalty must be defended. It is not enough that he be a great teacher; it is not enough that he possess the most worthy character; it is not enough that he have power to work miracles; or that he be lineally descended from David; that he appear at the right epoch, and be born in the predicted place. It must also be demonstrated that Jesus of Nazareth is *a King*.

It is evident that if we understand the word "king," in its ordinary acceptation, the past history of Jesus cannot maintain his claims to that office. His appearance was more that of a beggar than of a king, and his end was more that of a criminal, than of one possessed of supreme authority.

Yet, Jesus of Nazareth was a *King*.

He was so recognized by many during his earthly life. Say the wise men from the east, "Where is he that is born *King* of the Jews?" Matt. ii. 2. Says Zacharias, "Blessed be the Lord God of Israel, for he hath raised up an horn (that is, *king*) of salvation for us in the house of David." Luke i. 69. Nathanael also said to him, "Rabbi, thou art the Son of God; thou art the *King* of Israel." John i. 49. The multitude, too, who attended Jesus to Jerusalem, just before his crucifixion, sang as he entered the city, "Blessed be the *King* that cometh in the name of the Lord; peace in heaven and glory in the highest." Luke xix. 38. The thief on the cross speaks of his *kingdom;* and when Jesus himself was interrogated by the Roman governor: "Art thou a king then;" his reply was, "Thou sayest, *that I am a king.*" John xviii. 37. The superscription, too, written on his very cross was, "Jesus of Nazareth, *the King* of the Jews." John xix. 19.

From the manger, then, to his cross, Jesus of Nazareth was considered by many as a *King*. They respected him as such; they sang his praises as such. This truth, too, was his dying confession; and was even written over his head when suffering the agonies of crucifixion.

The kingly character of Jesus may also be defended upon another principle, often asserted and invariably recognized in the New Testament. This principle is, that in Jesus of Nazareth there was the actual *indwelling* of the great *Theocrat* of the previous dispensation.

This truth is taught in such passages as the following: "In the beginning was the Word, and the Word was with God, and the Word was God. And the *Word was made flesh and dwelt among us.*" John i. "And without controversy great is the mystery of godliness. *God was manifest in the flesh,* justified in the Spirit, seen of angels, preached unto the Gentiles, believed on in the world, received up into glory." 1 Tim. iii. 16. "God, who, at sundry times, and in divers manners, spake in times past unto the fathers by the prophets, hath in these last days spoken unto us by his Son, whom he hath appointed heir of all things, by whom also he made the worlds, who being the brightness of his glory, and the express image of his person, and upholding all things by the word of his power, when he had by himself purged our sins, sat down on the right hand of the Majesty on high." Heb. i. The sublime vision, too, which Isaiah had of the glory of Jehovah, is in the New Testament ascribed to Jesus. "These things said Esaias, when he saw his glory and spake of him." John xii. 41.

Now, if it be admitted, that in Jesus of Nazareth there was an indwelling Divinity—yea, that the very same illustrious Being, who appeared to Abraham, who spake to Moses, who delivered the law from Sinai, who dwelt in the Shechinah, was actually manifested in the person of Jesus; if, we say, this be admitted, then is the royalty of Jesus established beyond all doubt. For if the Jehovah of the Old Testament was in reality the King of Israel, the Jehovah of the New, must also be in like manner Israel's King. The difference in the form under which he appeared at these two different periods, cannot change either his character or his rights. Hence the complaint alleged by John against the Jews for not receiving Jesus—"He came unto his own, but his own received him not." John i. 11.

The New Testament, however, expressly declares that Jesus is not only a King, but the greatest of all Kings. He is said to be—"Head over all things."* "Lord of all;"† "the Head of the corner;"‡ "both

* Eph. i. 22.   † Acts x. 36.   ‡ Acts iv. 11.

Lord and Christ;"* a prince and a Saviour;"† "King of kings and Lord of lords."‡

The kingly character and office of Jesus, however, not only differ from those of all earthly monarchs, but far excel them. His character as sovereign is far superior. Most earthly kings have been not only of inferior, but even of base character. Many of them have been ambitious, many tyrannical, many weak, and many addicted to the foulest vices. On the contrary, the royalty of Jesus is tarnished by no misdeed, but adorned with every virtue. He is possessed of infinite wisdom, absolute purity, unerring justice, and boundless benevolence and sympathy towards his subjects. What renders his kingly character, too, infinitely attractive, is, that it is blended with that of *Saviour*. He has *redeemed* with his own blood the subjects he rules, and with a mighty arm is leading them from under the bondage of the great oppressor, to a place of absolute security and peace.

His right to rule is also differently established from that of mere earthly sovereigns. Many earthly kings are usurpers; or are the exponents of faction; or at most, hold their thrones by established usage or the popular will. Not so with Jesus. He is the *anointed of God.* Jehovah has placed him upon his holy hill; has "constituted him the heir of all things;" and "given him a name that is above every name."

The throne, too, which Jesus occupies is far more glorious, than that of the kings of the earth. He is seated "on the right hand of the Majesty on high;" "he has sat down with his Father in his throne." Earthly monarchs dwell in earthly palaces, they occupy thrones of ivory, of cedar, or of some costly materials. Jesus, however, has passed into heaven itself, and occupies the throne of the Eternal.

The extent, too, of his dominion is far greater than theirs. They rule earthly kingdoms, composed sometimes of one country, and sometimes of several countries put together. The greatest of them have not

* Acts ii. 36. † Acts v. 31. ‡ Rev. xix. 16.

ruled even one entire continent. On the contrary, the dominion of Jesus is literally over "all things." "God," says an Apostle, "has set Jesus at his own right hand in the heavenly places, far above all prinpality, and power, and might, and dominion, and every name that is named not only in this world, but also in that which is to come, and hath put all things under his feet." Eph. i.

The kingdom of Jesus, too, is far more permanent than that of earthly kings. Earthly kings are mortal, and even though they build great pyramids, as the receptacles of their royal persons after death, still those very pyramids but proclaim with a louder tongue the truth of their unabiding mortality. The pyramid remains, the rock of which it is composed withstands the ravages of time, but the body of the king, where is it? The traveller looks, and finds where once it was; but where it is, he cannot augur.

How different is the reign of Jesus! "Christ," says an Apostle, "being raised from the dead, dieth no more; death hath no more dominion over him." Rom. vi. 9. He is emphatically, "The King Immortal." Earthly thrones may crumble, earthly kings may die, human generations may waste away; yea, the solid earth, and the firm heavens may depart; still, however, will it be true of Jesus, that "his throne is for ever and ever." Heb. i. 8.

But we must speak more particularly of the *nature* of the kingdom of Jesus.

This kingdom is a *spiritual* one. This feature of it is very much insisted on both by Jesus and his Apostles. " My kingdom," said Jesus to Pilate, "is not of this world." John xviii. 36. Again, he affirms, " The kingdom of God is within you." Luke xvii. 21. The Apostle Paul also asserts, that " The kingdom of God is not meat and drink, but righteousness and peace and joy in the Holy Ghost." Rom. xiv. 17. The Apostle Peter, too, calls Jesus a " living stone," and represents all believers as " lively stones, built up into a spiritual house, to offer up spiritual sacrifices, acceptable to God." 1 Pet. ii. 5.

By the spirituality, however, of the kingdom of Jesus, is not meant a sort of mystical kingdom, which consists principally in contemplation, which sets aside the ordinary duties of life, and which seeks a sort of mysterious absorption into the divine nature. The doctrines of Jesus are eminently practical, and they are designed to penetrate and control every part of human life. They regulate business, they direct friendship, they diffuse themselves through society, pervading all its springs, and doings, and history.

Nor is the spirituality of the kingdom of Jesus inconsistent with the external organization of his church. "God," says an Apostle, "is not the author of confusion, but of peace." When we look into the kingdom of nature, we see universal arrangement. Place, office, destiny, is assigned to every thing. When we contemplate the polity set up under Moses, there is an exact system almost universally observed. So, in the Christian church; its spiritual character does not exclude its visible organization.

By the spirituality of the kingdom of Jesus, we mean that it is created by a spiritual agency, that it consists of spiritual subjects, that it is governed by spiritual laws, and that it awaits a spiritual destiny.

This kingdom is created by a spiritual agency. "Verily, verily," says Jesus, "except a man be born of water and of the Spirit, he cannot enter into the kingdom of God." John iii. 5. John also describes the subjects of this kingdom as "born, not of blood, nor of the will of the flesh, nor of the will of man, but of God." John i. 13. And the Apostle Paul says of all true saints, that they are God's "workmanship, created in Christ Jesus unto good works." Eph. ii. 10.

Men then are, or are not, the subjects of the kingdom of Jesus, as they are, or are not created anew by the power of the Holy Ghost upon their hearts. Neither birth nor baptism, priest nor church, self-exertion nor dependence upon others, can produce the spiritual character. It comes of God, if it comes at all; it is heaven-sent, if ever enjoyed on earth.

The subjects of the kingdom of Jesus are also spiritual. Like begets like. And as all the subjects of the kingdom of Jesus are begotten anew by the Holy Ghost, so do they resemble in their character the Author of their regeneration. One point of such resemblance is *vitality*. Previously to this Divine operation, the subject of it was "dead in trespasses and sins." Upon its occurrence he becomes "quickened," he is made to possess spiritual life. Other points of similarity refer to traits of moral character. "The fruit of the Spirit," says the Apostle Paul, "is love, joy, peace, long-suffering, gentleness, goodness, faith, meekness, temperance." Gal. v. 22, 23. Thus does the subject of "the renewing of the Holy Ghost" receive upon his own nature, in the very act of his renewal, the impress and moral image of the Spirit by which he is quickened. Hence such are said to "live in the Spirit," to "walk in the Spirit," and "to be spiritual."

The kingdom of Jesus is also governed by spiritual laws. Natural laws refer to physical bodies, civil laws to men in their relations to human governments. Spiritual laws are those which regulate the heart and conduct of men toward God. Owing to the natural depravity of men, such laws have but little influence over them, previously to their renovation by Divine power. But after that power has been exerted, the spiritual subject is then prepared to be put under this spiritual administration. The laws of God then have force and influence with him, and nothing delights him more than to obey them. This is what is meant by the Apostle, where he says, "For the law of the Spirit of life in Christ Jesus hath made me free (or delivered me) from the law of sin and death. For what the law could not do, in that it was weak through the flesh, God, sending his own Son, in the likeness of sinful flesh, and for sin, condemned sin in the flesh, that the righteousness of the law might be fulfilled in us, who walk not after the flesh, but after the Spirit." Rom. viii. There is also an allusion to this spiritual subjection to the Divine law in the following passage, "For this is the covenant that I will make with the house of Israel after those days, saith the Lord: I will put my laws into their mind, and write them in their hearts, and I will be to them a God, and they shall be to me a people." Heb. viii. 10.

The kingdom of Jesus also awaits a spiritual destiny. "But we are come," says the Apostle Paul, "unto Mount Zion, and unto the city of the living God, the heavenly Jerusalem, and to an innumerable company of angels, to the general assembly and church of the first-born, which are written in heaven, and to God the Judge of all, and to the spirits of just men made perfect, and to Jesus the Mediator of the New Covenant, and to the blood of sprinkling, that speaketh better things than that of Abel." Heb. xii. Again, the same Apostle says, in allusion to the resurrection of the bodies of the saints, "It is sown a natural body, it is raised a spiritual body." 1 Cor. xv.

It is true, there may be much of materiality in the heaven that awaits the saints. This, however, will not prevent their ultimate and glorious spiritual destination. "The spirits of just men will then be made perfect." Every citizen of the New Jerusalem will resemble Jesus in his glorified state. None will possess "spot or wrinkle or any such thing;" but all will be perfectly holy, and eternally blessed.

Such is the nature of the kingdom of Jesus, as to its internal and essential part. It is pre-eminently a spiritual kingdom. Hence it is entirely diverse from all the kingdoms and organizations of men. It is truly "a stone cut out of the mountain without hands." Hence, too, its real character and excellencies have never been perceived, and cannot be perceived by the men of the world. The Jews did not perceive it when first set up among them. Nor have the nations of the earth yet perceived it, though it has been set up in their midst for eighteen centuries past. It is this character of the kingdom of Jesus, too, which makes it so odious to those who can conceive of Christianity only in its external organization and forms. Hence, "he that is born after the flesh," now as formerly, persecutes, and will ever persecute "him that is born after

THE MESSIAH. 115

the Spirit." It is upon this principle we are to account for the antipathy of the Jews against the Apostles; of the ancient Romans against the early Christians; and in later times, of Romanists against the Reformers. It all results from the general truth, that the carnal mind perceiveth not the things of the Spirit.

We have already said, that the spiritual character of the kingdom of Jesus is not incompatible with a visible and external organization. What is this organization, and how far did it displace the one previously existing? We proceed to answer the latter question first.

The Christian organization, then, did not destroy the original covenant between God and Israel. This covenant was not Mosaic, but Abrahamic. It is also uniformly mentioned in Scripture as an "everlasting covenant." The present dispersion of the Jews, too, does not prove the non-existence of this covenant; for under the circumstances, the covenant itself requires such dispersion in fulfilment of one of its conditions. Besides, the Jews are to be gathered in; they are to be brought again into their own land. " The wastes of Canaan are again to be builded, and that desolate land to be tilled." Exod. xxxvi. How can such a restoration take place, unless the provisions of "the everlasting covenant" secure it? Hence, the apostle Paul says: " Blindness in part (or for a limited time) is happened to Israel, until the fulness of the Gentiles be come in; and so (or afterwards) all Israel shall be saved. As it is written, There shall come out of Zion the Deliverer, and shall turn away ungodliness from Jacob; for this is my covenant unto them, when I shall take away their sins." Rom. xi.

Nor did the new organization abolish the rite of circumcision. This rite was the *seal* of the covenant made with Abraham. If then the covenant continue, so must also its seal. It is true, that the Apostles would not impose this rite upon believing Gentiles. Acts xv. The reason of this, however, is obvious. The covenant and circumcision were national; they referred to the Israelites as a people. Inasmuch, then, as Christianity was not destined to *Judaize* the nations, not designed to make Jews of them, it was proper that peculiarities belonging to the Jews as a people should not be imposed upon those who were not by nature the descendants of Abraham.*

Nor was the new system designed to interfere with the civil or national laws of the Jews. Being a spiritual system, Christianity did not directly oppose any existing forms of political government. It might modify all, but it could exist under any.

Much less did Christianity subvert the moral part of the previous dispensation. Its position on this point is, " Till heaven and earth pass, one jot or tittle shall not fail from the law." All the morality then of the Old Testament still abides, and receives additional sanctions from the New.

What changes then, were effected by the Messianic kingdom? These four—the temple, the priesthood, and the ceremonial law were abolished, and the

---

* The opinion seems generally to prevail, that circumcision as a Jewish seal was abolished by Christ. Besides, however, the spiritual blessings embraced in the Abrahamic covenant for the world at large, were there not certain peculiar blessings designed for the Israelites as a people? Certainly, all those who consider them at present as in any sense God's peculiar people, must so understand this covenant. Why are they still a distinct people? Why are they to be converted *as a nation?* How is it, that so many believe in their literal restoration to Canaan? All these views seem to rest upon some Jewish peculiarity in the Abrahamic covenant. And if such a feature still 'exist in that covenant, why is not circumcision still a seal to Israel?

The author was apprehensive that he would be almost alone in his opinion. Upon examination, however, he finds himself sustained by several judicious and eminent critics. Grotius and Michaelis, as quoted by Bloomfield, use the following language: " The Jews (i. e. in the days of the Apostles) might adopt circumcision as a national rite; but the Gentiles having no such political reason, could only use it as necessary to justification; which would make void faith and grace, and is therefore strictly forbidden:" (on Gal. v. 2.) Macknight, on the same passage, says: "As the preservation (i. e. after Christ) of Abraham's posterity as a distinct people from the rest of mankind answered many important purposes in the Divine government, their observance of the rite of circumcision, declared by God himself to be the seal of his covenant with Abraham, was necessary to mark them as his descendants, as long as it was determined that they should be continued a distinct people." Dr. Doddridge also expresses a similar sentiment.

blessings of salvation were extended to the rest of the world.

Said Jesus to the woman of Sychar—" The hour cometh, when ye shall neither in this mountain, nor yet at Jerusalem, worship the Father." John iv. 21. He also said of the temple itself, " There shall not be left here one stone upon another, that shall not be thrown down." Matt. xxiv. 2. When the body of Jesus, of which the temple was a type, was "destroyed," the purposes of the temple were answered, and a new one was to be raised without hands.

But not only was the temple abolished, the Jewish priesthood shared the same fate. This priesthood was typical of that of the Messiah. When, therefore, the latter began, the former ended. Hence, at the death of Jesus, the veil of the temple was rent in twain from the top to the bottom. This was significant, not only of the abolition of the types and shadows, but of the appointment of a new High Priest. Hence the Apostle Paul says, " But Christ being come, a High Priest of good things to come, by a greater and more perfect tabernacle, not made with hands, neither by the blood of goats and calves, but by his own blood, he entered in once into the holy place, having obtained eternal redemption for us." Heb. ix. 11, 12. Again, the Apostle says expressly, that the Aaronic "priesthood was changed," (vii. 12.,) from the sons of Levi to Christ.

If then, the temple be abolished and the priesthood, of course, the ceremonial law departs with them. This is the reasoning of the Apostle. " For the priesthood being changed, there is made of necessity a change of the law;" that is, of the ceremonial law. Indeed, the entire Epistle to the Hebrews exhibits in the clearest manner, that the temple, priesthood and sacrifices of the ancient dispensation were all abolished by the new system. We there learn, that the Christian Jerusalem is a heavenly one; that his temple is above, that his High Priest is Christ, that the shedding of *his* blood is the only sacrifice for sin; and that the ancient Jewish ceremonies are now a mere nullity, except as they may be used to illustrate the "good things" of the new dispensation.

The other change effected by Christianity, and which the Apostle Paul considers a "great mystery," was, the extension of the blessings of salvation to the world at large. No language can better describe this than that of the Apostle himself—" For he is our peace, who hath made both one; and hath broken down the middle wall of partition between us; having abolished in his flesh the enmity, even the law of commandments, contained in ordinances, for to make in himself, of twain, one new man, so making peace; and that he might reconcile both unto God, in one body by the cross, having slain the enmity thereby; and came and preached peace to you which were afar off, and to them that were nigh. For through him we both have an access by one Spirit unto the Father." Eph. ii. 14—18.

Such were the effects of the new system upon that which pre-existed. It abolished its temple, priesthood, and ritual, as of no longer use; it also so extended the blessings of salvation, as to embrace the world in general, according to the promise given to Abraham, that "in his seed all the nations of the earth should be blessed."

We now proceed to the other inquiry, What is the organization of the new system, as a distinct establishment from that which preceded it?

This question, we are aware, is thickly set with difficulties, and is also associated in the minds of most men, with more or less of prejudice. It is not intended, however, to go into details, or to advocate any particular system.

The organization of the Christian Church may be divided into three periods—that of Jesus himself, that of the Apostles, and that which has taken place since. The part accomplished by Jesus in person, consists of the four following particulars—the communication of its moral truths, the delineation of its moral character, the appointment of its teachers, and the institution of its ordinances.

THE MESSIAH.

The doctrines, or moral truths of the new system, were placed by the Founder of Christianity, as the basis of the new establishment. These were the rock on which the Church was to be built, secure from all the devices of the gates of hell.

These truths were to be employed by the agency of the Spirit, both in the production and sustentation of the Church; eternal life was placed in the proper knowledge of God and of his Son, and the truth was ordained as the means of sanctification.

The truth, being thus essential both to the existence and development of the new system—being its heart, or vital part, was made by Jesus the *great idea* in Christianity. His disciples were to illustrate this truth in their lives; it was the message which his ambassadors were to publish; the ordinances appointed by him were to cherish it; and, in its rejection, there could be neither discipleship nor salvation.

Hence, Jesus spent his life, not in organizing a system, but in publishing the truth. "To this end," says he, "was I born, and for this cause came I into the world, that I should bear witness unto the truth." John xviii. 37. Again he exclaims, "I am come a light into the world, that whosoever believeth on me should not abide in darkness." John xii. 46. Upon the reception, or rejection of this truth, too, has he suspended the eternal destiny of all to whom his gospel should be made known—"Go ye into all the world and preach the gospel to every creature; he that believeth and is baptized shall be saved, but he that believeth not shall be damned." Mark xvi.

The fundamental idea then, in the organization of the Christian Church is, the moral truths of the gospel. The Church is where these are; it is not, where these are excluded.

The second step in the organization of the Church was, the distinct delineation of the character of its members.

Jews were made by birth, or by circumcision; not so Christians. Men could become real subjects of the kingdom of Jesus, only by the cordial reception of its moral truths in their spiritual renovation. The preparation of the soil, and the implantation of the seed, were alike a divine work. Hence the importance of describing those in whom this change was wrought, and by whom this truth had been received. These were not simply Israelites, or hearers, or professors, or preachers, or apostles; they were "the poor in spirit," "the meek," "those that hunger and thirst after righteousness," "the merciful," "the pure in heart," "the peacemakers," "the persecuted for righteousness' sake." Matt. v. The cordial reception of the moral truths taught by Jesus, produced traits of character like these; the renewing of the Holy Ghost, and his holy guidance, led to a life like this. Hence, they and they only are the subjects of the new kingdom, who thus exemplify the gospel, and thus exhibit before men its great cardinal virtues.

This is the second step of Jesus in organizing his Church. He first delivers its doctrines—he next describes its members.

The third step was, the consecration and mission of men who should publish these great moral truths, and thus disciple others, to whom the teachings of Jesus himself did not extend.

Men were to be made converts after Jesus left the world, just as they had been previously. It was his preaching, accompanied by the Holy Ghost, which had converted them during his life. It was by preaching, accompanied by the same power, that they were to be converted after his departure from the world. Hence the necessity for preachers, and for the continuance of preachers, as long as men were to be converted to God. This necessity led to the great commission given to the eleven, "Go ye into all the world and preach the gospel to every creature."

The last part of the work of Jesus in the organization of his Church, was the appointment of the ordinances of Baptism and the Supper. The former was designed to indicate publicly his disciples—the latter, to keep ever before the minds of these disciples, the one great truth of the new system, the *vicarious suf-*

ferings of Jesus for his people. The one was to express, that the moral truths of the system had been embraced; the other was to strengthen and invigorate the faith of disciples in those truths. The one was to separate Christians from the world; the other was to bind all Christians together, by uniting them more closely to their common Head.

Such was the organization of the Christian Church, as left by Jesus himself. There was no general and systematic organization of the Church as a whole; nor was there the regular constitution of one individual congregation. Its great foundations were laid; the sort of materials to be placed on these foundations were described; the master-builders were appointed, and its simple, but significant ceremonies, were instituted.

Jesus left, then, but two classes of persons in his Church—teachers and disciples; baptizers and the baptized—administrators and communicants—or, in other words, the preachers and the receivers of the word. The preachers were all on a perfect official equality; the disciples were so likewise. The former had been called and commissioned by the same Master, and they were to accomplish the same work; the latter had been converted by the same grace, and baptized with the same baptism. The one class were ministerial, the other Christian brethren. Nor was the officer to exalt himself above the member; but he was to be greatest in the estimation of his Master, who had a spirit to be accounted least, and servant of all.

How far the Apostles modified these great essential principles of the Christian Church, it now remains to inquire.

The Apostolic Church was first organized in the city of Jerusalem. It was not, however, done at once. For a considerable time, no officers but the Apostles were known. These and the membership composed the Church. Hence, when a new Apostle was to be chosen, the election was made by the disciples,[*] under the management of the eleven Apostles.

[*] Barrow, 327.

Acts i. Nor was there any ordination, but a simple enrolment, after the lot was cast, of the name of Matthias with the other Apostles. Even the temporalities of the new society were under the care of the Apostles. Acts iv. 35; v. 2; vi. 2. When, however, these temporalities became too burdensome, they were committed to a set of men chosen by the disciples for that purpose, and who, through prayer and imposition of hands, were ordained to the new office by the Apostles. Acts vi. The church now consisted of three classes of persons—apostles, deacons, and the membership. This membership, though very large, was still not as yet divided into separate societies; but constituted one united body now called the Church. Acts ii. 47; v. 11; viii. 1. About this time a great persecution arose. Stephen, one of the deacons, was stoned, and the members, with the exception of the Apostles, were driven into other countries and cities. This persecution, however, served greatly to enlarge the Church—for "they that were scattered abroad, went every where preaching the word." Not that they were all regular preachers; but they published the gospel in every practicable and prudent method.

About this time a new set of officers was introduced into the Christian society. These were Elders. The name implies *ruling;* especially among the Jews, where it was applied both to the general rulers of the nation, and to the particular rulers of each synagogue or religious assembly. We must suppose, therefore, that either the office in the synagogue was transferred to the new church; or, that an analogous office was instituted in the new society. The first mention of these new officers is made in Acts xi. 30, where the Christians of Antioch are said to have transmitted to "the elders" in Jerusalem, certain funds to supply the necessities of the poor saints there, and who seem not to have left the city with their wealthier brethren during the persecution. The next allusion to this office, not only refers to it as an office well understood, but also casts light upon the manner of its creation—" And when they had ordained them elders in every church, and had prayed with fasting, they commended them to the Lord on whom they believed." Acts xix. 23. The word ($\chi\epsilon\iota\rho o\tau o\nu\eta\sigma a\nu\tau\epsilon\varsigma$) which is here translated "ordained," is used but in one other instance in the New Testament. In 2 Cor. viii. 19, it is applied to Luke's being "chosen of the churches" to travel with Paul and others. It means literally to lift up, or extend the hand; which was an ordinary mode of taking a vote. Hence the Genevan version, Tyndal and Cranmer, all render the passage thus: "And when they had ordained them elders by election."* As, too, the deacons had been chosen by the members; and as these elders were put into this office from among the brethren over whom they presided, there can be no doubt, that they were elected by the popular vote. The conclusion then to which we come is, that these primitive elders were grave and judicious men, elected by each Christian congregation from among their own number, to superintend their spiritual interests, and to preside in their religious assemblies; and that they were solemnly consecrated to that office by prayer and fasting.

Whether these elders were really preachers, or simply rulers in particular congregations, has been much debated. The objections to their being strictly preachers are such as these. They were elected by their brethren, and from among themselves, as their spiritual guides. Now, it seems incredible, that an election of the brethren should make a preacher. Nor can we conceive, how the new churches planted by the Apostles could have had men, fitted at so early a date, to be preachers of the word. The locality too of these officers is an objection. Regular preachers were to "go into all the world and

* See Mezeray, Abrégé de l'Histoire de France, (Vol. i. p. 41, A. D. 400, to A. D. 500,) who expounds the words *vox populi vox Dei* to signify the election of bishops by the people. After alleging that bishops, during this period, were elected by the people, he adds, "La voix du peuple passoit en cela, pour une vocation de Dieu."—[*Ed. Presb. Bd. of Pub.*

preach the gospel to every creature." Their commission was general, their mission was to the world at large. These primitive elders, however, seem to have been entirely local. We find no instance of their exercising their gifts or office, beyond the churches over which they presided. The name too, is an objection. Why are they called *elders?* The term *evangelist* means a *gospelizer*, or one who preaches the gospel. The term *prophet* refers to *speaking*. The term *elder*, then, can awaken no other idea, than that of ruling, or of one, who manages the affairs of a Christian congregation.

On the contrary, there are some things to favour the position, that these elders were preachers. Who were to instruct these new churches, if they were not? The Apostle Paul also exhorts those of Ephesus. "To feed the church of God," Acts xx. 28; which seems to refer to the *preaching* of the word. The same Apostle also says that Elders must be "apt to teach," 1 Tim. iii. 2; and that they should be able "by sound doctrine both to exhort and to convince the gainsayers." Tit. i. 9.

The conclusion then, to which we come in relation to these officers is, that their original designation was that of exercising spiritual supervision, and authority in individual congregations; that to render them competent to such supervision, they needed themselves to be well instructed in the Christian doctrine, and that when no apostle, evangelist, prophet, or regular teacher, was present, it was their duty to instruct their several congregations. "Certainly," says the learned Neander, "it is not capable of proof that the teachers always belonged to the presbyters. This much only is certain, it was a source of great satisfaction, when among the rulers of the church there were men qualified also for teachers."*

Besides elders and deacons, whose offices confined them to individual churches, there were many others associated with the Apostles in their labours. Barna-

* Hist. Christian Religion and Church.

bas, Silas, Luke, Philip, Mark, Timothy, Titus, Apollos, and many others were of this number. These all appear to have been regular preachers of the word. It is true, nothing is said of the ordination of any of them except Timothy, and of Barnabas when appointed missionary to the Gentiles. How they were inducted into office, or whether any regular mode was used, we know not.

That there was no regular general government of the church instituted by the Apostles, is evident from the history of the facts left us. The only case which has the appearance of such a general government is, the reference of a particular question, by the church at Antioch, to the church at Jerusalem. Acts xv. This reference however was altogether voluntary, on the part of the church at Antioch; and it was decided at Jerusalem, not by an Apostle, or by a council of Apostles; but by the Apostles, Elders and "whole church." Acts xv. 22.

Such was the Apostolic Church. The disciples, who had previously existed in common, were by them distributed into separate congregations; and two new sets of officers were appointed, *deacons* and *elders*. The bond which held all their separate churches together was not authority or system, but the truth and mutual love. Never were churches more closely united, and yet never were churches less forced into union.

If it be asked, what was the umpire in cases of doctrinal or other controversies, the answer is, the *word of God*. This word, otherwise that it was recorded in the Old Testament Scriptures, was at first delivered by inspired men. As these inspired men were mortal, their instructions were committed to writing, and in that form were always afterwards to control the churches.

If it be still asked, who was to decide in controversies which should arise as to the meaning of these apostolical writings, the answer is, every church for itself, every teacher for himself, every man for himself. To place uninspired authority over inspired, and to require one church, preacher, or disciple, to yield absolutely to the decision of some other church, preacher, or disciple, is at once to overthrow the authority of God by establishing that of man; and to subvert the decision of one man or set of men, by the decision of some other men or set of men.

Nor is there the least shadow of proof that any such human umpire was either appointed by Jesus, or sanctioned by his Apostles. It is true, that in forming opinions about controverted points, some deference was due to those men who had the best opportunities for knowing what was true; or to those churches that had been most under apostolical teaching, or which had best preserved apostolic practices. All this, however, was but secondary and auxiliary; and in all matters of faith and practice, the apostolic writings, and these alone, were to govern. Not man, but God, was to be the only "Lord of conscience."

We come now to the third and last part of the organization of the Church. This has occurred since the days of the apostles; is merely human, and therefore exceedingly imperfect.*

---

* At the close of the first six centuries, the change, though great in some particulars, was small compared with that which followed. See Fleury's Second Discourse on Ecclesiastical History, Art. V. "The bishops," he says, " did not give great attention to the *temporel* of their church, but left the care of it to deacons and stewards, but they did not discharge themselves of the *spirituel* upon any body. Their occupation was prayer, instruction, and correction. They entered into every possible detail, and it was for this reason that the dioceses were so small, that one single man might suffice for them, and by himself know the whole of his flock. There would be no need for more than one bishop, to do every thing by another and from a distance. It is true, they had priests to relieve them in the *spirituel*, to preside at prayers, and to celebrate the holy sacrifice in case of the absence or sickness of the bishop, to baptize or give penance in case of necessity. Sometimes the bishop even confided to them the ministry of the word; for regularly there was only the bishop who preached. The priests were his council and the senate of the church, elevated to this rank for their ecclesiastical knowledge, their wisdom, their experience."

Abating some of this author's ecclesiastical technicalities, (such as holy sacrifice, penance, &c.) we may see more of the Presbyterian than of the Papal organization in these churches. Such small dioceses remind one of parishes; such minute primeval oversight of the flock, strongly resembles the duties of a parish clergyman. Priests who do

That the state of things left by the Apostles, continued for a considerable time, is evident from the Epistle of Clement to the Corinthians. In that epistle there is not the least intimation given, that Rome had any authority over Corinth. It also distinctly states, that Presbyters or Elders were chosen by the people, and that the subjection of the people to them was voluntary, not forced. "Wherefore we cannot think that those may be justly thrown out of their ministry, who were either appointed by the Apostles, or afterwards chosen by other eminent men, with the consent of the whole church." Again, says Clement, "It is a shame, my beloved, yea, a very great shame, and unworthy your Christian profession, to hear that the most firm and ancient Church of the Corinthians should, by one or two persons, be led into a sedition against its Presbyters."

The changes which were afterwards introduced into the apostolic organization of the Church are principally these three: The presbyterial feature was overshadowed by the episcopal, the episcopal by the patriarchal, and the patriarchal by the papal. The spirit of domination began with the rulers of each particular church, and ceased only, when every church, yea, the whole world, was subject to *one man!** Authority was thus substituted for truth, and the will of man for the will of God! These changes, it is true, were effected only gradually, and through many centuries; still, however, they were effected, and became alike destructive to the purity and the freedom of the

not preach, but serve as a council for the bishop, are not very unlike the eldership of Presbyterian churches. And the practice of confining the duty of preaching to bishops exclusively, would tend to multiply them so that each congregation might have one.—[*Ed. of Presb. Bd. of Pub.*

* Mezeray, speaking of the Church in France, under the reign of Clovis, says, "The titles, *Pope, Father of the Church, Beatitude, Most Blessed, Holiness, Sovereign Pontiff, Servant of the Servants of God, Apostolical,* were common to all bishops." Abrégé Chronologique de l'Histoire de France, Vol. i. p. 41. A. D. 400 to A. D. 500. The appropriation of these titles to the bishop of Rome exclusively, was the fruit of the ambition of the bishops of that city, which appeared at a later age.—[*Ed. Presb. Board of Pub.*

Church. And it is remarkable in this extraordinary drama, that one man, the Pope, has been made to hold a place of power, such as no one of the Apostles, nor all of them together ever held; indeed, such as Jesus himself never exercised while here on earth!

The diversities which now exist among various Protestant sects, on the subject of church government, may be traced to the prominence which they respectively give to certain parts of the original organization. It is likely that no one of them, in all particulars, agrees with the apostolic model. Some of them by giving great prominence to the independence of the churches in the days of the Apostles, have gone into pure congregationalism. Others by magnifying the prerogatives of the church rulers and teachers have approached an ecclesiastical hierarchy. Others, again, in consideration of the plurality of elders in each church, and of their being elected by their brethren, have adopted the presbyterial system. Doubtless, there are some things in which all these are right, and there are also some things in which they have all departed from apostolic practice.

These churches, however, may all sufficiently adhere to the original constitution, to render them brethren in the kingdom of one common Lord and Saviour. Do they attach the chief importance to the moral truths of the new system? Do they place discipleship in the cordial reception, and the proper manifestation of those truths? Do they receive and maintain a set of preachers and teachers under the sanction and upon the authority of Jesus? Do they administer the Christian sacraments? Are the writings of the Apostles their only umpire in all matters of faith and practice? Do they allow to each other the rights of conscience and of personal judgment? If so, they all rest upon the foundation laid by Jesus for his Church. If so, they are all sufficiently apostolic, to live together in peace on earth, and to reign together in glory hereafter.

We have dwelt the longer upon the kingdom of Jesus, because it is a matter of deep interest to Chris-

THE MESSIAH.

tians. Let us then apply this argument to his Messiahship. According to ancient prophecy, the Messiah was to be a king, indeed he was to be the greatest of kings. But we have seen, that these predictions have all been fulfilled in Jesus. By all who receive his doctrines, he is considered as possessed of the very highest possible royalty. Though crucified, he yet lives, and though assigned to the greatest ignominy once, yet does he now sit upon a throne " high and lifted up." The crown of power is on his head, the sceptre of dominion in his hand, and his name is " King of kings, and Lord of lords."

CHAPTER XIII.

THE RESURRECTION OF JESUS.

There are three sources of evidence to the Messiahship of Jesus, derived from his resurrection. It fulfils several ancient prophecies concerning the Messiah, it confirms the testimony given by Jesus to his own Messiahship, and it proves that he has power to exercise all the prerogatives of the Messiah.

In the 16th Psalm, are the following expressions concerning the future Deliverer. "My flesh shall also rest in hope. For thou wilt not leave my soul in hell, neither wilt thou suffer thy Holy One to see corruption. Thou wilt show me the path of life: in thy presence is fulness of joy; at thy right hand are pleasures for evermore." This psalm evidently refers to the Messiah. Hengstenberg says of it, "We must nevertheless assert, that every impartial critic must regard the Messianic interpretation of verses 9—11, as the easiest and most natural, and that it would be universally adopted, were it not for the influence of doctrinal views."* If, then, these verses of the psalm be applicable to the Messiah, they embrace his resurrection from the grave, and his exaltation to the right hand of God in the heavens.

The same truth is taught in the 22d Psalm. After a most vivid description of the cruel sufferings of the Messiah, the writer represents him as being remarkably delivered, by special Divine assistance. "Thou hast heard me from the horns of the unicorns. I will declare thy name unto my brethren. My praise shall be of thee in the great congregation. All the ends of the earth shall remember and turn unto the Lord,

*Christology, vol. i. p. 123.

THE MESSIAH. 131

and all the kindreds of the nations shall worship before thee. For the kingdom is the Lord's, and he is the Governor among the nations. A seed shall serve him; it shall be accounted to the Lord for a generation." Here, the same person, who, in the previous part of the sacred poem, is described as enduring the most dreadful agonies, is exhibited as rising above his sorrows; as entering the great congregation, and as exercising sovereignty over the nations. These facts never occurred, all of them, in the life of David; but were predictions concerning his *illustrious Son.*

In the 53d chapter of Isaiah the resurrection of the Messiah from death is also foretold: "When thou shalt make his soul an offering for sin, he shall see his seed; he shall prolong his days, and the pleasure of the Lord shall prosper in his hand. Therefore will I divide him a portion with the great, and he shall divide the spoil with the strong; because he hath poured out his soul unto death." Here, the same person, whose "soul was made an offering for sin," and whose "soul was poured out unto death," is represented subsequently as living, reigning, and triumphing. If then the psalm refer to the Messiah, it of course teaches his resurrection from the grave.

The author above quoted, makes the following judicious observations in reference to the three passages of Scripture above referred to. "Whoever had learned from Isaiah liii., to know the servant of God, who after having died for us, should be exalted to the highest glory, and enjoy a never ending life; or from Psalm xxii, had become familiar with the thought of a Messiah, who should pass through suffering to glory, and at the same time had perceived that the speaker in a psalm, was not always of course its subject, might easily come to the conclusion, that not David, but the Messiah, in the expectation of whose advent the whole spiritual life of the people entered, here appears as speaker, and foretells his own resurrection. And even granting that no one under the Old Testament attained to this knowledge, it is yet so obvious to us, who can institute a far more extensive comparison of the prophecies illustrated by the fulfilment, that we must regard the Messianic interpretation, as at least the most probable, even without the evidence of the New Testament." *

If then it was foretold that the Messiah was not only to die, but also to arise again from the grave; and if it be proven, that Jesus of Nazareth after his crucifixion, did thus arise by the special energy and interposition of God, then is it clear, that in this particular, the history of Jesus also fulfils prophecy concerning the promised Deliverer, and shows that he was indeed the Son of God.

But Jesus himself not only asserted his Messiahship as we have already seen, but predicted his resurrection after three days. "From that time forth began Jesus to show unto his disciples, how that he must go unto Jerusalem, and suffer many things of the elders and chief priests, and scribes, and be killed, and be raised again the third day." Matt. xvi. 21. Now, if in accordance with this and similar statements, he actually did arise from death, not only is his testimony to his resurrection to be believed, but also his more important testimony, that he was the Messiah, is established. This truth he often asserted, this truth he always admitted. If then, by the direct concurrence of heaven, he was actually raised from the tomb, his Messiahship is confirmed by God himself, and illustrated by a miracle the most remarkable, of which we have any knowledge.

Equally evident is it, that if Jesus was raised from the dead, and if he did ascend up into heaven, according to the testimony of the Evangelists; and if especially, the concurrence of his own will was employed in this resurrection and ascension, then must it be admitted, that Jesus has all those attributes and qualifications, which peculiarly and exclusively adapt him to the Messianic kingdom and throne.

Is the resurrection of Jesus then, a well authenticated fact? This will depend of course, upon the number, the competency, and the credibility of the

* Chris. i. 124.

witnesses, who have testified to the rest of the world on the subject.

The number of witnesses is sufficient. The Jewish law, and the laws of other nations, require even in capital offences, the testimony of but two or more witnesses. "At the mouth of two witnesses, or three witnesses, shall he that is worthy of death, be put to death." Deut. xvii. 6. The witnesses to the resurrection of Jesus are the eleven Apostles, together with a large number of others. " He was seen of Cephas, says the Apostle Paul, then of the twelve; after that he was seen of above five hundred brethren at once; after that he was seen of James; then of all the Apostles, and last of all, he was seen of me also, as of one born out of due time." 1 Cor. xv. 5–8.

These witnesses were also competent. The competency of a witness in this case depends upon three things;—upon his knowledge of Jesus before his crucifixion; upon his personal observation of his death; and upon personal interviews with him after his resurrection. The witnesses were acquainted with Jesus previously to his crucifixion. They had been intimate with him, many of them, even from his childhood. Others had been his constant companions for several years; they knew no one more certainly than they had known him.

They were also the personal spectators of his crucifixion and death. This scene took place at the feast of the Passover, when Jerusalem was crowded with Jews from every part of Judea, and almost of the world. It was exhibited in the most public manner. If, therefore, the Apostles felt any interest in the fate of their Master, they could not avoid witnessing it. It is impossible to deny that they felt the deepest interest in him. They must therefore have had the most certain knowledge, of the issue of his crucifixion. Hence, they have detailed with the greatest accuracy every event which occurred, from the bloody sweat of Gethsemane, to his expiring cry upon the cross. When the soldiers drove the nails, and lifted up the cross, they saw it; when the multitudes derided him, wagging their heads, they saw it; and when Jesus exclaimed, "Father, into thy hands I commit my spirit," and immediately expired, they witnessed it. And when, after his death, "a soldier with a spear pierced his side, and forthwith came thereout blood and water," they saw it. In recording his personal testimony to this fact, John says, "and he that saw it, bare record; and his record is true, and he knoweth that he sayeth true, that ye might believe." John xix. 35. The certainty of his death was also conveyed officially to Pilate. Nor could Joseph and Nicodemus, who were rulers, and who buried him, be deceived. And even if it were possible for all these to be imposed upon, can we imagine, that "the chief Priests and Pharisees," who had his sepulchre sealed, could have been mistaken? Indeed, the reality of his death was never questioned by the Jews, or by any one in that day; it was in reference to his resurrection only, that they disbelieved.

The Apostles also had, not one, but many personal and protracted interviews with Jesus, after his resurrection. He not only appeared to Mary Magdalene, but conversed with her. He was not only seen by the two on the way to Emmaus, but entered into a long conversation with them. The very same evening, too, he entered the room where ten of the Apostles had assembled, and furnished them with the most indubitable proof of the reality of his resurrection. "And he said unto them, why are ye troubled? and why do thoughts arise in your mind? Behold my hands and my feet, that it is I myself: handle me and see, for a spirit hath not flesh and bones, as ye see me have. And when he had thus spoken, he showed them his hands and his feet, (that is, the marks of the nails.) And while they yet believed not for joy, and wondered, he said unto them, Have ye here any meat? and they gave him a piece of broiled fish, and of an honey-comb, and he took it, and did eat before them." Luke xxiv. He next enters into a protracted discourse with them. In this case, the personal identity of Jesus, is submitted to the most minute and varied examination of ten men, for the space at least of several hours. How was it possible for them to be deceived?

One of their number, however, being absent, the interview was repeated a week afterwards. "And after eight days, again his disciples were within, and Thomas with them. Then came Jesus, the doors being shut, and stood in the midst and said, Peace be unto you. Then saith he to Thomas, reach hither thy finger, and behold my hands; and reach hither thy hand, and thrust it into my side, and be not faithless, but believing. And Thomas answered, and said, "My Lord and my God!" John xx. Another discourse of considerable length also follows, during which the Apostles had every possible opportunity for ascertaining the truth of his resurrection. The interview, at the sea of Galilee, was also of the same convincing and irresistible character. Jesus not only appears to seven of the Apostles, but works a miracle for them, eats before them, and converses with them for a considerable time. John xxi.

It is impossible therefore, for the witnesses to this fact, to have been deceived. They had every opportunity that men could have, to know the truth in the case. They knew Jesus before his crucifixion most intimately; they were spectators of his crucifixion, and they had several protracted interviews with him after his resurrection, during which he not only exhibited the very marks of his execution, but both ate in their presence, and conversed freely with them.

Are these witnesses then credible? This question is to be decided by a reference to their moral character. It is impossible for a good man, and especially for a number of good men, to impose a deliberate falsehood upon others. Were the Apostles then good men?

The first evidence to this fact is to be adduced from the doctrines and precepts which they promulged, and which it is certain they believed. Now, character is the result of certain truths upon the heart. If then the Apostles published to the world, and really embraced, themselves, a set of doctrines, and a code of morals, the most pure and heavenly, that the world has ever known, how is it possible for them to have been wicked or deceitful men?

The publication of these truths, too, and especially their public testimony to the resurrection of their Master, subjected them to every sort of indignity and persecution. It was at the peril of their lives, that they bore such testimony. And yet they bore it, not only in the temple, but in the presence of the very murderers of Jesus.

The spirit, too, which these witnesses exhibit, demonstrates their sincerity. What brotherly love reigned among them, what benevolence toward mankind! What an absence of resentment, what a calm submission to injuries! What adherence to truth! What love of principle! There is, indeed, not the least evidence against the moral character of even one of them. Their reputation was above suspicion. Look at the charges, brought occasionally against them by their enemies! What are they? They all lie against the very truth they were publishing, and in the publication of which they jeoparded their lives. The only crime is, that they teach the people, that Jesus was alive, and that he was indeed the Messiah!

If then, these witnesses were of sufficient number, if they were competent to judge as to what they testified, and if they were credible witnesses, being all of them men of the greatest integrity of character, then, does the resurrection of Jesus, as a matter of fact, rest upon a foundation the most solid of which we can conceive. No other truth in history is more clearly attested—no other truth in history possesses higher claims upon our belief.

Now, whether we consider Jesus as raised by the Father, according to several Old Testament prophecies, or by the Spirit, according to the testimony of Paul, or by himself, according to his own testimony, it alters not the case. There doubtless are senses in which the Three Persons of the Trinity were all concerned in his resurrection to life. The reality of his resurrection is the main point in the argument. This we have fully proven. If then, he really arose from the dead, there are several prophecies referring to the resurrection of the Messiah fulfilled in him. Then is his own testimony to Messiahship confirmed; and then, may we readily believe, that, in as much as he triumphed over all the powers of death, so he possesses all those powers and prerogatives that are appropriate to the Messiah, and that he is able to save and deliver all who put their trust in him.

There is one other source of evidence to the reality of the resurrection of Jesus, which must not be altogether omitted. Jesus had promised to his disciples "the Comforter." He had assured them, that after a few days, they would be endued with extraordinary power from on high. This promise was fulfilled in the most public and extraordinary manner. About ten days after the ascension of their Master, and in the midst of the feast of Pentecost, the Holy Ghost was poured out upon the Apostles. They were at once endued with the knowledge of foreign languages. They received power to work miracles. They had also such spirit and energy imparted to them, as rendered them willing to face either danger or death, in their extraordinary mission.

Now, it is impossible for such an event as this to have taken place, without Divine approval. And it is equally impossible for that approval to have been given, and yet the Apostles to have been bad men, and engaged at the time in fabricating a pernicious delusion for the rest of mankind. This extraordinary effusion, then, of the Spirit upon the witnesses, so publicly given, must be considered as the sanction of Jehovah to the truth of their testimony, as a Divine attestation to the resurrection of Jesus.

CHAPTER XIV.

THE BLESSINGS CONFERRED ON THE GENTILES BY JESUS.

In the ancient predictions concerning the Messiah, it was foretold, that the Gentiles should derive great benefits from his advent. To punish the nations for their idolatry, God had been pleased to confine his revelations and covenants, for many centuries, to the descendants of Abraham. But when the Great Deliverer should appear, and should give to the world new and fuller exhibitions of the Divine character and government, then, the nations of the earth were to be recalled from their idolatries, and restored to the worship of the true God.

This fact is intimated in the primary call given to Abraham; "In thee shall all families of the earth be blessed." Gen. xii. 3. Besides other and similar announcements of this truth to Isaac and Jacob, the latter patriarch makes a very striking allusion to it in the benediction pronounced upon Judah—"The sceptre shall not depart from Judah, nor a lawgiver from between his feet until Shiloh come; and unto him shall the gathering of the people be." Gen. xlix. 10. Hengstenberg paraphrases this passage thus—"Judah shall not cease to exist as a tribe, nor lose its superiority, until it shall be exalted to higher honour and glory, through the great Redeemer, who shall spring from it, and whom not only the Jews, but all the nations of the earth shall obey."*

Similar predictions are also to be found among the inspired songs of ancient Israel. In the 2d Psalm, Jehovah addressing his Son, or the Messiah, says— "Ask of me, and I shall give thee the heathen for

* Chris. i. 59.

thine inheritance, and the uttermost parts of the earth for thy possession." In the 22d Psalm it is also said, that in the days of the Messiah, "All the ends of the world shall remember and turn unto the Lord: and all the kindreds of the nations shall worship before thee." In the 72d Psalm, it is predicted of the Messiah, "He shall have dominion also from sea to sea, and from the river, unto the ends of the earth."

The Prophets too, of ancient Israel, predict the conversion of the Gentiles under the Messiah. "And in that day," says Isaiah, "there shall be a root of Jesse, which shall stand for an ensign of the people; to it shall the Gentiles seek: and his rest shall be glorious." Isa. xi. Again, the same Prophet says, "I the Lord have called thee in righteousness, and will hold thine hand, and will keep thee, and give thee as a covenant for the people; for a light of the Gentiles." Isa. xlii. 6. Jeremiah also predicts, "The Gentiles shall come unto thee from the ends of the earth, and shall say, Surely our fathers have inherited lies, vanity, and things in which there is no profit." Jer. xvi. And Malachi also declares, "For, from the rising of the sun, even to the going down of the same, my name shall be great among the Gentiles." Mal. i.

It is evident, that these predictions do not refer to those incidental blessings, which the Israelites, from age to age, may have conferred upon some Gentiles. These blessings were to be general—they refer to a particular period—they centre in a special person. It was in the Messiah, and from the Messiah, that the nations were to be blessed.

Have these predictions, then, any fulfilment in Jesus the son of Mary?

It is noticeable, then, I remark first, that even the birth of Jesus was attended with circumstances which seem to point him out as the appointed means of converting the Gentiles. " Glory to God in the highest, and on earth peace, good-will toward men," Luke ii., sang the celestial multitudes at the birth of the infant Jesus. This natal song evidently points out Jesus, as the means of blessing to the world at large. The visit of the Eastern Magi was also indicative of the same thing. Matt. ii. The venerable Simeon, too, as he held this remarkable babe in his arms, predicted that he was to be, not only "the glory of Israel," but "a light to lighten the Gentiles." Luke ii.

Many things also occurred during the ministry of Jesus, which demonstrated that these prophecies were about being fulfilled in him. Thus, when he was about to heal the centurion's servant, he said to those around him, "And I say unto you, that many shall come from the east and west, and shall sit down with Abraham, and Isaac, and Jacob in the kingdom of God." Matt. viii. His healing also of the Samaritan leper, Luke xvii.; his casting out the devil from the daughter of the Syrophenician woman, Matt. xv.; the parable of the good Samaritan, Luke x.; that also of the prodigal son, Luke xv.; his remarks to the woman of Sychar, John iv.; his observations at the feast when certain Greeks desired to see him, John xii.; and especially his declaration to the chief priests and elders, that " the kingdom of God should be taken from them, and given to a nation bringing forth the fruits thereof," Matt. xxi., all teach, that the Gentiles were to be blessed in the mission of Jesus.

After his resurrection, however, this truth was made more plain. Although the Apostles were "to tarry in the city of Jerusalem until endued with power from on high," (Luke xxiv,) yet, he commanded them to "go into all the world and preach the gospel to every creature." Mark xvi. Here, the partition wall between Jew and Gentile was cast down, and "all the families of the earth were to be blessed," in this illustrious son of Abraham.

Nor was this commission an idle ceremony. It is true, that, even after the Apostles were endued with power from on high, they lingered in the city of Jerusalem. It is true, that, even in them, the appropriating spirit which confined the blessings of the Messiah to the Jews exclusively, with great difficulty yielded to the new commission. Still, however, God's purpose prevailed. Peter is sent to Cæsarea, by express revelation. Acts x. A persecution disperses the brethren at Jerusalem, and they are sent abroad to publish the glad tidings. Acts viii. The preaching of Philip is made instrumental in the conversion of the Samaritans. Acts viii. An Ethiopian is brought in by the same means. Acts viii. But what hastened this result more than any thing else, was the conversion of Saul of Tarsus. His conversion was miraculous, and his character and history altogether extraordinary. More than any other, he had persecuted the Church; more than any other, he was opposed to the new sect. But God, who had assigned him a special and important field of labour, at the predetermined moment, and in the pre-arranged manner, arrested the bold persecutor, and makes him not only a disciple of Jesus, but a publisher of his gospel.

Not long after his conversion, Saul was specially designated by the Holy Ghost, as a missionary to the Gentiles. He and Barnabas laboured first in Asia Minor, but were afterwards directed to go into Europe. In a few years, they visited the principal cities of the two continents, and established churches at Ephesus, at Philippi, at Corinth, and in most of the cities of the then known world.

In reference to the labours of the other Apostles, and also of the very large and numerous ministry which existed in those days, we have but partial accounts. The hints, however, given us in the various epistles, together with the known fact, that very shortly afterwards, Christians were scattered throughout the Roman empire, prove, that the early preachers of the word must have been exceedingly diligent in the propagation of the new faith. Even the Roman capital became the seat of a Christian church; while Spain and other remote countries are spoken of as scenes of these benevolent efforts.

Upon the conversion of the Gentiles to the doctrines of Jesus, a new question arose, which for a time much agitated the Christian Church. This question referred to the necessity of circumcising the new converts, and thus making them Jews as well as Christians. The

Synod assembled at Jerusalem, decided this question in the negative, and thus freed the Gentile Church from this painful, and unnecessary yoke. Acts xv.

About forty years after the resurrection of Jesus, an event took place, deeply painful in itself, yet of great advantage to the new faith. This was the overthrow of the Jews by the Romans, together with the destruction of their temple, and the practical abolition of their ritual services. These events had been most graphically and mournfully foretold by Jesus. Matt. xxiv. Luke xxi. Considered as judgments upon the nation, they were inflicted as a punishment for his crucifixion. Luke xix. 44; xxiii. 28—31. But there was another design. It was in the temple-service chiefly, that the old and new systems clashed. In order, therefore, to the full development and general triumph of Christianity, it was necessary that the temple-service should cease. Indeed, the very existence of the temple, its canonical priesthood, its altar of incense, its holy of holies, its entire rites and ceremonies might all be pleaded, while they stood, especially by the Jews, as so many evidences, that that dispensation was still in operation, and that Jesus was rather an impostor, than the Messiah. When, however, the providence of God concurred with the mission and doctrines of Jesus, to abolish the ceremonial law and priesthood; when the spires of the temple no longer glittered over the spiritual worship of the new economy, nor the sword of the temple was seen any more to shed the blood of unoffending Christians; when the strong walls of Jerusalem were crumbled, and her turrets were in the dust; when the Jew was a captive, and his holy of holies defiled and destroyed, then did Christianity arise upon the world as a new sun, and the unpretending mission of Jesus receive a sanction which incredulity itself could scarcely doubt.

This captivity of the Jewish nation still continues. Eighteen centuries have passed away. Generations have been born, and generations have died. Still, however, is the Jew an exile from the land of his

THE MESSIAH. 143

fathers, and the home of his fathers' sepulchres. Still too proud to acknowledge Jesus as the Messiah; still raising the cry of his crucifiers, "away with him, away with him," the child of Abraham even yet perpetuates the cause of his exile, and by rejecting Jesus, excludes himself from the richest blessings of the Abrahamic covenant! Other nations have bowed to his standard; even the most barbarous tribes have received him as their Hope. The Indian and the African, the Chinese and the Hottentot; nations the most polite, and nations the most savage, have all been rendering homage to the son of Mary, the Son of God. Still, however, the Jew disbelieves—disbelieves and wanders on in darkness and exile, the object of deep interest to the true Christian, the object of ridicule, it may be, to the infidel or scoffer, a living proof, however, of the truth, both of the Mosaic and Christian Scriptures. Still he wanders, and seems destined to wander, until the time shall come, that their Messianic captivity shall cease, and the sons of Jacob shall once more cluster around Sion, and there worship Him whom their fathers pierced, and there receive as their King, Him whom their fathers crucified as a malefactor.

This diffusion and triumph of the doctrines of Jesus in Gentile countries, besides being the fulfilment of prophecy, is proof of the Messiahship of Jesus, on two other grounds—in its cause, and in its results. Whatever importance we may attach to the zeal, or even to the alleged fanaticism of the early preachers of the gospel, whatever power we may ascribe to their principle of brotherly love; and whatever influence we may attribute to the performance of miracles by them; still, we must introduce another and a more efficient cause for the results which followed. Christianity is pre-eminently a spiritual system. And besides the war which it waged with kings and emperors, with priests and worshippers, with the customs and habits of men, it carried on a still fiercer conflict with the passions and prejudices of the human heart. It sought to revolutionize society by revolutionizing individual man. It called for a new heart, for a renovated character. And until this primary demand was granted, nothing was gained. It was to triumph, not over the bodies, but over the souls of men. It sought a recognition, not in the decrees of senates, but in the inward approval of the human will. Its temple was to be a temple of regenerated hearts; its dominion, the subjection of converted men to its authority.

Now, to accomplish this, a divine agency was necessary. Zeal might spread the message to the ends of the earth; miracle might attract attention to the message thus diffused; eloquence and argument might convince the judgment and sway the passions in its favour; but to effect a conversion, to seat that message permanently in the soul, to make it the oracle of sound doctrine, and the umpire of pure morals, was a work which Omnipotence alone could accomplish.

To send forth, therefore, the fishermen of Galilee on the high mission of converting the world, unaccompanied with the aid of a higher power, would have been a vain and futile undertaking. This, however, was not done. "And lo! says Jesus, I send the promise of my Father upon you." Luke xxiv. In these words the necessary divine help is both promised and pledged. The Holy Ghost was to accompany these humble instruments; he was to enlighten their minds; he was to work in them and by them, and they were to suspend the entire success of their mission upon his accompanying power.

Now, if the truths delivered by the Apostles of Jesus, were thus attended by the Spirit of God; if he so far approved their work, as to render it effectual to the conversion of men, then is there in this very fact the most convincing proof, that Jesus of Nazareth was the Messiah. Can we believe, that the Holy Ghost would give his sanction to imposture? Can we imagine, that God would co-operate with deluded enthusiasts? Certainly not.

Consider also the moral results of this new faith.

The Jew is withdrawn by it from his traditionary forms and ceremonies. The Gentile relinquishes the religion of his ancestors, and the temple of his gods. The disciples of Plato, of Aristotle, and of Zeno, lay aside their metaphysical jargon. The proud and the revengeful are made humble and forgiving. All these unite in the maintenance of a pure and simple faith; in the exhibition of a holy and blameless life. No matter what had been the previous character of men, the result of the new system was always the same. It allied men to God through the mediation of a common Saviour; it bound them together as a holy brotherhood; it filled them with compassion and goodwill toward the rest of mankind; and it produced in them all, a morality before unknown; a holiness to which, previously, they were utter strangers.

The same effects, too, produced by this new faith on individuals, extended to nations. National character, national laws, national feelings, national destinies, were all changed by it. It revolutionized senates, it changed the decrees of emperors and kings, it impressed a new character upon the face of society.

The history of the world, too, proves, that in proportion as nations have been under the legitimate influence of these new doctrines, have they been exalted and happy. New securities have been furnished by them to governments; new motives of obedience to subjects; new bands applied to all the domestic and social relations of life. The spread of the new system has also been favourable to mental improvement and science. It has especially been a protective to youth against innumerable dangers and evils. It has diffused a spirit of peace and forbearance among mankind. It has referred the nations to a common origin, to a common humanity, to a common Saviour. Its tendency is to destroy war, to establish peace, and to make of all mankind one great and loving family.

Now, can it be true, that results like these are the fruits of imposture? Can a system, founded in error, promoted by fraud, and accompanied by the Divine abhorrence, thus exalt the soul of man—thus elevate the social condition of the species? Can holiness result from falsehood, or benevolence be the fruit of fanatical ambition? Has the world received its greatest blessings from the greatest of impostures, or society its highest elevation from the worst of causes? Surely, the judgment of mankind must be in the negative. So much of good could not arise from so much of evil; so much of elevation from a system of mere fraud and delusion.

The doctrines of Jesus then are proved to be divine, by their fruits. Their results are such, as can only spring from a system founded in truth and approved by God. The fact, too, that they are accompanied by a Divine agency, and thus rendered effectual to salvation, also demonstrates their Divine origin. God can have no copartnership with error, nor would the Holy Ghost co-operate with wicked men.

The point, however, on which we desire here chiefly to fix the attention is, that these doctrines have so completely revolutionized the face of the Gentile world. Idolatry, with its long train of superstitions, has been swept away. The dogmatism of ancient philosophers has been destroyed. The mythological charm of the poets has been broken. The customs, and rites and ceremonies of ages have been supplanted. All these things have passed away, while the gospel of the great Nazarene is now enshrined, where pagan temples, and altars, and rites once stood ! What magic wand, what mysterious cause has effected all this? At the very time, too, when the Gentiles are enjoying such rich blessings, the Jews are without a king, without a sceptre, without a throne ! Why such a change, such a transfer of blessings? Evidently, because the seed of Israel, stumbling at the humility of a crucified Messiah, have been the occasion of extending the blessings of his kingdom to the other nations of the earth. "I say, then," says an Apostle, "have they stumbled that they should fall? God forbid; but through their fall salvation is come unto the Gentiles."

How strongly then does the existing state of things

prove the Messiahship of Jesus! According to the prophecy of Jacob, the sceptre was not to depart from Judah till Shiloh had come. But this sceptre has long since forsaken that tribe. Must not Shiloh then, already have appeared? There is also another proof of this: to this Shiloh the nations were to be gathered. They were to receive him as their King and Redeemer. Has not this been fulfilled in Jesus? Let the last eighteen centuries answer; let the existing state of the world reply.

Thus have we sought to prove, from his ancestry, from his miraculous birth, from the place of his nativity, from the epoch of his appearance, from the testimony of inspired witnesses, from his own testimony, by testimony from Heaven, by miracles, by his character, by his teachings, by his sacrifice and priesthood, by his kingly authority, by his resurrection, and by the blessings he has conferred upon the Gentiles, that JESUS IS THE CHRIST. More proof is unnecessary— further demonstration useless. For if men " hear not Moses and the Prophets, neither will they be persuaded, though one arose from the dead."

PART II.

ANTICHRIST;

OR

THE PAPACY PROVED TO BE THE ANTICHRIST

PREDICTED IN THE

HOLY SCRIPTURES.

INTRODUCTORY REMARKS.

We have already remarked upon the importance of ascertaining the personal identity of *Christ*. Of corresponding importance is it, to discover the personal identity of *Antichrist*. Antichrist is the enemy of Christ. As therefore, our salvation is secured through personal union by faith with Christ, so our destruction is made certain, if at last we are found on the side of Antichrist. Here, we cannot serve two masters. If we adhere to the cause of Christ, we cannot promote that of Antichrist; and if we maintain the cause of Antichrist, we cannot promote that of Christ.

Nor is there between these two any neutral ground. " He that is not for Christ, is against him;" and he that is not against Antichrist, is for him. Christ and Antichrist are in open hostility. The struggle is great, and has been of long continuance. It is going on around us; and we cannot be idle spectators of the scene. Our views, our feelings, our conduct, must favour the one or the other of these contending parties. Let every man, therefore, select his position, and gird on his armour. Let him choose the one or the other of these two masters. Which will he serve? With which does he seek his destiny?

But how is Antichrist to be ascertained? The same way that we ascertain Christ. Search the Scriptures; examine facts. The Jews were condemned, because, with the Scriptures in their hands, they did not recognize, but rejected Christ. And so shall we be condemned and punished, if, with the same Scriptures in our hands, we do not recognize, but blindly follow Antichrist.

The times also require this investigation. Throughout Europe, throughout the world, there is a revival of the Papal system. True, this revival is not to be considered as indicative of any very great triumphs. The best days of Popery have been numbered. The notions which men now entertain of popular liberty, and of the rights of conscience, the general intelligence that prevails, the recorded history of Papal oppression, the circulation of the Holy Scriptures, and above all, the word of God, all lead to the belief, that no efforts of the crafty agents of this crafty system, can ever give it the influence it has once exerted. "Tekel" is inscribed upon it; and some Cyrus will, ere long, be raised up, who shall dry up its waters, break down its gates of brass, and let oppressed humanity go free. No; it is not the ultimate triumph of this system we fear; it is the harm it may do in its death-struggle; it is the unnatural energies of its spasmodic dissolution, that we dread.

In America, particularly, is this investigation important. In all the countries over which it has triumphed, Popery, like the anaconda, has wound around its folds of art, of cunning, of superstition and of power, until, enclosing every thing in its too friendly embraces, it has, with one tremendous effort, crushed the nation to death. It sends forth its missionaries; it gathers its schools and colleges; it erects its cathedrals and builds its churches; it is patriotic, benevolent, charitable. Its alms and offerings attract the vulgar, its austerities and penances convince the sceptical. It is at first tolerated; then approved; next obeyed! But now come the dread realities of the system, taxation, passive submission, excommunications, interdicts, crusades, the inquisition, destruction. Yes, Popery has well nigh destroyed every country in which it has been predominant. The liberties and national prosperity of a people cannot co-exist with such a system.

Let then, Americans—Americans, who have never witnessed a Court of Inquisition, or an Auto-da-fé, on their virgin soil; Americans, whose national liberties are still fragrant with the blood of revolutionary fore-

INTRODUCTORY REMARKS.

fathers; Americans, whose proud eminence in the civilized world, gives them more to lose than other nations; let Americans especially examine this subject well. And if, in such an examination, the following pages shall contribute but a mite to the discovery of the truth, the author will feel himself more than compensated for the labour they have cost him.

THE PAPACY PROVED TO BE THE ANTICHRIST.

CHAPTER I.

THE SEAT OF ANTICHRIST.

The same inspired word, which has revealed to the Church an Antichrist to come, has also specified the seat of his power: that seat is the city of Rome.

In Daniel's vision of the four beasts, is the following language: " I considered the horns, and there came up among them another little horn, before whom there were three of the first horns plucked up by the roots: and behold in this horn were eyes, like the eyes of man, and a mouth speaking great things." Dan. vii. 8. The beast upon whose head Daniel saw the ten horns, is generally supposed by commentators to symbolize the Roman government; the ten horns, the ten kingdoms by which that government was succeeded; and the little horn, the Papacy. The reasons, upon which this interpretation is founded, are the following:

The scope of the vision requires it. This vision was given to Daniel, to portray before his mind, those great empires, or governments, which were to precede the everlasting kingdom of the Messiah. These governments were four. The first, under the symbol of a lion, was the Assyrian. The second, under the symbol of a bear, was the Persian. The third, under the symbol of a leopard, was the Macedonian or Grecian. The fourth, which was represented by " a beast dreadful and terrible, and strong exceedingly," must, of course, be the Roman.

To apply this last symbol as some have done, to the kingdom of the Seleucidæ, is to commit two fatal errors. That kingdom is represented in the vision, by one of the heads of the third beast, the symbol of the Grecian empire; for it is expressly said, "the beast had four heads." These four heads were, the Egyptian, Syrian, Thracian, and Macedonian divisions of the great Alexandrian empire. If, then, the kingdom of the Seleucidæ, or Syria, were included under the third symbol, it certainly would not be also exhibited by the fourth.

The other fatal mistake is, that this hypothesis makes Syria a greater and more notable kingdom, not only than the Assyrian, the Persian, and the Grecian; but than even the Roman empire itself! It is expressly said, by the angelic interpreter of the vision, that this fourth beast "shall devour the whole earth, and shall tread it down, and break it in pieces." This was never true of Syria, nor has it been of any other kingdom since, but that established by Romulus.

The ultimate dismemberment of the Roman empire, and the formation from its fragments, of ten separate states, also agree with this interpretation.*
"The ten horns out of this kingdom," says the angel, "are ten kings (i. e. kingdoms) that shall arise." Now it is a notorious fact, that when the Roman empire was overrun and subverted by the northern nations of Europe, ten kingdoms arose out of its fragments. The following are the names of those kingdoms, as given by Machiavel, himself a Roman Catholic. "The Ostrogoths in Mœsia; the Visigoths in Pannonia; the Sueves and Alans in Gascoigne and Spain; the Vandals in Africa; the Franks in France; the Burgundians in Burgundy; the Heruli and Turingi in Italy; the Saxons and Angles in Britain; the Huns in Hungary; the Lombards, at first upon the Danube, but afterwards in Italy."†

This interpretation is also supported by the very extraordinary agreement between "the little horn" and the Papacy. This little horn "came up among" the other horns; "it was diverse from the rest;" "it plucked up three of them by the roots;" "its look

* See Appendix, Note A. † His. Flor. i. 1.

was more stout than its fellows; "it had eyes like the eyes of man;" it had also "a mouth that spake very great things;" it made war with the saints, and prevailed against them, till the Ancient of days came, and judgment was given to the saints." The length of time, too, during which this "little horn" should oppress the saints, is expressly stated to be, "a time, times, and the dividing of time;" that is, twelve hundred and sixty years.

All these marks indicate the Papacy so strongly, that it is difficult to conceive how they could ever have had a different application. The Papacy arose among the ten Gothic kingdoms of Europe: it was, however, diverse from all those kingdoms, being an ecclesiastical sovereignty; in its rise, it subverted three of those kingdoms, those of the Heruli, Ostrogoths, and Lombards; its "look" too, has always been more "stout," than that of any other European kingdom; it is distinguished for craft and cunning; it is more ambitious and boastful than its neighbours, pretending to exercise absolute sovereignty over them; it has ever been a persecuting power; and it is long-lived; having not even yet exhausted the twelve hundred and sixty years of its predicted existence. What a remarkable agreement between prophecies and facts! What a perfect symbol is the "little horn," of the Papal power! Probably, no one Messianic type in the Old Testament scriptures, is more perfectly fulfilled in Jesus, than is this little horn in the Papacy.

The commentator on the Doway Bible admits that "the little horn" is a symbol of Antichrist. "This," says he, "is commonly understood of Antichrist. It may also be applied to that great persecutor Antiochus Epiphanes, as a figure of Antichrist." But who is Antichrist? According to Romanists, some great enemy of Christianity, who is to arise at some future period, who will dreadfully oppress the Church, and whose duration will be very brief. Upon the expression in this vision, "a time, times, and half a time," the same commentator says, "this means three years and a half, which is supposed to be the length of the duration of the persecution of Antichrist."

That this papal interpretation of the symbol is incorrect, is evident. The fourth beast is admitted, even by this same authority, to be the "Roman empire." The ten horns are also said to represent "ten kingdoms, among which the empire of the fourth beast shall be parcelled." Now, the Roman empire has ceased to exist for many centuries past. If, then, it ever could be divided into ten kingdoms, such division must already have taken place. The "little horn," then, or Antichrist, must, of course, have been in existence long since; for it was to "spring out of the midst" of the other horns, or kingdoms. And, here, I cannot but remark upon the unfairness of this papistical commentary. The beast, it states, represents the Roman empire; the ten horns, the ten kingdoms, into which that empire was divided. And yet, the "little horn," which is admitted to be a symbol of Antichrist, and which was to exist among the ten horns, or kingdoms, is said to be a figure of some malignant power not yet in existence!

We have not, however, located Antichrist at Rome. Daniel places him among the ten horns; that is, among the nations of Southern Europe. He does not, however, inform us of his precise locality. This is done by the Apostle John. "And I saw a woman sit upon a scarlet-coloured beast, full of names of blasphemy, having seven heads and ten horns. And the woman was arrayed in purple and scarlet colour, and decked with gold and precious stones and pearls; having a golden cup in her hand full of abominations, and filthiness of her fornication. And upon her forehead was a name written—'Mystery, Babylon the great, the mother of harlots, and abominations of the earth.' And I saw the woman drunken with the blood of the saints, and with the blood of the martyrs of Jesus." In explaining these remarkable symbols, the angel said to John, "The seven heads are seven mountains on which the woman sitteth." And, as if this were not sufficiently distinct, he adds: "The woman which thou sawest is that great city which reigneth over the kings of the earth." Rev. xvii.

This passage may be considered both as a commentary upon, and an enlargement of, the vision of Daniel. Here, as there, is a beast having ten horns." The beast, in the vision of John, as in that of Daniel, symbolizes Rome; the ten horns, the ten kingdoms which succeeded the Roman empire. Rev. xvii. 12. While, however, Daniel's beast is represented as dreadful and terrible, and strong exceedingly," John's is said to be scarlet-coloured and full of names of blasphemy." The reason for this is, that Daniel referred principally to Rome Republican and Imperial, while John, as we shall see hereafter, describes chiefly Rome Papal. In Daniel's vision there is no mention made of the seven heads" of the beast. This figure is employed in the latter vision to identify the beast. The seven heads," says the angel, are seven mountains." This refers to the seven hills on which Rome is built. The grand distinction, however, between the two visions is, that while Daniel speaks of a little horn" rising up among the ten horns, John omits this figure, but introduces another of a different kind. He sees a woman arrayed in purple and scarlet-colour, and decked with gold and precious stones," sitting upon the beast. The reason for this difference is, that Daniel represents Antichrist as a political, while John exhibits him as an ecclesiastical power.

Nor will it appear upon examination, that the little horn" is a more significant type of the Papal state, than the woman arrayed in purple and scarlet" is of the Papal church. This woman was seen sitting upon the scarlet-coloured beast." This denotes that <u>union of church and state, which has so long existed between the Papacy and the civil governments of Europe.</u> It also indicates the authority which the Roman church has so absolutely wielded over these governments. The woman was also arrayed in <u>purple and scarlet-colour</u>." The Pope of Rome has for ages pretended to be emperor of the whole world. As such, he not only <u>dresses himself in purple and scarlet, but adorns with the same costly materials, all around him</u>— Even the mules and horses," says Bishop Newton, "which carry the popes and cardinals, are covered with scarlet cloth; so that they may be said, literally, to ride upon 'a scarlet-coloured beast.'"* This woman was also "decked with gold and precious stones, and pearls." This indicates the very great wealth and splendour of papal establishments. The following is an extract from a letter written by a traveller in Mexico: "In the cathedral of Puebla hangs a chandelier of massive gold and silver, of whole tons in weight. On the right of the altar stands a carved figure of the Virgin, dressed in beautiful embossed satin, executed by the nuns of the place. Around her neck is suspended a row of pearls of precious value; a coronet of pure gold encircles her brow; and her waist is bound with a zone of pure diamonds and enormous brilliants. The candelabras in the cathedral are of silver and gold, too massive to be raised by even the strongest hand, and the Host is one mass of splendid jewels of the richest kind. In the cathedral at Mexico, there is a railing of exquisite workmanship, five feet in height, and two hundred feet in length, of gold and silver; on which stands a figure of the Virgin, with three petticoats—one of pearls, one of emeralds, and one of diamonds; the figure alone is valued at three millions of dollars." If such be papal worship in Mexico, what is it among the splendid capitals of Europe? What must it be at Rome?

This woman is also represented as a harlot; yea, as the greatest of harlots. This refers to the idolatries of papal Rome. That the fornication here alluded to is spiritual, that is, idolatry, is admitted by even Romanists themselves. "By Babylon," says the commentator on the Doway Bible, "is meant either the city of the devil in general, or pagan Rome, which was the principal seat of empire and idolatry." Here, however, a great mistake is committed, in supposing, that the prophecy alludes to pagan Rome. This harlot, or adulterous woman, is evidently the type of

* On Proph. 568.

a false church. But when was any church whatever in alliance with pagan Rome? In the days of pagan Rome, the church, so far from riding on the beast, was trampled under foot, and almost destroyed by him. Evidently the reference is to papal Rome. And are there no such idolatries practised in this apostate church, as correspond with the figure so graphically drawn by the Apostle? Is not the Pope himself worshipped? Is not the Virgin worshipped? Do not churches and altars, relics and crucifixes, pictures and statues, saints and angels, all receive divine honours? Never did pagan Rome excel professedly Christian Rome in these particulars. The papacy is the fountainhead, the source of these abominations, which from the Roman metropolis, extend almost to the whole world.*

This woman was also "drunk with the blood of saints and of the martyrs of Jesus." It it said of the " little horn," in Daniel's vision, that " he made war upon the saints and prevailed against them." We have already mentioned, that this "little horn" was a type of the papal state, while this woman is a type of the papal church. In popery, however, both church and state are employed, in the work of persecution. The spiritual court first tries and condemns the criminal; he is then delivered over to the civil authority to be executed. The venerable council first determines upon a crusade; the next step is, the enlistment in the enterprise, of the kings and potentates of the earth. In this way has the papal church been "drunken with the blood of saints." And has not this prediction been fulfilled, to the very letter fulfilled? " Not to mention," says Bishop Newton, " other outrageous slaughters and barbarities, the crusades against the Waldenses and Albigenses, the murders committed by the duke of Alva in the Netherlands, the massacres in France and Ireland, will probably amount to ten times the number of all the Christians slain, in all the ten persecutions of the Roman emperors put together."† The same sentiment is expressed by

* See Appendix, Note B.   † On Proph. 571.

Gibbon as we shall see hereafter in his history of the Roman empire.

Such are the correspondencies between "the woman arrayed in purple and scarlet," and the papal church. Evidently then, the one is the type of the other. But if so, the city of Rome itself was to be the spot where that antichristian power was to be enthroned upon the nations of Europe.

That Rome is the head of the papal world, and that a great autocrat has been presiding there for many centuries past, are facts of general notoriety; indeed it is fundamental in the whole papal scheme, that the seven-hilled city should be the metropolis of this strange and wonderful empire. Should Rome be displaced, the whole fabric would fall. Hence the seventy years, during which, through the influence of the French kings, the popes were made to reside at Avignon, are considered by all good Catholics, as a Babylonish captivity.

The radical doctrine of this system, as expressed by the Florentine Synod is, "That the Apostolic chair and the Roman high priest doth hold a primacy over the universal church; and that the Roman high priest is the successor of St. Peter, the prince of the Apostles; the true Lieutenant of Christ, and the Head of the Church; that he is the Father and Doctor of Christians; and that unto him in St. Peter, full power is committed to feed, and direct and govern the Catholic church."*

Daunau, in his Court of Rome, represents this as "a controverted point" among Roman Catholics.— "Not one word," says he, "in the gospel, nor even in the writings of the Apostles, indicates the city of Rome as the indispensable capital of Christendom."† This is very true; but it is neither the doctrine nor the practice of the Romish Church. "That the primacy of the Church is of divine right," says Dens, "and that this primacy should continue in the Roman bishop, or pope, are points that are considered settled in the

* Barrow. † P. 155.

faith."* This doctrine may be briefly expressed thus: Christ delegated his authority to Peter; Peter established his seat at Rome; upon his decease, he transferred his office to a Roman successor: hence these Roman successors of the Apostle, are, to the end of the world, the vicegerents of Christ, and the head of his Church. In all this, locality at Rome is essential. Withdraw that idea, and the primacy falls.

It need not be mentioned here, upon how many false premises this doctrine is based. It need not be affirmed, that Peter held no office higher than the other Apostles. It need not be asserted, that the very peculiar offices of Christ, could not be conferred on Peter, or on any other. It need not be maintained, that Peter's office, as Apostle, could not be transferred to Linus. It need not be stated, that the New Testament does not even allude to the fact, that Peter ever saw Rome. It need not be suggested, that Eusebius, when mentioning the visit of Peter to Rome, although he refers to his labours and martyrdom, says not a word about his primacy in that city. It is not necessary to assume the ground, that for three or four centuries after the martyrdom of Peter, the Roman See exercised no special sovereignty over the general Church. These things need not here be affirmed. It is enough to fulfil the prophecy under consideration, that the reverse of all this has been maintained; and that upon these false premises, a potentate of extraordinary character, wearing at once mitre and crown, wielding together sword and Bible, presiding alike over politics and religion; it is enough, we say, that such a potentate has for ages, and in the face of the whole world, occupied his seat upon the ashes of old Rome. Had the supreme pontiff of Christendom been located any where else; had he lived at Alexandria, Jerusalem, Paris, or London; had he been further removed from the power-spot of the old empire— there had at least, been one argument less in establishing his antichristian character. But, by an awful

* Theol. c. xxiv.

infatuation, and with a pertinacity bordering on madness, the great father of Christians has taken his seat, just where it was predicted beforehand that Antichrist should reign!

We employ then the very seat and chair of St. Peter, the ashes of old Rome, and the superstitions of the new, the Vatican, the Roman tiara, and the Roman crown, Roman bulls and Roman interdicts, Roman bibles and Roman prayers; we urge all this Romanism as evidence conclusive, as proof irrefragable, that the Papacy is the Antichrist predicted in the Holy Scriptures. The seat of the Pope condemns him, and the very walls of the "eternal city," proclaim his antichristian character.

CHAPTER II.

THE TIME OF ANTICHRIST.

Not only the seat, but the time of Antichrist is foretold in the word of God. True, there are several events which strongly indicate the rise of this power, and which have therefore occasioned a variety of opinions among the learned, as to the precise epoch of its commencement. Like the various edicts, however, of the Persian kings, from which the seventy weeks of Daniel have been calculated, these events are, for the most part, so near to each other, as to leave but little, if any doubt, as to the proper application of the prophecies.

Those portions of Scripture which most clearly designate the rise of Antichrist, are the following. "I considered the horns," says Daniel, "and behold, there came up among them another little horn, before whom there were three of the first horns plucked up by the roots." Dan. vii. 8. In explaining the vision to the prophet, the angel said: "The fourth beast shall be the fourth kingdom upon earth. And the ten horns out of this kingdom, are ten kings that shall arise; and another shall arise after them; and he shall be diverse from the first; and he shall subdue three kingdoms." Dan. vii. 24. The Apostle Paul also says concerning the same power, "And now ye know what withholdeth, that he might be revealed in his time. Only he who now letteth will let, till he be taken out of the way. And then shall that wicked be revealed, whom the Lord shall consume with the spirit of his mouth; and shall destroy with the brightness of his coming." 2 Thes. ii. 6–8. In explaining the symbol of the scarlet-coloured beast on which the woman was sitting, the angel said to John: "The beast that thou sawest was, and is not, and shall ascend out of the bottomless pit, and go into perdition. The seven heads are seven mountains on which the woman sitteth. And these are seven kings: five are fallen, and one is, and the other is not yet come: and when he cometh, he must continue a short space. And the beast that was and is not, even he is the eighth, and is of the seven; and goeth into perdition. And the ten horns which thou sawest are ten kings, which have received no kingdom as yet; but received power as kings one hour with the beast. These have one mind and shall give their power and strength unto the beast. For God hath put in their hearts to fulfil his will, and to agree, and give their kingdom unto the beast until the words of God shall be fulfilled." Rev. xvii. The following passage is also believed by some writers on prophecy to mark more definitely than any of the preceding, the precise period of the rise of Antichrist. "And they (the saints) shall be given unto his hand, until a time, times and the dividing of time." Dan. vii. 25.

That the eleventh, or little horn of Daniel, the wicked power, or man of sin of Paul, and the eighth king or the beast of John, all refer to the same thing, is generally conceded by commentators, and must appear evident to any one who carefully considers these prophetic symbols. Daniel's little horn arose among the ten horns upon the head of the fourth beast, the symbol of the Roman empire. Paul's man of sin was to arise when that empire ceased to "let;" or, when "it was taken out of the way." And John's eighth king or beast, was that peculiar power which should succeed the seventh form of government at Rome. As, therefore, the little horn, the man of sin, and the eighth king, were all predicted to arise about the same time; as they were all to succeed imperial Rome, and as similar characteristics are ascribed to them all, they must mean the same thing.

But there is another reason for this conclusion, equally strong. Each of these symbols denoted a power, which was to continue the same length of time. The little horn of Daniel was to continue until "the judgment was set, and his dominion was taken away to be consumed and destroyed to the end." Dan. vii. 26. The man of sin was to exist until he should become the son of perdition, that is, until he should be "consumed by the Lord, and destroyed by the brightness of his coming." 2 Thess. ii. 8. And the eighth king, or the beast of John, was that which was to tyrannize "until the words of God should be fulfilled;" that is, until the twelve hundred and sixty years, so often alluded to, should end; and then it was to "go into perdition." Rev. xvii. The "little horn," therefore, "the man of sin," and "the beast," were not only to begin, but they were to end at the same time; viz. at some future coming of Christ. This also proves that they are the same.

As this is a point of some importance in our future calculations, it will not be amiss to introduce here the testimony of two of the ancient fathers. Irenæus says: "Daniel, respecting the end of the last kingdom, that is, the last ten kings, among whom that kingdom should be divided, upon whom the son of perdition shall come, saith, that ten horns shall grow on the beast, and another little horn shall grow up among them, and three of the first horns shall be rooted out before him." Of whom also, Paul the Apostle speaketh in his second Epistle to the Thessalonians, calling him the son of perdition, and 'the wicked one.' St. John, our Lord's disciple, hath in the Apocalypse still more plainly signified of the last time, and of these ten kings, among whom the empire that now reigneth shall be divided; explaining what the ten horns shall be which were seen by Daniel."*

The following is the statement of Cyril of Jerusalem in the fourth century: "The first kingdom that was made famous was the kingdom of the Assyrians: and the second was that of the Medes and Persians together; and after these the third was that of the Mace-

* Iren. 1, 5.

donians; and the fourth kingdom is now that of the Romans. Afterwards, Gabriel interpreting, saith, Its ten horns are ten kings that shall arise; and after them shall arise another king, who shall exceed in wickedness all before him: not only the ten, he saith, but all who were before him. And he shall depress three kings. But it is manifest that of the first ten he shall depress three, that he himself might reign the eighth."* These quotations will show that the interpretation above given is neither modern nor protestant, but ancient and patristic.

Admitting, then, that these various symbols designate the same power, there are several strong marks furnished in these prophecies for ascertaining the period when that power should arise.

1. The first of these is, the dissolution of the western Roman empire. The propriety of restricting these prophecies to the western empire will appear from the following judicious remarks of Sir Isaac Newton: "All the four beasts are still alive, though the dominion of the three first be taken away. The nations of Chaldea and Assyria are still the first beast. Those of Media and Persia are still the second beast. Those of Macedon, Greece, and Thrace, Asia Minor, Syria, and Egypt, are still the third. And those of Europe on this side Greece, are still the fourth."† As therefore the prophecies refer to the fourth, and not to the other three beasts, our business is with the Latin and not with the Greek empire. Now it was some time after this Latin or western empire was subverted, that the man of sin, according to Paul, was to make his appearance. When he that was then *letting* (κατεχων) should be taken out of the way, "then shall that wicked be revealed."

The western empire was overthrown by those northern barbarians, whose ravages are so significantly exhibited in the 8th chapter of the Apocalypse, under the sounding of the first four trumpets. Alaric and his Goths besieged and plundered Rome about the

---

* Cyrilli Hieros Catech. 15, c. 6.   † Observations on Daniel.

THE ANTICHRIST. 169

year 410. Attila and his Huns devastated a great part of the empire and invaded Italy about the year 452. In 455, Genseric, king of the Vandals, not only captured but pillaged Rome, for the space of fourteen days. And about the year 476, Odoacer, king of the Ostrogoths, terminated the imperial authority at Rome, by the conquest of the city, and the banishment of Augustulus to the castle of Lucullus, on an annuity of six thousand pieces of gold.* Now it was, that "the third part of the Roman sun was smitten, and the third part of the moon, and the third part of the stars." Rev. viii. 12. Antichrist then, according to Paul, was not to arise till some time after the year 476 or 479, as the event above alluded to is differently estimated.

2. A second epoch, furnished us in the prophecy, is the time when the western empire was succeeded by ten new kingdoms. The beast had ten horns, and these horns were the symbols of ten kingdoms. Antichrist, however, was not to arise at the same time precisely with these kingdoms, but shortly afterwards; "and another shall arise after them."

The following is a list of these ten European kingdoms, given by Bishop Lloyd, together with the dates of each: Huns, about 356; Ostrogoths, 377; Visigoths, 378; Franks, 407; Vandals, 407; Sueves and Alans, 407; Burgundians, 407; Herules and Rugians, 476; Saxons, 476; Lombards in Hungary, 526; in Germany, 483."† According to these calculations, the rise of Antichrist cannot precede the year 483 or 526.

3. Another mark by which the time of Antichrist is designated, is when Rome should be under its eighth form of government. "And there are seven kings: five are fallen, and one is, and the other is not yet come, and when he cometh, he must continue a short space. And the beast that was and is not, even he is the eighth, and is of the seven, and goeth into perdition."

* Gibbon's Rome.   † Newton on Proph., Dis. xiv.

The expression here used, "the beast that was and is not," is thus interpreted by Bishop Newton: "A beast in a prophetic style is a tyrannical idolatrous empire. The Roman empire was idolatrous under the heathen emperors; it then ceased to be so for some time under the Christian emperors; it then became idolatrous again under the Roman pontiffs, and so hath continued ever since."* The beast then "that was and is not," denotes Rome imperial in its three successive conditions of Rome pagan, Rome Christian, and Rome papal. Rome papal is that which the angel terms the eighth, and which he says, "is of the seven" —εκ των επτα εστι. This last expression is rendered by Doddridge thus, "he ariseth out of the remainders of this people." The correct interpretation, however, seems to be, that he is to succeed the seven in a regular line; he is to arise from them. But where shall we find the eight successive Roman sovereignties, referred to by the Apostle? According to most commentators, in the kings, consuls, dictators, decemvirs, military tribunes, emperors,† exarchs, and popes, by which Rome has been governed. Rome was originally governed by kings for more than two hundred years. It was then under the control of consuls, dictators, decemvirs, and military tribunes, about the space of five hundred and thirty years. The reign of the emperors lasted about five hundred, and that of the exarchs about two hundred. There are some writers, who prefer to substitute the Italian Gothic kingdom, which lasted over sixty years, in the place of the exarchate; considering the latter as the instrument merely of the sixth or imperial government. It is quite certain, however, from history, that the Pope did not begin to exercise political power, until the overthrow in Italy of the exarchate.

This event occurred under very peculiar circumstances. The emperor Leo the Third, usually termed the iconoclast, had ordered all sacred images and figures to be removed from Christian churches. Gre-

---

* On Proph. Dis. xxv.   † Tacitus i. 1.

gory the second, who then filled the papal chair, wrote him a letter of severe remonstrance. Among other things, we find the following sentiments in this papal epistle. Advocating the use of pictures and images, he says, "The idols of antiquity were the fanciful representations of phantoms or demons, at a time, when the true God had not manifested his person, in any visible likeness. The latter are the genuine forms of Christ, his mother and his saints, who have approved, by a crowd of miracles, the innocence and merit of this relative worship." In censuring Leo for rebelling against papal authority, he says: "Are you ignorant that the popes are the bond of union, the mediators of peace between the east and the west? The eyes of the nations are fixed upon our humility, and they revere as a God upon earth the Apostle St. Peter, whose image you threaten to destroy. The remote and interior regions of the west present their homage to Christ and his vicegerent. Abandon your rash and fatal enterprise, reflect, tremble, repent. If you persist, we are innocent of the blood that will be spilt in the contest: may it fall on your own head."*

Matters soon came to a crisis. By the counsel and authority of Gregory, the Exarchate was armed against the emperor; the exarch who espoused the cause of Leo, was killed by popular fury. A battle was soon fought between the army of the emperor and that of the pope. The latter was victorous. "The strangers," says Gibbon, "retreated to their ships; but the populous sea-coast poured forth a multitude of boats; the waters of the Po were so deeply infected with blood, that during six years the public prejudice abstained from the fish of the river; and the institution of an annual feast perpetuated the worship of images, and the abhorrence of the Greek tyrant. Amidst the triumph of the catholic arms, the Roman pontiff Gregory III., convened a synod of ninety-three bishops against the heresy of the iconoclasts. With their consent, he

* Gibb. xlix.

pronounced a general excommunication against all, who by word or deed, should attack the traditions of the fathers, and the images of the saints." *

Surely here are events, which seem almost precisely to fulfil the predictions of John. A Roman bishop, not only reprimanding an emperor, and acknowledging, that he receives through St. Peter, co-ordinately with Christ, the homage of the nations; not only considering himself as the bond of union between the east and the west, but actually arming his subjects for battle, fighting, conquering! And for what? To establish the worship of images! To declare as heretics, all who should renounce such worship! Does not this look like the literal revival of the sixth or idolatrous beast? Does it not occur, too, at the proper period? The seven preceding administrations had all passed away. The imperial arm was broken; the exarchate subverted. Surely then, this was the time, this the occasion for the rise of the eighth Roman power, or "the beast."

The author above quoted, gives the following account of the new organization, which succeeded the Exarchate. "By the necessity of their situation, the inhabitants of Rome were cast into the rough model of a republican government: they were compelled to elect some judges in peace and some leaders in war. The style of the Roman senate and people was revived, but the spirit was fled. The want of laws could only be supplied by the influence of religion, and their foreign and domestic counsels were moderated by the authority of the bishop. His alms, his sermons, his correspondence with the kings and prelates of the west, his recent services, their gratitude and oath, accustomed the Romans to consider him as the first magistrate or prince of the city. The Christian humility of the popes too, was not offended by the name of Dominus, or Lord; and their face and inscription are still apparent on the most ancient coins."†

The termination of the Exarchate and the establish-

* Gib. xlix.   † Ibidem.

ment of political power in the hands of the Popes, occurred about the year 730. True, the exercise of such power was disturbed by the Lombards, their former allies. The interference however, of the French kings soon subdued these troublesome neighbours, and secured the popes in the privileges, which by rebellion and war, they had obtained.*

4. A fourth sign of the rise of Antichrist is, the subjugation or rooting up of three of the ten kingdoms, in the midst of which he was to arise—" before whom there were three of the first horns plucked up by the roots." The following extract from Professor Gaussen, will sufficiently illustrate this point. "Take now," says he, "the map of Italy, and look for the dominions of the Pope; and see of how many of the ten first kingdoms, the pontifical territory occupies the site at this day. You will see that it has supplanted these three; the Herules, the Ostrogoths, and the Lombards. And go to Rome itself, and see the Pontiff on the banks of the Tyber in all his sovereign pomp, trampling under foot the ashes of Romulus in the Basilica of St. Peter's, or in his own palace of the Vatican. You will see on his brow that Babylonish tiara, surmounted by the three crowns of the three horns, "plucked up by the roots before him;" those of Odoacer, Theodoric, and of Alboin, he the only king in the world who wears this prophetic head-dress."†

These three kingdoms virtually fell into the hands of the Pope, when the Exarchate was wrested from the eastern emperor. The northern portion of this Exarchate however, being invaded by the Lombards, a fit occasion was furnished, for the interposition of some foreign prince. This prince was Pepin, king of the French. The Pope had confirmed a doubtful sovereignty on Pepin and his descendants. To reward him for this service, as well as to atone for his personal sins, the son of Martel invaded Lombardy, and compelled Astolphus to transfer his territory to

* See Appendix, Note C. † Geneva and Rome.

the occupant of the chair of St. Peter. This event occurred in the year 754. "The Pontiff," says Daunau, "Stephen II., enters France, and there as minister of the Greek emperor, gives in 753 to Pepin and to his sons the title of Roman Patrician, which Charles Martel had borne before him; and receives, it is said, in exchange, the gift of the provinces which Astolphus occupied and which the Emperor claimed. In 754, Pepin crossed the Alps, besieged Pavia, and forced Astolphus, to promise the restoration of the Exarchate and the Pentapolis, not to the emperor of Constantinople, but to St. Peter, to the church, and the Roman republic."* Gibbon speaks of this grant in the following language:—" The splendid donation was granted in supreme and absolute dominion; and the world beheld for the first time a Christian bishop invested with the prerogatives of a temporal prince; the choice of magistrates, the exercise of justice, the imposition of taxes, and the wealth of the palace of Ravenna."†

It is wonderful how ingeniously, and how gradually the successor of St. Peter became possessed of his temporal estates and influence. When the Exarchate fell, deference was still paid to the eastern emperor; the new government, too, was made to assume a sort of republican aspect, and was controlled at first only indirectly by the Pope. Even after the grant, too, of the French kings, those kings held the title of Patricians of Rome! "Such a course" says Daunau, "was in fact a method of entering furtively into the number of independent states, and of attenuating more and more the thread by which the Popes were connected with the Byzantine empire. Commonly, the Pope did not fill the first magistracy of this republic. He abandoned the insignia of power to a prefect, a duke, or to a patrician; and prepared himself to substantiate soon, for undecisive forms, a definite and pontifical form of government."‡ This mode of obtaining

* Court of Rome, i. † Rome, ch. xlix.
‡ Court of Rome.

political power, is what some understand by the little horn's rising "after," that is behind, or unobserved by, the other ten kingdoms.

5. A fifth sign of the rise of Antichrist is, the deliverance into his hand of the saints of the Most High. " And they shall be given into his hand, until a time, times and the dividing of time." " For God hath put in their hearts to fulfil his will, and to agree, and give their kingdom unto the beast, until the words of God shall be fulfilled."

There are two methods in which the saints may be delivered into the hand of Antichrist. The one is, by constituting him the sole head of the church; the other is, by subjecting political governments to his will, so that they shall execute the anathemas which he from time to time may pronounce. In both of these ways have the people of God been delivered into the hand of the Papacy.

The time when the Pope was constituted the sole head of the church, has, by many, been computed from the edict of the emperor Phocas in 606. The following is the statement of Baronius on that subject. " Hinc igitur, anno Christi 606, in Cyriacum Phocas exacerbatus in ejus odium imperiali edicto sancivit, nomen universalis decere Romanam tantummodo ecclesiam, tanquam quæ caput esset omnium ecclesiarum; solique convenire Pontifici." " Hence, therefore, in the year 606, Phocas provoked with Cyriacus, through hatred to him confirmed by an imperial edict, that the name universal became the Roman church only, as that which was the head of all the churches; and could only be properly ascribed to the Pontiff."

Hallam, in a note appended to his Middle Ages, for several reasons which he specifies, gives it as his opinion, that too much importance has been ascribed by many writers to this testimony of Baronius. He believes, that the edict of Valentinian III. in 455, can be better authenticated, and is more to the point than this of Phocas. It may, however, be questioned, whe-

* Eccle. An. Anno 606.

ther either Phocas, or Valentinian, or any other emperor, had either the right or the power to deliver the saints into the hands of the Papacy. Though joined to the state, still the church had, even in those ages, much power of her own. Such, too, was the influence of bishops and of ecclesiastical institutions, that we doubt, whether the will of any one emperor could have brought the church into absolute subjection. Nor could the edict of one emperor be perpetual: it might be abrogated even in the next reign. The prophecy evidently requires, that this subjection should be the result of many and conspiring providential causes. The spirit of the age must be such, the instruction of the people such, their passive submission such, and even their apparent necessities such, as to lead to a result of this kind. The bishop of Rome was to be constituted the sole head of the church, not by any one arbitrary act, but by the general consent of Christendom, arising from the existing state of the world. The matter of inquiry then becomes, not *who* did it, but *when* have we evidence, that the Church became subject to the Roman bishop as its supreme head?

The prophecies require, that the spiritual and temporal power of Antichrist should begin at the same time. The "beast" was to rule the nations, during the same period that he was to oppress the church. Nor is there any distinction made in the vision of Daniel, between the duration of the temporal and spiritual power of the "little horn." They appear to be contemporaneous. If, too, the spiritual power of Antichrist should be dated from one period, and his temporal power from another, then would there be two periods of twelve hundred and sixty years, during which he was to exist! It is evident, however, that this prophetic age of the beast and little horn, is to extend over but one such period. The spiritual and temporal power, therefore, of Antichrist, must begin and end at the same time.

We have already noticed, that the temporal and political power of the popes, began at the time when these pontiffs cast off their allegiance to the eastern emperors. The cause of this rebellion was image-worship. The emperor prohibited the worship of images as idolatry; the popes maintained the propriety of such worship as sanctioned by tradition and miracles. This was the point at issue between them; and it was the means of severing for ever the tie which bound the bishops of Rome to the court of Byzantium.

The result in this case, however, was not simply political; it was also religious. If the bishop of Rome was bound as a subject to obey the court of Constantinople, much more was he bound as a Christian to keep the commandments of God. These commandments, however, forbid image-worship in every form. The law is express, and often repeated. At the same time, therefore, that the Pope set up a political supremacy for himself, did he erect also, an independent spiritual dominion.

We invite particular attention to this remarkable coincidence. In the Apocalypse it is said, "And the beast is the eighth, and is of the seven, and goeth into perdition." The easiest and most natural construction of this passage is the following: "The beast will be the eighth power at Rome; he will immediately succeed the seven preceding powers; and he will continue till Rome shall have no government at all: the power-line, the Roman succession, will end in him. When, then, did the Roman pastor or bishop become the "beast?" Precisely then, when he began to wield a political and an idolatrous sceptre. Now, this event took place, when the popes, by rebellion against the eastern court, set up virtually a kingdom of their own upon the basis of idolatry. Then were the foundations of the Apocalyptic Babylon laid; then did Rome become "the mother of harlots, and abominations of the earth." This event occurred near the middle of the eighth century.

But to place the saints effectually in the hands of Antichrist, it was necessary, that the political governments of Europe should also be under his control.

Without this he could not enforce his will as law throughout the Christian world. As a local prince, he might rule his own Italian subjects. As the accredited head of ecclesiastical polity, he might have influence in the church. But to render his authority absolute and universal, the independence of states must bow to his will, and the kings of the earth stand ready to execute his pleasure.

And here again, we are called upon to notice the extraordinary fact, that just about the time that the popes became independent princes, and began also to exercise superior spiritual control, a sort of imperial power fell into their hands. The crown was transferred from Childeric to Pepin, but a year or two before the Pope was made supreme proprietor of Lombardy!

At some period then, between the rupture of the Pope with Leo III., and his decision in the case of Pepin, that is, somewhere between the year 730 and 753, we may safely locate the rise of the political, imperial, and supreme spiritual power of the popes.

As further proof of this, it may be proper here to notice the decisions of two ecclesiastical councils, which sat within or near this period. By the council of Francfort, A. D. 742, it was decreed, "that as a token of their willing subjection to the See of Rome, all Metropolitans should request the pallium at the hands of the Pope, and obey his lawful commands."*
"In the second Nicene council, says Mosheim, held in the year 786, "the imperial laws against the new idolatry were abrogated, the decrees of the council of Constantinople reversed, the worship of images and the cross restored, and severe punishments denounced against such as maintained that God was the only object of religious adoration."† The object of this council was, to suppress in the east, as had already been done in the west, all opposition to image-worship. Surely this looks as if the saints, all who abhorred idolatry, had now been given into the hand of the

---

* Middle Ages, xvii. † Cen. viii.

THE ANTICHRIST. 179

beast. The universal law was, image-worship or punishment, idolatry or death.

Thus have we noticed five prophetic marks or evidences of the rise of Antichrist. This malignant power was to arise, after the dissolution of the western Roman empire. It was to arise among the ten new kingdoms, by which that empire was to be succeeded. It was immediately to succeed that brief administration, whatever it was, Exarchate or Gothic kingdom, which was to constitute the seventh form of government at Rome. In its rise, it was to root up three of the ten kingdoms around it. The saints were also to be put in its power, for a period of twelve hundred and sixty years. Now, these events as above shown, all fall within the compass of two hundred and seventy-eight years; this being the space of time from the dethronement of Augustulus to the grant of Pepin. Within this period then, are we to find the rise of Antichrist. According to prophecy, his rise could not take place earlier, nor was it to be later. We are then limited to this period; and within it somewhere, are we to find the origin of that great enemy to the church, which so filled the minds of Daniel, of Paul, and of John.

But this period may be reduced to still narrower limits. The dissolution of the western empire was to be succeeded by another political power, which was "to continue a short space." This political power must be, either the kingdom of Odoacer, or the Exarchate. If the former, then are sixty years to be deducted from this period; if the latter, two hundred and sixty. We have already assigned reasons why we suppose the latter to be meant. This period then, will be narrowed down to the space of twenty-four years, within which we are to find the rise of Antichrist. This short period extends from the year 730 to 754.

What power, then we ask, arose within this period to which the characteristics of Antichrist may be established? Not the Mohammedan surely. Mohammed arose in Asia, not in Europe; he was too, an enemy to idolatry, not its patron; he appeared also in the seventh century, not in the eighth. Nor can Antichrist be Pepin, Charlemagne or any of the French kings. France was one of the ten horns of the beast; it could not therefore be another power rising among them. Nor have we any evidence, that even one of the traits of Antichrist was ever developed in the character of these kings! Who then we ask is Antichrist? Let history, let universal history reply. He is the Pope. No other answer can be given. It was at this very period, that the Papacy arose, as an independent and sovereign power in Europe. It was at this very time, that the Pontifical mitre began to be seen among the crowns of European kings. It was precisely here, that idolatry was set up again, as the religion of the Roman world.

If then, Jacob's prediction concerning Shiloh, and the seventy weeks of Daniel, are evidence conclusive, that Jesus of Nazareth is the Christ, so also are the predictions, concerning the time of the "little horn," of "the man of sin," and of "the beast," proofs irrefragable, that the Papacy is Antichrist. And as it may be proved, that any one hereafter pretending to be the Messiah, is not such, because he appears out of time, so may it be demonstrated, that any one hereafter who may be thought to be Antichrist, is not, for the very same reason. The time, then, as well as the place, determines the antichristian character of the papal throne. The Pope is Antichrist, so says prophecy; so says history; so says his own fully developed character.

CHAPTER III.

ANTICHRIST A PECULIAR POWER.

In designating the person of Christ, the Holy Scriptures have specified, not only the place and time of his birth, but have also furnished certain traits of character, by which he might be distinguished from all others. The same course has been pursued in this holy volume in its description of Antichrist. Not only are the place and time of this extroardinary power given, but certain peculiar and characteristic marks are furnished, by which he may be distinguished from all other powers. In the present chapter, it is our design to consider the peculiarity of the power of Antichrist; or, some of those things in which he differs from all other political governments.

In explaining to Daniel the symbol of the " little horn," the angel said, "he shall be diverse from the rest." Dan. vii. 24. As the word which is here rendered diverse is variously translated, it will be proper, first to settle its import. The original is—וחוא ישנא מן־ קדמיא— and he shall be hated more than the first. So the word is literally translated, and so it is uniformly rendered in almost every instance in our English version. The seventy have rendered the passage thus, " ὁς ὑπεροισει κακοις παντας τους εμπροσθεν "—who shall excel in wickedness all that were before him. The Apostle Paul seems to refer to this version, where he calls the same power, ὁ ανθρωπος της ἁμαρτιας, and ὁ ανομος; " that man of sin" and " that wicked." The Vulgate renders the phrase in the following Latin : " Et ipse potentior erit prioribus "—"and he shall be more powerful than his predecessors." This version is followed by the Doway Bible; "and he shall be mightier than the former." Luther also adopts the same sense—" der wird mächtiger seyn denn der vorigen keiner "—" he will be more powerful than any that were before him." The French agrees with our English version—" qui sera different des premiers;"—" who shall be diverse from the first."

Probably the context will furnish us with a clew to the right meaning. The little horn is represented as having "eyes like the eyes of man, and a mouth speaking great things;" as being "more stout than his fellows," and as "subduing three kings." A horn is a scriptural symbol for a king or kingdom. Eyes denote cunning and craft, and a mouth speaking great things, indicates boastful pretensions and ambitious designs. Certainly a kingdom of this sort, growing up among other kingdoms, must be very dissimilar to its neighbours; it is likely to be more powerful, and in the end it must be hated. All these translations therefore substantially agree; and they all indicate certain peculiarities in which the power foretold, differs, not only from those around it, but from all preceding forms of government. This power we have already asserted to be the Papacy, which differs from other European governments in several respects.

The Papacy is a spiritual power. Other European governments profess to be spiritual only in the sense, in which Paul asserts that "the powers that be are ordained of God;" that is, they are providentially appointed. Not so the Papacy. Its authority is professedly derived immediately from heaven. "The Pope receives power and jurisdiction," says Dens, "immediately from Christ." (Theol. xxiv.) "The authority given to St. Peter and his successors," says the bull of Sixtus V., "excels all the powers of earthly kings and princes."* "One sword," says Pope Boniface VIII., "must be under another, and the temporal authority must be subject to the spiritual power."† Again, Dens, in his Moral Theology, in answer to the question, "Has the supreme Pontiff a certain temporal and civil power?" gives the following an-

* Barrow. † Idem.

swers: "There have been those, who ascribed to the Pontiff by divine right the most plenary and direct power over the whole world, as well in temporal as in spiritual things." Others, he says, maintain that, "when the spiritual power cannot be freely exercised, nor the Pope's object be obtained by spiritual, then he may have recourse to temporal means; and thus it has been done by Pontiffs more than once." Here, according both to popes and doctors, the papacy is supreme in one way or another, and that by divine right, over all the kingdoms of the earth. This is certainly, one point of diversity, between this power and all others. No European kingdom, no kingdom that has ever existed, has assumed so much as this.

Another peculiarity of this power is, its awfully despotic character. In other governments there are privileges, there are checks upon power. But what privileges have Papists? What checks are there to papal tyranny? None, whatever. The supreme pontiff domineers over all. Having on his head Christ's crown, and in his hand his rod of iron, he sets absolute defiance to all inferior orders and ranks of men. "Go and contemplate him in the Vatican," says Gaussen, "as I have done; you will there see the painting which represents the Emperor Henry the Fourth, stripped before Gregory the Seventh, placed in the royal saloon, through which the ambassadors of all the powers of Europe pass; and in another, the heroic and powerful Emperor Frederick Barbarossa, on his knees before Pope Alexander the Third, in the public square at Venice. The Pope's foot is on his shoulder; his sceptre is thrown upon the ground, and underneath are these words, *Fredericus supplex adorat, fidem et obedientiam pollicitus—* "Frederic, having promised faith and obedience, as a suppliant adores," (the Pope!) Where is the king of the west, who is carried on men's shoulders, and surrounded by peacock's feathers? Incense is burnt before him as an idol; he is knelt to on both knees; his slipper is kissed on his foot; and he is adored.

Venite, adoremus—"Come, let us worship," exclaim the cardinals, when they go to him.*

The following are extracts from the bishops' and archbishops' oath. "I, N., of the church of N., from henceforth will be faithful and obedient to St. Peter the Apostle, and to the Holy Roman Church, and to our Lord, the lord N., Pope N., and to his successors, canonically coming in. Heretics, schismatics and rebels to our said lord, or his aforesaid successors, I will to my power persecute, and oppress. The possession belonging to my table, I will neither sell, nor give away, nor mortgage, nor grant anew in fee, nor any wise alienate, no not even with the consent of the chapter of my church, without consulting the Roman Pontiff."†
Surely, if kings and emperors, cardinals, archbishops and bishops, are thus miserably enslaved, the people cannot know what freedom is. A tyranny like this, has positively never existed besides it, on the earth. And the only wonder is, that men can be found so blinded by priestcraft, so passively tame in their tempers, as to submit to such an arbitrary and unnatural domination. And yet for ages on ages, not only the ignorant and the ignoble, but the proud and the great in Europe, have lain submissively under this galling yoke of bondage. The will of the Pope has been the fiat of the Almighty, and kings and emperors have trembled before him, as they would beneath the thunders of Jehovah.

The government of the Pope is also diverse from all other governments in the extent of its domination. Most governments have been satisfied with comparatively contracted territorial limits. Even those which have been the greatest and the most ambitious, have ruled over but a part of mankind. Neither the Assyrian, the Persian, the Grecian, nor the Roman empire filled the world. The pretensions, however, of the successors of St. Peter, have uniformily extended to the entire globe. That Christ possessed "all power on earth," none can deny who receive the New Tes-

* Geneva and Rome. † Barrow.

tament as of divine authority. But Christ gave his power to St. Peter, and St. Peter left it to his successors in the papal chair at Rome. Whatever of power therefore, Jesus Christ has over the nations, the same has the Pope.*

Nor has this result of the papal system been denied by the abettors of popery. On the contrary, they constantly maintain it. The following is the established doctrine on this point as derived from their own divines. *Prima sententia est, summum Pontificem jure divino habere plenissimam potestatem in universum orbem terrarum, tam in rebus ecclesiasticis quam civilibus.*† "The primary doctrine is, that the chief pontiff possesses by divine right, plenary power throughout the whole world both in ecclesiastical and civil matters."† In one of the canon laws of popery, it is affirmed that, "The Roman Pontiff bears the authority, not of a mere man, but of the true God upon earth." (*Veri Dei vicem gerit in terris.*‡) "Under the Pope's nose," says Barrow, "and in his ear, one bishop styled him, 'prince of the world;' another orator called him, 'king of kings and monarch of the earth;' another great prelate said of him, that 'he had all power above, all power in heaven and earth!'"§

Presumption like this, we hesitate not to say, has not a parallel in the history of our race. No government has aspired to a dominion so great as this, nor has the most ambitious conqueror ever conceived, that a domain so vast, was to lie beneath his victorious

---

* Some may suppose that the former pretensions of the occupants of the chair of St. Peter, have been relinquished by his more modern successors. Such, however, is by no means the case. In a letter to his brothers, Counts Gabriel, Joseph, and Gaetano Mastai Feretti, dated Rome, June 16, 1846, the recently elected Pope, Pius IX., uses the following language—" The blessed God, who humbles and exalts, has been pleased to raise me from insignificance to the most sublime dignity on earth." It is evident, therefore, that however weak the more modern Popes are in reality, their opinions as to the exalted dignity of their stations, are perfectly coincident with the views of a Gregory VII. or Innocent III.

† Barrow. ‡ Church of Rome compared, p. 29.
§ Supremacy, 17.

sword. No; such ambition, such claims were left alone for the bishops of Rome to exhibit.

Another grand peculiarity of the papal power is to be found in the nature of the sanctions by which its laws are enforced. In all other human governments, offences are punished by ordinary and temporal punishments. A man is fined, is deprived of certain privileges, is imprisoned, or is executed. In this case, a civil offence is followed by a civil punishment. But the Papacy is a spiritual, as well as a temporal power. It draws out offences from the conscience and the heart. Its inquisitorial confessions and courts, employ their interrogatories and their *irons*, as a sort of priestly omniscience, to survey all the secret chambers of the soul. When, too, the crime is ascertained, it is visited not simply with confiscation and burning, but with anathema. The temporal power of the ecclesiastical monarch enkindles the fires of the *auto-da-fé*, while his spiritual power consigns him to those of hell.

As the power of Christ was supreme, not only on earth, but also "in heaven," the legal heir of this power is not satisfied with a divided patrimony; he must have all. Hence his keys, his masses, his prayers, open and shut the invisible world at pleasure. "He openeth and no man shutteth, he shutteth and no man openeth." Leo X., one of the best of the Roman pontiffs, uses this language: "The Roman pontiff, the successor of Peter, in regard to the keys, and the vicar of Jesus Christ on earth, possessing the power of the keys, may, for reasonable causes, by his apostolic authority, grant indulgences out of the superabundant merits of Christ and the saints, to the faithful, who are united to Christ by charity, as well for the living as for the dead. Wherefore, all persons, whether living or dead, who really obtain any indulgences of this kind, are delivered from so much temporal punishment, due according to divine justice for actual sins, as is equivalent to the value of the indulgence bestowed and received."[*]

[*] Le Plat. quoted by Cramp, 341.

'You may buy," says Dr. Sturtevant, "as many masses as will free your souls from purgatory for twenty-nine thousand years, at the church of St. John's Lateran, on the festa of that saint. Those that have interest with the Pope may obtain an absolution in full, from his holiness, for all the sins they ever have committed or may choose to commit."* "Because private believers," says Dens, "may apply their own satisfactions to souls in purgatory, therefore the Pope may apply to them the satisfaction of Christ and the saints from the treasury of the church."† How long, therefore, a soul shall remain in purgatory, or whether it shall ever get out, depends upon the will of the Pope, exercised either by himself, or by some of his vicegerents. And when we remember, that purgatory is one of the four divisions of hell, and that Bellarmine and others maintain, that its fires are of the same nature as those of hell, the power of the keys must surely give to the successors of St. Peter no ordinary influence over the fears, the purses, and the persons of his widely extended flock.

Now, all other kings and sovereigns have left the infliction of such punishment with God only. They have punished men but as the subjects of civil law, and as amenable to civil penalties. They have not followed the departed spirit to eternity, and there also haunted it with their chains and instruments of torture. They have usually supposed that their work was ended at death. Not so the Pope and his priesthood. The iron grasp of their tyranny is not broken even by the power of the grave. They hold their subjects amenable even beyond time. They torture or bless them even in eternity itself. Surely, a government like this, cannot be found besides it, in the history of the world.

The possession of absolute infallibility is another peculiarity of the Papacy. The old Latin adage, " humanum est errare"—it is human to err—has so commended itself to the experience of mankind, that it

* Letters from Rome. † Theol., chap. xl.

has been converted into a sort of moral axiom, which no one doubts, and every one believes. Nor is it human for individuals simply to err; governments also err. Hence, in every wise civil constitution, there is always an article provided against the mistakes which may have crept into such constitution, even despite the wisdom of its framers. And in all courts of law, even in those from which there is no appeal, it is yet believed, that there may be erroneous decisions and that the condemned must sometimes look, not to the tribunals of man, but to the judgments of God for ultimate justice. Nor can there be found in the history of the world, a solitary king, sovereign, or saint, in whom there have not been either the ebullitions of passion, or the mistakes of the understanding. One perfect or infallible man has never yet existed, save the Lord Jesus Christ, and he was more than man. Adam, Noah, Abraham, Moses, David, Paul, and Peter, plead no exemption from universal human frailty. Yet, this is the boast of the Roman Pontiff! As a man, it is allowed, even he may err; but as the vicar of Christ, like Christ himself, his judgments are infallible. "The supreme Pontiff," says Dens, "determining from the throne, matters relating to faith or customs, is infallible: which infallibility proceeds from the especial assistance of the Holy Ghost."* Blessed Spirit of the living God! one is ready to exclaim—are all the blunders, the errors, the follies, the madness, the persecutions, the bloodshed, of the Roman Pontiffs, many of which have disgraced mankind, are all these to be ascribed to thy direction and counsel! Yet, such are the pretensions of the Pope, such is the creed of Romanists! Poor pitiable sovereigns of Europe! How unfortunate is your condition! Ye are guilty of errors. Your blunders are on the page of history. But your venerable father, your endeared brother, the Pope, has none of your frailties, none of your human weaknesses! Why, then, do ye not all seek wisdom from him; take counsel from him? Why

* Theol., ch. xxiv.

debate so long in your national legislatures? Why not send an express to Rome to gain infallible decisions?

Thus stands the Roman pontificate—a *sui generis* in fact, as well as a *sui generis* in vision. Well might Daniel gaze in astonishment, " because of the voice of the great words which the horn spake!" It is worthy of notice here, that this ancient seer expresses no astonishment whatever at the appearance of the other horns. Each one of them was the symbol of a kingdom as well as " the little horn." Yet the attention of the prophet is wholly turned to the contemplation of " the little horn." This horn was to him a matter of the greatest wonder. Unlike the other horns, it had "eyes and a mouth speaking great things." Though little, "its look was more stout than its fellows." It seemed, too, to be filled with the most inveterate hatred to the saints. The prophet gazed and wondered when he contemplated this horn; because, while the other horns were the symbols of ordinary, political kingdoms, the little horn, in which so many contraries met, was the symbol of a kingdom, the like to which had never existed, either in the heaven above or on the earth beneath. It was to be diverse from all kingdoms.

Now, where is the king or kingdom, in which the peculiarities of the little horn are to be found? Not in Antiochus. Not in Julius Cæsar. Not in Mohammed. None of these men were so peculiarly distinguished from their fellow men; nor did any of them, save Cæsar, have any connexion with the Roman beast. Where then shall we find the reality of which "the little horn" is the symbol? In Antichrist, says the Romanist; but Antichrist has not yet come. In Antichrist, we say; but Antichrist has already been in the world for more than a thousand years.

Thus does the anomalous character of the Papacy prove it to be the antitype of "the little horn." This power is unlike all others; is uncongenial with all others. It is a usurper, a supplanter. We can readily conceive, how a spiritual power, either associated with the state, or entirely independent of the state, may exist without discord or collision. If the church be entirely distinct from the political institutions of a people, there can of course be no disturbance, as there is no contact. And if a church be established by law, as the operations of the religious and the political systems are kept in distinct spheres, there may be but occasional evils growing out of such union. But for a government that claims its existence *jure divino*, that sets up a universal empire, that arrogates to itself supremecy in all civil, as well as ecclesiastical matters—for a government that considers itself infallible, and which requires absolute submission in all its subjects—for such a government to exist in the midst of other governments; in its very principles trampling upon their rights and privileges; wielding both a temporal and a spiritual sword; punishing offenders both in this world and the next—for such a government to exist in harmony with other governments, is impossible, absolutely impossible. The papal system can harmonize with no other, whether religious or political. To the religious world, it exhibits one supreme pontiff of Christendom, and requires for him universal obedience. To the political world, it presents one great monarch, whose throne is above every throne, and whose will is law throughout the globe. No: the Papacy is a unit, and presents the front of positive hostility to every thing that is not consolidated in itself. It may not be able to carry out its principles and wishes, but this is its nature. It is "diverse" from all other governments; it is the adversary of all other governments.

CHAPTER IV.

ANTICHRIST AN APOSTATE FROM THE CHRISTIAN FAITH.

ANOTHER mark of Antichrist as given in the Scriptures is, apostasy from the Christian faith. "For that day shall not come, except there come a falling away (ή αποστασια) first, and that man of sin be revealed, the son of perdition." 2 Thess. ii. 3.

Several distinguished commentators, as Grotius, Whitby, Le Clerc, and Wetstein, have interpreted "the day of Christ,"—(ή ήμερα του Χριστου) in this passage as applicable to the destruction of Jerusalem, and have consequently referred the term — ή αποστασια— "the apostasy," to the revolt of the Jews against the Romans, previously to the destruction of that city. This opinion, however, will appear, from even a brief reflection upon this passage, to be wholly untenable. It is evident from the whole scope of the passage, that the future coming of Christ is meant; and that the apostasy referred to, is of a religious, and not of a political character. Indeed the Apostle explains his own meaning, "Now the Spirit speaketh expressly, that in the latter times some shall depart from the faith." 2 Tim. ii. 1—αποστησονται τινες της πιστεως.

Other commentators, who understand by "the day of Christ" the future coming of the Saviour, yet apply the term αποστασια, "apostasy," to something which has not as yet occurred. Roman Catholic writers are generally of this opinion. Bloomfield, too, in his notes on the New Testament, has maintained the same sentiment. "Upon the whole," says he, "there seems good reason to suppose, with many eminent expositors for the last half century, that what is here spoken of, has not yet taken place. "The man of sin," says the commentator on the Doway Bible, "agrees to the wicked and great Antichrist, who will come before the end of the world."

If it were meant by this, that the Papacy, the real Antichrist, will assume a more malignant and desperate character anterior to the coming of Christ, we would freely yield to this interpretation. This fact appears to be definitely and clearly revealed in the 16th chapter of the book of Revelation, verses 13, 14. But if such interpreters mean, that Antichrist is yet to arise, that he is but one person, that his dominion is to be brief, and that he is immediately to precede the coming of Christ, then do we differ from them *toto cœlo*. The Roman Catholic comment on this passage is strangely inconsistent with itself. "This revolt (apostasy) is generally understood by the ancient fathers, of a revolt from the Roman empire, which was first to be destroyed before the coming of Antichrist." According to this statement, if Antichrist be not already come, the prophecy must be false ; for the Roman empire was subverted in the year 476. Antichrist was to succeed that empire; and yet, although more than thirteen centuries have passed, he has not appeared ! The error here consists, in making Antichrist one person. It is certain, that Antichrist is to continue to some future coming of Christ. It is equally certain, that he was to arise directly after the fall of the Roman empire. He cannot therefore be one person ; but must be a succession of persons filling the same office.

Our Roman Catholic annotator has also another opinion. "This revolt (apostasy) may perhaps be understood also, of a revolt of many nations from the catholic church; which has in part happened already, by the means of Mahomet, Luther, &c., and it may be supposed, will be more general in the days of Antichrist." Mohammedanism is certainly neither an apostasy from the faith, nor a revolt from the Romish church. The Arabians were not professing Christians, nor was Mohammed a member of any Christian society whatever. It is absurd therefore, to suppose, that Mohammed, or Mohammedanism is the subject

THE ANTICHRIST.

of these prophecies. Besides, where this delusion is evidently predicted under the fifth and sixth trumpets, it is not described as a departure from the faith, or a revolt from Christendom, but as an invasion of the faith, and an assault upon Christendom.

As to the reference of these predictions to the Reformers and their adherents, it is enough to answer in the language of Bishop Newton : " Who, then, is the man of sin ? Luther and his followers, or Calvin and his followers ? Or, who ? for the Protestants are far from being united under one head. Which of the Protestant churches exalts herself above every God and magistrate ? Which of them arrogates to herself divine honours and titles? Which of them pretends to establish her doctrine and discipline by miracles ? These things would be ridiculously and absurdly objected to the Protestant churches, and more ridiculously and absurdly still by the members of the church of Rome."* If, too, Christian faith be contained in the Holy Scriptures, it certainly must be most preposterous to imagine, that those men who are doing all in their power to scatter the Holy Scriptures throughout the earth, have departed from the faith.

There is a power, however, already existing, and which is destined to exist until the coming of Christ, which this prophetic description does suit, and it suits no other. " The usurpation of the Papacy in divine things is so unparalleled," says Doddridge, " that if these words are not applicable to it, it is difficult to say, who there ever has been or can be to whom they should belong."

If Romanism be not the apostasy ($\dot{\eta}$ $\alpha\pi o\sigma\tau\alpha\sigma\iota\alpha$) here mentioned, and the papacy "the man of sin" ($\dot{o}$ $\alpha\nu\theta\rho\omega\pi o\varsigma$ $\tau\eta\varsigma$ $\dot{\alpha}\mu\alpha\rho\tau\iota\alpha\varsigma$), then may we conclude certainly, that no parade of facts whatever, can prove a prophecy to have been fulfilled. With a mode of interpretation which would lead to the denial of such an application of these predictions, it would be impossible to demonstrate the Messiahship of Jesus, or the

---

* On the Prophecies, Diss. xxii.

truth of the Christian dispensation. This will appear more evident, however, when we shall have shown, that the Papacy, including the whole system of Romanism, is not only an apostasy, but *the apostasy*, from the Christian faith. And here we lay it down as self-evident, that any body of men denying that the Holy Scriptures are the only standard of faith and practice; or, that Jesus Christ is the sole Head of the Church, and of each believer; or, that there is but one Mediator between God and man; or, that sinners are justified by faith, and solely on account of the righteousness of Christ—any set of men, we say, denying these things, must be, and are apostate.

Romanists deny that the Holy Scriptures are the only rule of faith and practice. The Council of Trent, in determining the proper standard of faith and practice, uses the following language: "That this truth and discipline are contained in the written word, and in the unwritten traditions, which were received by the Apostles from the mouth of Christ himself, or from the Apostles themselves as the dictate of the Holy Ghost to them, and delivered as it were from hand to hand, have come down to us."* In Dens' Moral Theology, are these statements: "Divine tradition has equal authority with Holy Scripture; for both are truly the word of God!" "The church, however, has not framed a catalogue of divine traditions, but sets forth, sometimes one, and sometimes another, as occasions demand." "Divine tradition is truly a rule of faith, as it is the word of God, not less than Holy Scripture." "There is more need of divine tradition than of Sacred Scripture, as Scripture cannot be known without tradition." Then under the question, "Are there any special rules for ascertaining traditions?" The following answers are given: "Whatever the Roman Church holds as tradition is to be regarded as such. Whatever the Catholic Church holds or declares as such, is to be regarded as tradition."† These extracts are sufficient to show, that the Romish church

* Council of Trent, Sess. iv.   † Theol., chap. xviii.

feels herself fully competent to give a rule of faith, not only equal, but superior to the word of God! Well has an Apostle said, "Beware, lest any man spoil you, after the tradition of men." Coloss. ii. 8. And well has the Saviour declared concerning such, "Full well ye reject the commandment of God, that ye may keep your own tradition." Mark vii. 9.

Romanists have also exalted over the church, and over the consciences of men, another head than Christ. The scriptural doctrine on this subject is, that "Christ is the head over all to his church;" Eph. i. 22; and that "the head of every man is Christ." 1 Cor. xi. 3. Jesus Christ, speaking to every individual congregation of believers, and to each individual believer, through the Holy Scriptures, is alone Lord of conscience, and Head and Umpire of faith. A congregation or individual may be instructed and reasoned with, as to what Christ in the Scriptures has made known. But every attempt to interpose another authority between the congregation of the Lord, or any individual believer, and Christ, his supreme Judge, supplants the authority of Christ, and substitutes that of man in its stead. This the Romanists do, over the general church, over each congregation, and over each individual member. Over the general church, there is the Pope, deciding, determining, settling all things. Over the congregations, there is the Bishop, exercising a similar, but subordinate authority. And over each member, there is the Priest, controlling the consciences of men, and occupying a place between each member and Christ. The authority of Christ is thus removed from the church and its members, and the authority of the priesthood substituted.

No better evidence need be adduced on this point than the fact, that the Romish church is so extremely unwilling that either churches or individuals should either hear, or read the Holy Scriptures. The following is a decree of the Council of Trent, in full force at the present time—"As it is manifest by experience, if the Holy Bible in the vulgar tongue [the only way in which the people can read it] be every where indiscriminately permitted, more injury than advantage would accrue, on account of the temerity of the people, let it abide in this point by the judgment of the bishop or inquisitor, that with the advice of the priest or confessor, the reading of the Bible in the vulgar tongue, translated by Catholic authors, may be conceded to those, who, they apprehend, can derive no injury, but an increase of faith and piety from such reading: *which permission they must have in writing.* But whosoever shall presume, without such permission *to have,* or *to read it, cannot obtain absolution of his sins, unless the Bible be first returned to the ordinary.* But regulars may neither purchase nor read it, except by permission obtained from their prelates."* Commenting on this decree, Dens says: "This law has been received and hitherto kept, in the whole purely Catholic world: more indulgence has been granted *only* when it was necessary to live among heretics." Again he says: "Observe, the power of granting permission to read the Sacred Scripture in the vernacular tongue, belongs to the *bishop,* or *inquisitor,* not to the *priest,* or *confessors,* unless this power has been conceded to them." Again, he says: "It must be said, that in this point the discipline of the church has been changed; just as communion under both kinds, and daily communion have been changed. For formerly the faithful, more submissive to their pastors, humbly and faithfully derived the sense of Scripture from them, without danger of perverse translations; but now, through the example of the heretics, the lust of dissenting from the pastors has arisen; and it is manifest from experience, that by the promiscuous reading of the Sacred Scripture, men are made more proud, more discontented, and universally more conceited."† Probably, no language could more certainly express the fact, that the Holy Scriptures and the Romish priesthood are at variance, than this above quoted. Every one who prayerfully searches the Scriptures to learn the mind and will of

---

* Decrees of Trent. † Moral Theol. 140–142.

Christ, as a necessary consequence, perceives and forsakes these "doctrines of men" by which he was previously held. Hence the law to prohibit, except in very peculiar cases, and under a written permission, the perusal of the sacred word ! This fact alone proclaims, as in letters of fire, that Christ's Headship has been supplanted in the Romish church.

Romanists also deny the sole mediatorship of Christ. The Apostle teaches, that "there is one mediator between God and man, the man Christ Jesus." 1 Tim. ii. 5. And Jesus himself says—" I am the way, the truth, and the life; no man cometh to the Father but by me." John xiv. 6. It is also said of Christ—"Because he continueth ever he hath an unchangeable priesthood; wherefore he is able also to save them to the uttermost that come unto God by him, seeing he ever liveth to make intercession for them." Heb. vii. 24, 25. The Scriptures universally represent Christ's mediation, as one, alone, and all-sufficient. The Romish doctrine, however, represents it as insufficient, and as needing auxiliary intercession.

The annotator on the Doway Bible admits that "Christ is the only mediator of redemption;" and that "he stands in need of no other to recommend his petitions to the Father." At the same time, however, he asserts " that this is not against our seeking the prayers and intercessions of the saints and angels in heaven, for obtaining mercy, grace and salvation through Jesus Christ !"*

The Council of Trent passed the following decree on this subject —" The holy council commands all bishops and others who have the care and charge of teaching, that they labour with diligent assiduity to instruct the faithful, concerning the invocation and intercession of the saints, teaching them that the saints, who reign together with Christ, offer their prayers to God for men; that it is a good and useful thing suppliantly to invoke them, and to flee to their prayers, help, and assistance."† In reference to the

* On 1 Tim. ii. 5. † De Invocatione.

nature of this worship, Dens says: "It is absolute, because it is exhibited on account of the excellence, intrinsic and peculiar to the saints; yet, it may also be called respective, inasmuch as God is honoured in the saints." Again he says: "But that we implore the clemency of God through the saints, is not through the defect of the power or mercy of God; but because God is willing to grant certain blessings only through the saints."*

The practical effect of such a tenet may be learned from the following extract taken from the Catholic Manual used in the United States. "Holy Mary, pray for us. All ye holy angels and archangels, pray for us. St. Abel, all ye choirs of just souls, St. Abraham, St. John the Baptist, pray for us: St. Peter, St. Paul, St. John, pray for us. All ye holy disciples of our Lord, pray for us. St. Sylvester, St. Gregory, all ye holy monks and hermits, pray for us. All ye holy virgins and widows; all ye saints of God, make intercession for us."†

These extracts are enough to show that, in the doctrine and worship of Romanists, the creature is associated with the Creator, and the sole mediation of Christ is subverted through the invocation of saints.

Papists are also in error on the subject of a sinner's justification before God. The following are decrees of the Council of Trent. "Whosoever shall affirm that the ungodly is justified by faith only, (*sola fide impium justificari*,) so that it is to be understood that nothing else is to be required, to co-operate therewith in order to obtain justification; and that it is on no account necessary that he should prepare and dispose himself by the effort of his own will, (*suæ voluntatis motu*) let him be accursed, (*anathema sit.*) Again, "Whosoever shall affirm, that men are justified solely by the imputation of the righteousness of Christ, (*sola imputatione justitiæ Christi;*) or, that the grace by which we are justified is only the favour of God (*esse tantum favorem Dei,*) let him be accursed." "Whosoever shall affirm, that justification received is not

* Moral Theol. c. xxxiii.   † Ib. page 276.

THE ANTICHRIST. 199

preserved, and even increased in the sight of God, by good works, (*per bona opera;*) let him be accursed." " Whosoever shall affirm, that he who has fallen after baptism, cannot by the grace of God rise again; or, that if he can, it is possible for him to recover his lost righteousness by faith only, without the sacrament of penance, let him be accursed." "Whosoever shall affirm, that when the grace of justification is received, the offence of the penitent sinner is so forgiven, and the sentence of eternal punishment reversed, that there remains no temporal punishment to be endured before his entrance into the kingdom of heaven, either in this world, or in the future state in purgatory, (*vel in hoc seculo, vel in futuro, in purgatorio,*) let him be accursed." "Whosoever shall affirm, that the good works of a justified man, are in such sense the gifts of God, that they are not also the worthy merits of the justified person, (*ut non sint etiam bona ipsius justificati merita;*) or, that he being justified by his good works, which are wrought by him through the grace of God, and the merits of Jesus Christ, of whom he is a living member, does not really deserve, (*non vere mereri,*) increase of grace, eternal life, the enjoyment of that eternal life if he dies in a state of grace, and even an increase of glory; let him be accursed."*

Any one acquainted with the Scriptures will readily perceive that these anathemas of the celebrated Council of Trent fall primarily upon the head of Christ and his Apostles! The doctrine of Paul is, that "a man is justified by faith without the deeds of the law."* And Christ has taught us to say, after we have done all commanded us: "We are unprofitable servants; we have done that which was our duty to do." Luke xvii. 10. All ideas of human merit are entirely excluded by the teachings both of Christ and his Apostles. "Where is boasting then?" asks an Apostle, " It is excluded. By what law? Of works? Nay, but by the law of faith." Rom. iii. The anathema of Paul, then, and those of the Romanists, are hurled at

* De Justificatione. † Rom. iii. 28,

precisely opposite persons. Romanists affirm, "If any man exclude works in our justification, let him be accursed." Paul declares, If any man put them in, let him be accursed. "If any man preach any other gospel unto you, than that ye have received, let him be accursed." Gal. i. 9. Whose anathema, then, are we most to dread, that of the Council, or that of Paul? Whose doctrine are we to receive, that of Christ? or, that of the Pope?

Romanism, then, denies that the word of God is the sole rule of faith and practice. It denies that Jesus Christ is the sole Head of the Church. It denies that the mediation of Christ is one and exclusive. It also denies the justification of a sinner by faith only, and wholly on account of the righteousness of Christ. For these its denials of fundamental scriptural doctrines, it is, and must be apostate. Its teachings and those of Christ are at variance; its doctrines and those of the Apostles are directly opposite. Nor is this all. We hesitate not to affirm, that the papal system is *the apostasy*, predicted by Paul; and that in it we will find all the facts, which the Apostle to the Gentiles so graphically places upon the inspired page.

Here, then, is another mark by which the Papacy and Antichrist are proved to be identical. Antichrist was to be a great apostate; he was also to preside over a great apostasy. The Pope is an apostate, and he presides over an apostate church. His system excludes that of Christ, his doctrines subvert the doctrines of Christ. He is emphatically Antichrist, the opponent of Christ; and his system of doctrine is anti-christianity, displacing absolutely and entirely, those doctrines of grace of which Jesus was the Herald and the Author.

CHAPTER V.

ANTICHRIST AN IDOLATER.

Another mark of Antichrist, is idolatry. "Now the Spirit speaketh expressly, that in the latter times, some shall depart from the faith, giving heed to seducing spirits, and doctrines of devils." 1 Tim. iv. 1. (διδασκαλιαις δαιμονιων.) That this passage is to be applied to Antichrist, or the Papacy, is evident from two facts. The persons, who are here represented as giving heed to "seducing spirits, and doctrines of devils," are those who have departed from the faith; that is, they are those who constitute the great apostasy already alluded to. The species, too, of idolatry here spoken of, is precisely that which Romanists practise; it is "the doctrines of demons;" that is, it is worship rendered to the souls of departed men.

A more explicit account, however, of this Romish idolatry, is given in the following text: "And the rest of men, which were not killed by these plagues, yet repented not of the works of their hands, that they should not worship devils (demons, i. e. departed souls) and idols of gold, and silver, and brass, and stone, and of wood; which neither can see, nor hear, nor walk." Rev. ix. 20. That the reference here is also to Rome, is evident. The fifth trumpet describes the rise and progress of Mohammedanism. The sixth, the incursions of the Turks upon countries nominally Christian. "The rest of the men, therefore, which were not killed by these plagues," must refer to those portions of nominal Christendom, which were not subdued by the followers of the Arabian prophet. These countries were precisely those occupied by the Papacy.

Other passages of Scripture, charging idolatry upon the Papacy, may be found in the 17th and 18th chapters of the book of Revelation. In these chapters, this apostate church is called, in reference to these idolatries, "The great whore," "The mother of harlots;" and it is said of her, that "all nations have drunk of the wine of the wrath of her fornication." That whoredom and fornication refer to idolatry, any one, at all acquainted with the writings of the ancient prophets, must know. If, then, as we have already proven, these passages refer to modern Babylon, that is, to Rome, then is the sin of idolatry predicted, as one of the strongest marks by which Antichrist may be distinguished.

It is well known, that no charge brought against Papists, is more offensive, than that of idolatry. Gregory the Second, in his letter to the emperor Leo, in which he undertakes to repel the charge of idolatry, says, "The former idols were the fanciful representations of phantoms, or demons, at a time when the true God had not manifested his person in any visible likeness. The latter are the genuine forms of Christ, his mother, and his saints, who had approved, by a crowd of miracles, the innocence and merit of this relative worship."* Here, this kind of worship is called relative; and is said to be both innocent and meritorious. The opponent, also, of McGavin, uses the following language: "No one is ignorant, that the heathens worshipped Diana and Venus with divine honours, as deities; but, to say that the Church of Rome pays the same adoration to the blessed Virgin Mary, is contrary to truth."†

Such statements as these, however, can deceive no one acquainted with either pagan or Jewish antiquity. It is entirely certain, that the ancient pagan idolaters uniformly recognized one Supreme Being. The gods, therefore, which they worshipped, were subordinate deities; indeed, they were, for the most part, the souls of departed sages and heroes. In speaking of the

* Gibbon's Rome, ch. xlix.   † Protestant, vol. ii. ch. clix.

idolatry of the ancient Egyptians, from whom the Greeks borrowed most of their mythology, Shuckford says: "In time, they looked over the catalogue of their ancestors, and appointed a worship for such as had been more eminently famous in their generation; and having before this made pillars, statues, or images in memory of them, they paid their worship before these, and so introduced this sort of idolatry."* The following is the language of that ancient Greek poet, Hesiod : "After this generation (the primitive fathers of the human race) were dead, they were, by the will of great Jupiter, promoted to be demons, keepers of mortal men, observers of their good and evil works, clothed in air, always walking about the earth, givers of riches,"&c.† Plato also says, that "Hesiod and many other poets speak excellently, who affirm, that when good men die, they attain great honour and dignity, and become demons;" (objects of worship and veneration.) This philosopher also teaches, that "all those who die valiantly in war, are of Hesiod's golden generation, and are made demons (gods) and that we ought for ever after to serve and adore their sepulchres as the sepulchres of demons."‡

The following is Plato's explanation of what he means by demons: "Every demon is a middle being between God and mortals. God is not approached immediately by man, but all the commerce and intercourse between God and men is performed by the mediation of demons. Demons are reporters and carriers from men to the gods, and again from the gods to men, of the supplications and prayers of the one, and of the injunctions and rewards of devotion from the other."§

It is just as true, then, that the demons and idols of ancient paganism have a foundation in truth and reason, as that the saints (demons) and images of modern Rome have. The demons of Hesiod and Plato, and of the ancient world generally, were the souls of de-

* Vol. i. B. v. Refer. to Diod. Sic. i. sec. 11.
† Parkhurst's Lexicon in verbo. ‡ Ibidem. § Ibidem.

parted worthies. The images and statues, too, by which they were worshipped, were also the representations of these deceased heroes and sages. Their worship was also maintained to be respective—i. e. they were worshipped as mediators between the supreme God and mortal men. Pagan idolatry, therefore, can be defended upon the very same ground which is advocated for modern Romish idolatry. If, therefore, the one be condemned, the other cannot be justified.

Is it true then, that modern Rome maintains a worship of this kind? The following are some of the decrees of Trent on this subject. All Catholic bishops and priests are required to "instruct the faithful concerning the intercession and invocation of saints, the honour due to relics, and the lawful use of images, teaching that it is a good and useful thing suppliantly to invoke them, and to flee to their help, prayers and assistance." "Let them teach also, that the holy bodies of the holy martyrs and others living with Christ are to be venerated by the faithful, since by them God bestows many benefits upon men." "Moreover, let them teach, that the images of Christ, of the Virgin, mother of God, and of other saints, are to be had and retained, especially in churches, and due honour and veneration rendered to them. The honour, however, with which they are regarded, is referred to those, who are represented by them; so that we adore Christ, and venerate the saints, whose likenesses these images bear, when we kiss them, and uncover our heads in their presence, and prostrate ourselves." "Quas osculamur, et coram quibus, caput aperimus, et procumbimus."* This council proceeds however still farther; it authorizes representations or images of the invisible God!! It gives however this caution, "that when the Deity is thus represented, it is not to be supposed, that the same can be seen by our bodily eyes, or that a likeness of God can be given in colour or figure;" "non propterea Divinitatem figurari, quasi coloribus

---

* Sessio xxv. De Invocatione, &c.

aut figuris exprimi possit." Strictly in accordance with this permission of the council, papists frequently represent God the Father as an old man, God the Son as a young man, on his right, and God the Spirit, as a dove hovering over them ! ! !

The following is the language of Dens.

" What is meant by an image ?

" A similitude or representation of some existing thing, expressed for that thing as a copy.

" How does it differ from an idol ?

" Because an idol is a likeness representing that, which either simply does not exist, or certainly is not such as that which is worshipped; but an image is a similitude of a thing which really exists, as of a man.

" Prove that the images of Christ and of the saints are to be worshipped.

" It is proven in the first place from the council of Trent." He afterwards asserts, " however this may be, it is sufficient for us against sectarians to state, that all Catholics teach and prove that the images of the saints are to be worshipped."

In speaking of the kind of worship to be rendered the saints, &c., Dens says, " the images of the saints are worshipped with the respective veneration of *dulia;* of the Divine Virgin, with the relative worship of *hyperdulia,* of Christ and of God, with the respective worship of *latria.*"

Besides, then, the decrees of Trent, which are binding upon all Catholics, here is one of their distinguished theologians, as composedly defending and illustrating the duty of image and saint-worship, as the sincerest Protestant would illustrate and enforce the duties of faith and repentance !

The late Pope Gregory the XVI. in one of his encyclical letters uses the following language. " Now, that all these events may come to pass happily and successfully, let us lift up our eyes and our hands to the most holy Virgin Mary, who alone has destroyed all heresies, and is our greatest confidence, even the whole foundation of our hope ! " *

* Papal Rome as it is, page 136.

When such sentiments are advocated and published by councils, doctors, and popes, it is not wonderful that the same idolatry should pervade the mass of the people. In the Ursuline Manual, designed "for forming youth to the practice of solid piety," and having the sanction of the "Right Rev. Bishop Hughes," among others are the following prayers. "A prayer to St. Augustine"—"O glorious St. Augustine! the light and oracle of the faithful! penetrated with veneration for thy virtues, I choose thee for my Father, my Protector, and my Advocate. I most humbly beseech thee to have compassion on my youth, and to protect me in those dangers which thou well knowest, are attendant on my inexperienced age," &c. Next follows, "A prayer to St. Angela, Foundress of the Ursuline order." "Most blessed St. Angela, who art now in possession of that eternal crown which is promised to those who instruct others unto justice, permit me to have recourse to thee, as to my glorious patroness, and to choose thee for my special advocate before the throne of God. In union with all those happy souls, who, under God, are indebted to thee, for the glory they now enjoy in heaven, I thank God for having raised thee up, to provide for millions the great blessings of religious instruction. O glorious patroness and mother of the weakest portion of Christ's flock, do not abandon thy charge, now, that thou seest more clearly than ever the dangers to which youth is exposed."*

The following are prayers extracted from the Catholic Manual, having the sanction of Archbishop Whitfield, and designed "for the use of Christians in every state of life." "Holy Mary, Virgin, Mother of God! I this day choose thee for my Mother, Queen, Patroness and Advocate; and I firmly resolve never to depart, either by word or action from the duty I owe thee, or suffer those committed to my charge to say or do anything against thy honour. Receive me therefore as thy servant for ever, assist me in all the actions of

* Ursuline Manual, pp. 350, 351.

THE ANTICHRIST. 207

my whole life, and forsake me not at the hour of my death. The following prayer is addressed to "the Monthly Patron."* "O thou blessed inhabitant of the heavenly Jerusalem, who hast been appointed by the divine Goodness to be my patron during this month; defend me by thy intercession from all dangers of soul and body; obtain, that I may be a faithful imitator of thy virtues, and that the fire of divine love may be more and more kindled in my heart."†

Here then are manuals and prayer-books, putting into the lips of youth and Christians, direct addresses and supplications to mere creatures. The knee is bent, the lips opened, and petitions expressed to absent and distant saints! What is this? All, except papists, can see that it is not only idolatry, but idolatry in one of its worst forms.

It is sometimes attempted to justify this creature-worship, by comparing it with the petitions which believers offer for each other on earth. But nothing is more unlike. We may ask our friends to pray for us without idolatry, but we cannot pray to the saints without idolatry. In the former case we commune with creatures as creatures. In the latter, we ascribe to them divine attributes, and render to them divine homage. Hence, the opponent of McGavin does not hesitate to say: "I know that the saints in heaven are in a state of perfection and glory, and that they know what passes in the hearts of men upon earth; but how is not for me to inquire or explain."‡ Here the attribute of Divine omniscience is affirmed as the property of creatures. And if such creatures possess one such perfection, of course they possess others. Hence they are even in the highest sense deified!

If then there ever has been, or can be, a system of idolatry or creature-worship on earth, the Romish system is such. True, we are to expect those men who are engaged in such practices to defend and maintain them. And inasmuch as they profess to be Christians, we must, of course, expect them so to alter, change,

* Ursuline Manual, p. 258.   † Ib. p. 273.   ‡ Prot. ii., clix.

and interpret Scripture, as to make it consist in their view, with such modes of devotion and worship. In all this, however, Rome gives to the world the strongest possible proof of her judicial blindness, and only works out and proves the theorem, that she is "Babylon the great, the mother of harlots and abominations of the earth."

Another feature, therefore, of Antichrist is established upon Papal Rome. Antichrist was to be idolatrous. Papal Rome both is idolatrous, and has been for ages. Her system, of angel, saint, image, and relic-worship, exceeds even the grossest superstitions of ancient Greece or Rome.

CHAPTER VI.

ANTICHRIST A BLASPHEMER.

Another mark of Antichrist is blasphemy. Blasphemy refers both to the speech and actions of men. Thus the reproaches, cast by the Gentiles upon the name and character of God, are termed by the Apostle Paul, "blasphemy." Rom. ii. 24. And so also Christ's assertion, that he was the Son of God, was considered by the Jews as blasphemy. "For a good work," say they, "we stone thee not; but for blasphemy; and because that thou being a man makest thyself God." John x. 33.

Blasphemy is predicted of Antichrist in several passages of Scripture. It is said of the little horn, which is the symbol of Antichrist, "and he shall speak great words against the Most High." Dan. vii. 25. The beast also which John saw, and which is also a symbol of Antichrist, had upon his seven heads "the names of blasphemy." Rev. xiii. 1. It is also said of this same beast—"And there was given unto him a mouth speaking great things and blasphemies, and he opened his mouth in blasphemy against God, to blaspheme his name, and his tabernacle, and them that dwell in heaven." Rev. xiii. 5, 6. The Apostle Paul also gives us the following description of the same evil power: "For that day shall not come except there come a falling away first, and that man of sin be revealed, the son of perdition, who opposeth and exalteth himself above all that is called God, or that is worshipped; so that he as God, sitteth in the temple of God, showing himself that he is God." 2 Thess. ii. 3, 4.

Is there any thing then in the actual state of the

Papacy, corresponding to these predictions concerning the blasphemous character of Antichrist? To this I reply, first, that the very office of the Pope is blasphemous. What that office is, may be learned from the following Romish authorities. One of the canons of the papal Church says: "The Pope, by the Lord's appointment, is the successor of the blessed Apostle Peter, and holds the place of the Redeemer himself upon the earth." (Ipsius Redemptoris locum in terris tenet.) Again, "The Roman pontiff bears the authority not of a mere man, but of the true God upon the earth:" (sed veri Dei vicem gerit in terris.) "Christ, the King of Kings, and Lord of Lords, gave to the Roman pontiff, in the person of Peter, the plenitude of power;" (plenitudinem potestatis.) Again; the Doway catechism asserts, that "he who is not in due connexion and subordination to the Pope and general councils, must needs be dead, and cannot be accounted a member of the church, since from the Pope and general councils, under Christ, we have our spiritual life and motion as Christians." The following language is also used: "It was becoming, since the chief pontiff represents the person of Christ, that as, during Christ's earthly ministry, the Apostles stood around him, so the assembly of the cardinals, representing the apostolic college, should stand before the Pope." Again: "Whenever there is any question concerning the privileges of the apostolic chair, they are not to be judged of by others. The Pope alone knows how to determine doubts concerning the privileges of the apostolic seat."*

And who is the Pope? A man, a mere man; an uninspired man; often, an immoral and wicked man! And yet, such is his office, such his prerogatives, such his pretensions! Well has the Apostle said—"He, as God, sitteth in the temple of God, showing himself that he is God." Here is blasphemy, blasphemy of the blackest die.

The attributes ascribed to the Pope in this office

---

* Bishop Hopkins's "Church of Rome," chap. iii.

are also blasphemous. Among others, the Pope is considered as invested with the three following powers: inspiration, infallibility, and absolute authority. "The supreme pontiff," says Dens, "determining from the throne matters relating to faith or customs, is infallible; which infallibility proceeds from the special assistance of the Holy Spirit."* He also thus describes the authority of the Pope: "Hence it follows, that all the faithful, even bishops, and patriarchs, are obliged to obey the Roman pontiff; also that he must be obeyed in all things, which concern the Christian religion, and therefore, in faith and customs, in rites, ecclesiastical discipline, &c. Hence, the perverse device of the Quesnelites falls to the ground; namely, that the Pope is not to be obeyed, except in those things which he enjoins conformably to Scripture!!"† Strictly in accordance with this teaching of the theologian, is the published doctrine of the late Pope Gregory XVI.—"Let all remember," says he, "that the principle of sound doctrine, with which the people are to be imbued, must emanate from, and that the rule and administration of the universal church belongs to, the Roman pontiff, to whom was given the full power of feeding, ruling, and governing the universal church by Christ our Lord."‡

Here then is a frail, erring mortal, arrogating to himself, and that by virtue of office only, the attributes of the Deity! The Spirit of God is with him, infallibility is his; and he is to be obeyed, even where he enacts laws, and teaches doctrine contrary to Scripture! Surely this is blasphemy—this is "to speak great words against the Most High."

The homage rendered to the Pope is of the same blasphemous character. The following is the description of a scene, which took place a few years since at Rome, and which was witnessed by an American citizen. "A most superb procession took place on the morning of the festa of the annunciation, which I

* Mor. Theol. on Primacy.
† Ibidem. ‡ Voice from Rome, p. 14.

with thousands of others, ran to see. The Pope, riding on a white mule, (I suppose to imitate our Saviour's entry into Jerusalem,) came, attended by his horse-guards, who rode before to clear the way, mounted on prancing black horses; and accompanied by such a flourish of trumpets and kettle-drums, as to wear far more the appearance of a martial parade, than of a religious ceremony. All were dressed in splendid full uniform, and in every cap waved a myrtle sprig, the sign of rejoicing. The cardinals followed, and the rear was brought up by a bareheaded priest on a mule, with the host in a golden cup, the sight of which operated like a talisman on every soul around me, for every knee bent. The Pope himself was clothed in robes of white and silver, and as he passed along the crowds of gazing people that lined the streets and filled the windows, he forgot not incessantly to repeat his benediction, a twirl of three fingers, typical of the Father, Son and Holy Ghost; the little finger representing the latter. Many tiresome ceremonies followed his entry into the church. He was seated on his throne; all the cardinals successively approached, kissed his hand, retired a step or two, gave three low nods, one to him in front, as personifying God the Father; one to the right, intended for the Son; and one to the left for the Holy Ghost!" Speaking of another procession on Palm Sunday, the same writer says:—"The Pope was clothed this time in scarlet and gold, and a most sumptuous figure he made. The cardinals were dressed in their morning robes, of a violet colour, richly trimmed with antique lace, with mantles of ermine, and scarlet trains, but these were soon changed for garments of gold. The same round of ceremonies were performed as I related, on the festa of the annunciation. Two palm branches received the benediction of the Pope, after having passed through a cloud of incense. The procession then began to move off, two and two, beginning with the lowest clerical monk; and at last the Pope himself in his chair of state, under a crimson canopy, and borne

THE ANTICHRIST.

on the shoulders of four men. Great pomp and splendour marked this parade. The crowns and mitres of the bishops and patriarchs, white and crimson, glittering with jewels, and set with precious stones; their long, rich dresses, the slow and uniform march of the procession, and the gay crowds surrounding, presented quite an imposing appearance."*

And this is the vicar of Jesus Christ! this the successor of the laborious and self-denying Peter! One would think that the Pope much more resembles some image of the ancient Jupiter, than either Christ or his Apostle. But look at the worship rendered to the Pope on his throne! He is adored as the personification of the Holy Trinity! And this too, not by ignonant fanatics, but by illustrious cardinals! Nor does it occur privately, or occasionally; but in the most public assemblies, indeed before the world; and on all great and solemn occasions! And is not this blasphemy? What! shall a mortal, a sinner, thus receive the worship of Jehovah? Does a man pretend to be the representation of the Trinity? All this, however, but fulfils the extraordinary predictions of Paul, concerning this same wicked power:—" Who opposeth and exalteth himself above all that is called God, or that is worshipped."

The acts of the pontificate are of the same blasphemous character. Exalted as he is to the very acme of both temporal and spiritual jurisdiction, the Pope of Rome imagines himself to be a very god on earth. Bishops and kings are but his footstool, while even heaven and hell are locked or unlocked at his pleasure. The following are a few of the papal maxims ascribed originally to Gregory VII. " The Roman Church is the only one that God has founded. The title of universal, belongs to the Roman pontiff alone. He alone can depose and absolve bishops. He has a right to depose emperors. All princes must kiss his feet. No chapter, no book can be reputed canonical without his authority. His name is

* Dr. Sturtevant.

the only one to be uttered in the churches. It is the only name in the world. He alone has the right to assume the attributes of empire."* And in the exercise of these fearful prerogatives, see the Roman Pontiff, from his lofty balcony, pronouncing from year to year, the awful anathemas of the bull "In coena Domini." The following is one of these thundering curses: "We excommunicate and anathematize in the name of God Almighty, Father, Son and Holy Ghost, and by the authority of the blessed Apostles Peter and Paul, and by our own; all Hussites, Wickliffites, Lutherans, Zuinglians, Calvinists, Huguenots, Anabaptists, Trinitarians and apostates from the Christian faith, and all other heretics, by whatsoever name they are called, and of whatsoever sect they be; as also their adherents, receivers, favourers, and generally any defenders of them; together with all, who without our authority, as that of the apostolic see, knowingly read, keep, print, or in any wise, for any cause whatever, publicly or privately, on any pretext or colour, defend their books, containing heresy or treating of religion; as also schismatics, and those who withdraw themselves, or recede obstinately from the obedience of us, or of the bishop of Rome for the time being."

An Apostle has said, "judge nothing before the time:" and again—"vengeance is mine, saith the Lord." Here, however, we see the Pope of Rome thundering his curses upon his enemies with a liberal hand; yea, "cursing, whom the Lord has not cursed." This, however, has been predicted of this blasphemous power. "And he opened his mouth in blasphemy against God, to blaspheme his name, and his tabernacle, and them that dwell therein."

Here, then, is the antitype of the beast which John saw rising out of the sea, "having seven heads and ten horns, and upon his horns ten crowns, and upon his heads, the names of blasphemy." Here is another deep and prophetic mark of the great Antichrist. The very chair of the Pope, his high pretensions, his

* Court of Rome—Persecutions of Popery.

arrogance and pride, his anathemas and curses, the worship he requires from his subjects, and the false doctrines and rules, which in the name of God, and as God, he enforces upon men, all these things prove him to be the blaspheming king, of which Daniel and Paul, and John, severally speak; all proclaim him Antichrist.

CHAPTER VII.

ANTICHRIST AN INNOVATOR.

The introduction of changes in divine institutions and laws, is another prophetic feature in Antichrist. Thus Daniel predicts of him; " and he shall think to change times and laws"—ויסבר להושניה זמנין ורת. The Seventy render the passage into Greek thus—*και υπονοησει του αλλοιωσαι καιρους και νομους*. The Vulgate translates it into the following Latin: " Et putabit mutare tempora et legem." The following is the English of the Doway Bible—" And he shall think himself able to change times and laws." Daniel vii. 26.

The character of these times and laws is not only to be inferred from the context, but is distinctly taught us by the Apostle Paul. " He, as God, sitteth in the temple of God, showing himself that he is God." 2 Thess. ii. 4. The meaning of this passage is, that Antichrist, arrogating to himself divine authority and honours, hesitates not to make those changes and alterations in the institutions of heaven, which God alone has the exclusive right either to establish or annul. Some of these changes are definitely expressed by the same Apostle—" forbidding to marry, and commanding to abstain from meats, which God hath created to be received with thanksgiving of them which believe and know the truth." 1 Tim. iv. 3. These passages refer to Antichrist; and the latter teaches most clearly, who that Antichrist is. Who is it that forbids to marry? Who is it that commands a great variety of fasts and abstinences? It is the Church of Rome. While God has left both marrying and fasting as voluntary things to his people, and while the New Testament teaches that many of the Apostles, the brethren of the Lord, and even Peter (1 Cor. ix. 4,) had wives, the Papacy dares to step in between God and the consciences of men, and to interpose its authority as absolute and imperative! The following are some among the many changes which the Papacy has introduced in divine ordinances and laws. We have already noticed its denial of the Scriptures as the sole rule of faith, its perversion of the doctrine of justification by faith, its virtual subversion of the sole mediatorship of Christ, and its utter destruction of the Christian liberties of God's people; we now proceed to increase the catalogue of alterations in the divine economy and law, which this wicked power has made, during the lapse of past centuries.

The Papacy has virtually abolished the obligation of the moral law. Not only is the second commandment made a part of the first, in the more systematic arrangement of doctrines in the Romish Church, and the tenth divided into two, to complete the number; but in their catechisms for the young, the second is entirely omitted!* Their system too, of saint and image-worship, even where the literal law is retained, completely subverts its authority. The fourth commandment has shared a similar fate. True, it is retained verbally, but then its force and obligation are entirely destroyed. The multiplication of other holy days by this church, has caused the Sabbath as a divine institution, proportionably to sink in the estimation of all Catholic communities. Dens, in in his treatise on theology, on the fourth commandment asks this question—" What is taught by this third (4th) precept in the new law?" The answer given is, " Principally these three things—1. That certain specified days are to be kept holy. 2. That they are to be kept holy by external divine worship, by hearing masses. 3. That the same are to be kept holy by abstaining from servile labours." He next asks, " Which days are those appointed to be kept holy?" The answer is, " In the first place, are the Lord's days; next, festival days!" Here, saints' days and

* See Appendix, Note D.

other set days appointed by the Church of Rome, are actually placed in the Decalogue as of Divine appointment! More than one hundred of these human Sabbaths are imposed upon the dupes of Rome, under the authority of Him who spake from Sinai, and who said, "Remember the Sabbath day to keep it holy." Hence the ever occurring interruptions to weekly labour in Catholic countries, hence the declension in national prosperity of all those countries. , God's economy has been abolished, and man's substituted. But this evil also operates against the sanctity of the weekly Sabbath. This day is put on a footing with the other holy days; it is devoted to plays and sports, by those who should be taught, "not to think their own thoughts, or to speak their own words on God's holy day." "As to hunting, says Dens, and fishing, unless accompanied with great noise or fatigue, they are lawful recreations on the Lord's day! Many suppose that it is not unlawful to fish with a reed, hook, or small nets, for the purpose of recreation; and they think the same of hunting on a small scale."—He also introduces two other authorities as advocating the selling of clothes, shoes, and other things, to servants and labourers, on the Sabbath, and represents it as doubtful whether painting is not lawful on that day! If such be the teachings of sound Roman Catholic divines on the sanctity of the Sabbath, what shall be said of the practices of the people generally? Hence in all Catholic countries, after morning mass, and certain external forms of worship, the Sabbath is spent as a day of recreation and sport.*

The fifth commandment has been set aside by the Papacy in all those numerous cases in which children have been compelled by the church to inform against heretical parents, and in which parents have been constrained to turn the accusers of their own offspring. The following is the testimony of one who was born a Roman Catholic, and long continued such.† "Every year there is publicly read (in Spain)

---

* See Appendix, Note E. † Rev. Joseph Blanco White.

at church, a proclamation or bull from the Pope, commanding parents to accuse their children, children their parents, husbands their wives, and wives their husbands, of any words or actions against the Roman Catholic religion. They are told that whoever disobeys this command not only incurs damnation for his own soul, but is the cause of the same to those whom he wishes to spare. So that many have had for their accusers, their fathers and mothers, without knowing to whom they owed their sufferings under the Inquisitors; for the name of the informer is kept a most profound secret, and the accused is tried without ever seeing the witnesses against him."* Here, then, according to papistical policy, the obligations of the fifth commandment are subverted by the tyrannical and interposed authority of the priesthood.

It need scarcely be affirmed, here, what effects the imposition of celibacy upon the clergy is likely to produce in reference to the seventh commandment. When such celibacy is voluntary, there is but little danger; where, however, it is forced, there is always danger to the party upon whom it is thus laid. Even Christ said on this subject, " he that is able to receive it, let him receive it." Matt. xix. 12. The Apostle Paul also gives the following advice:—" to avoid fornication, let every man have his own wife." 1 Cor. vii. 2. A single life, according to Scripture, should be voluntary, wherever adopted. Every man, in this particular, is to judge for himself. But the Church of Rome forces celibacy upon her priesthood. Can any one believe, that this arbitrary law can extinguish the propensities of nature? or, that all who have professedly submitted to it, have really led chaste and virtuous lives? Impossible! And if the seventh commandment be violated by the priesthood, is it likely that it can have its proper influence among all the multitudes who constitute the entire Catholic community? At any rate, any one can see, that the tendency of this rule is to subvert the pure morality of the church.

* Preservative against Popery, p. 5.

The sixth and eighth commandments have both been trampled under foot by the Holy Inquisition. The great object of this court seems to be to enrich the church by murdering its enemies, or suspected friends. In Spain, this Holy Court directed its energies at first, principally against the Jews. "In one year," says McCrie," five thousand Jews fell a sacrifice to popular fury.*" These Jews were immensely rich, and their property became the possession of their malignant persecutors. In the very year in which Luther made his appearance (1517), in Spain alone, there were 13,000 persons burnt alive, 8700 burnt in effigy, and 169,723 condemned to various penances.† Is it possible to imagine that a body of men, who can, on slight pretexts, accuse, condemn, and burn worthy and industrious citizens, and then take possession of their property, can have any regard for either the sixth or the eighth commandment?

But this whole law is virtually abolished by the Tax-book of the Roman Chancery. Here crimes are reduced to a regular scale of pecuniary valuation. Of course, the idea that a transgressor has of the character of his sin, is the amount of money he has to pay for its pardon. The following are a few items from this Tax-Book: "Robbing a church, $2.50. Perjury, forgery, and lying, $2. Robbery, $3. Burning a house, $2.75. Eating meat in Lent, $2.75. Killing a layman, $1.75. Striking a priest, $2.75. Procuring abortion, $1.50. Priest to keep a concubine, $2.25. Ravishing a virgin, $2. Murder of father, mother, brother, sister or wife, $2.50. Marrying on a forbidden day, $10. All incest, rapes, adultery, and fornication, committed by a priest, with the joint pardon of the other parties concerned, $10. Absolution of all crimes together, $12."‡ According to this scale of the Roman Chancery, not only are human laws made equal, and even superior to the divine, but crimes the most atrocious are represented as venial; a

---

* Reformation in Spain, 71.
† Idem. p. 83.
‡ Text-Book of Popery, p. 263.

few dollars and cents cancel the account, and turn the transgressor forth to commit new depredations upon the law of God, and upon human society! Thus does the Papacy virtually abolish and set aside the moral law itself.

2. We notice next the interference of the Papacy with marriage; an institution appointed directly by God, older than any other, and one which lies at the basis of society, and which is essential to the purity of any community whatever. Every reader of church history will perceive an early tendency in the church to discountenance marriage in her clergy. This tendency was farther increased by the monastic life. It was afterwards converted into an ecclesiastical law, and marriage in a priest was considered a more heinous crime, than adultery in a layman.

That such an unnatural statute has no countenance in Scripture, is certain. God himself has said, "It is not good for man to be alone.", Gen. ii. 18. Even the high-priest among the Jews was expected to marry, "and he shall take a wife in her virginity." Lev. xxi. 13. The Apostle Paul also says, "a bishop must be the husband of one wife." 1 Tim. iii. 2. It is also manifest that Peter and several of the Apostles were married men. 1 Cor. ix. 4. True, Christ and Paul intimate, that under given circumstances it would be better for ministers not to marry. Neither, however, makes any law on the subject; but leaves it to the choice of ministers themselves; the Papacy, however, "forbids to marry."

Pope Gregory VII. assembled an ecclesiastical council at Rome, in the year 1074. In this council "it was decreed," says Mosheim, "that the sacerdotal orders should abstain from marriage; and that such of them as had already wives or concubines, should immediately dismiss them, or quit the priestly office. These decrees were accompanied with circular letters, written by the pontiff to all European bishops, enjoining the strictest obedience to this solemn council, under the severest penalties."—" No sooner was the law concerning the celibacy of the clergy published," remarks the same historian, "than the priests in the several provinces of Europe, who lived in the bonds of marriage with lawful wives, complained loudly of the severity of this council, and excited the most dreadful tumults in the greatest part of the European provinces. Many of these ecclesiastics chose rather to abandon their spiritual dignities, and to quit their benefices, that they might cleave to their wives." He also remarks: "The proceedings of Gregory appeared to the wiser part, even of those who approved of the celibacy of the clergy, unjust and criminal in two respects: first, in that his severity fell indiscriminately and with equal fury upon the virtuous husband and the licentious rake. Secondly, that instead of chastising the married priests with wisdom and moderation, he gave them over to the civil magistrate, to be punished as disobedient and unworthy subjects, with the loss of their substance, and with the most shocking marks of undeserved infamy and disgrace!!"* How powerless must have fallen upon the ear of such a Pope, the words of Christ—"Whom God hath joined together, let not man put asunder." Matt. xix. 6.

Here then we see the Papacy, true to the prophecy concerning it, but in direct violation of the laws of God and of society, among a large class of persons, annulling an institution, of which it is said, "marriage is honourable in all." The object of such a law is evident enough—it is to create the tools of papal power. By destroying all conjugal ties in her priesthood, by withering in the heart all domestic loves and affections, Rome seeks to ally to the chair of St. Peter, a vast number of willing minions, who will go at her bidding, and who shall seek in despite of all opposition, to establish her dominion over the nations of the earth. While, however, she thus seeks to increase her authority, she but exhibits her real character, and demonstrates to the world, that she is the Antichrist, predicted in the Holy Scriptures.

It has already been shown, in speaking of the

* Century xi. Part ii. Sec. ii.

apostasy of Rome, how the gospel, as a system of grace and salvation, has been corrupted by the Papacy. Rome has also perverted and changed every institution and ordinance connected with the gospel.

3. She has changed and corrupted the sacraments of the new dispensation. Any reader of the New Testament will readily perceive, that Christ appointed but two such sacraments, Baptism, and the Lord's Supper. Rome, however, has ordained seven—Baptism, Confirmation, the Eucharist, Penance, Extreme Unction, Orders, and Matrimony. The authority for such sacraments is thus expressed by Dens: "The primary reason of this, is the will of Christ, as made known by divine tradition! This number of seven is also insinuated in various passages of Scripture. Thus, Prov. ix. 1, it is said, 'Wisdom, which is Christ, has built a house for herself, that is the church, and she hath hewn out seven pillars,' doubtless the seven sacraments, which, like so many pillars sustain the church! So in like manner, (Exod. xxv.,) by the seven lamps, which were on one candlestick, this is implied: for there are seven sacraments, just so many as there are lamps, which illumine the church."* Such is the miserable foundation on which Rome rests her doctrine of seven sacraments!

But she has changed the design and character of a sacrament. The sacraments of the New Testament are but the external signs and seals of internal and spiritual grace. Rome, however, makes them the material causes of grace. The council of Florence uses the following language: "These our sacraments both contain and confer grace, upon such as worthily receive them." The council of Trent speaks in a similar manner—"If any one shall say, that grace is not conferred by the sacraments of the new law themselves by their own power—(per ipsa novæ legis Sacramenta ex-opere operato non conferri gratiam)—but that mere belief of the divine promise is sufficient to obtain grace; let him be accursed."† Dens explains

* Dens's Theol. ch. xxxiv. † De Sacramentis in genere.

the mode in which grace is conferred by these sacraments. "Sacraments act in the manner of natural agents, whose effect is more or less, according to the greater or less capacity or disposition of the subject: which disposition still has no efficiency; as it is plain in fire, which burns dry wood more effectually than green, although the dryness is merely the remover of a hindrance, or an indispensable requisite, and not the efficient cause of combustion."* Here, it is distinctly stated, that upon the same principle that fire burns wood, sacraments confer grace! Grace is inherent in the sacrament; consequently, the application of the sacrament to the subject, as naturally sanctifies, as the application of fire to wood burns! Hence the same author says: "The power of regeneration is attributed not less to the water, than to the Holy Ghost!!†

From the view thus taken by Rome, of the design of a sacrament, it is not wonderful that she considers the administration of her sacraments as essential to salvation. When his Jewish brethren placed the same false view upon circumcision, the Apostle to the gentiles exclaimed: "Circumcision is nothing, and uncircumcision is nothing, but the keeping of the commandments of God." 1 Cor. vii. 19. And when this view began to be taken also by Christians, of baptism, the same Apostle said: "I thank God, that I baptized none of you, but Crispus and Gaius." 1 Cor. i. 14. The plain and constant teaching of the New Testament is, that men are saved "by grace," and that the gift of this grace is not dependent upon human work or merit in any sense whatever. "The wind bloweth where it listeth," says Christ; and believers are said to be born, "not of blood, nor of the will of the flesh, nor of the will of man, but of God." John iii. and i. Rome, however, places the gift of grace in the hands of her priesthood, and not in the hands of a sovereign God. Nor is this all; the administration of her sacraments must be accompanied with the intention of the priest, otherwise the sacrament itself becomes ineffica-

* Theol. ch. xxxiv. † Ibidem.

cious. "The intention in the minister," says Dens, "consists in an act of his will, by which he wills the external performance of the sacraments, with the intention of doing what the church does." And Trent has decreed—" If any one shall say that the intention is not required in ministers, when they perform and confer sacraments, at least of doing what the church does, let him be accursed."* This of course places salvation in the intention of a priest. Who can ascertain that intention? Who, but God, can read the heart of a Catholic priest? How then can a communicant have any evidence of pardon, but the word of the priest? And yet this sort of sacrament is essential to salvation! "The effect of this sacrament," (baptism,) says the Council of Florence, "is the remission of all original and actual guilt; also, of all punishment which is due for that guilt." Trent decrees, that, "Whosoever shall say that baptism is optional, that is, not necessary to salvation, let him be accursed."† Hence the practice of this church, to allow midwives and others to baptize children in cases of emergency. Hence the directions given about baptizing children in the womb, and of opening mothers, who die in child-birth, in order to baptize the living offspring! Hence, too, that heathenish practice of excluding from consecrated burying places, not only heretics and others, but the children of Roman Catholic parents, provided they die before baptism can be administered!‡

The same necessity is held as to the other sacraments. "Whether confirmation," says Dens, "is necessary to salvation, is a disputed point; but the more probable opinion is the affirmative."§ It is rather wonderful that an infallible church should be held in doubt as to a matter of this kind. As to the necessity of the eucharist, however, there is no doubt. "While the other sacraments," say the Decrees of Trent, " then first possess the power of sanctifying, when they

* Dens',Theol., chap. xxxiv. † Dens' Theol. ibidem.
‡ Dens, ibidem. § Dens, ch. xxxvi.

are used by any one, the very Author of sanctity is in the eucharist before it is used."* This sacrament, thus changed into Christ himself, "is not," says the Roman Catholic catechism, "like bread and wine, changed into our substance, but in some measure changes us into its own nature." The same catechism affirms, that "it is an antidote against the contagion of sin;" and that "invigorated by the strengthening influence of this heavenly food, the recipient at death wings his way to the mansions of everlasting glory and never-ending bliss."† "The sin of its omission," says Dens, "is mortal."‡

The same necessity is placed upon penance and extreme unction. "Whosoever shall deny," says the Council of Florence, "that sacramental confession is necessary to salvation, let him be accursed."§ "Whosoever," says the same Council, "shall say that the sacred anointing of the sick does not confer grace, nor remit sins, nor raise up the sick, but that it has now ceased, let him be accursed."‖ Thus, these Romish sacraments are considered, all of them, and in every case, essential to salvation; a position contrary to Scripture, and which has no authority but the word of Rome.

The corruption which Rome has introduced into the simple, but significant ceremony of the Lord's Supper, deserves particular attention. Any plain and honest reader of the New Testament, must perceive at once, that the object of the Lord's Supper was to erect in the Church a memorial of that greatest of all events, the death of Christ upon the cross. That, as the feast of the passover was a memorial of the deliverance of the Israelites from the bondage of Egypt, when the first-born were slain, so this institution was designed to be a perpetual memento, or commemorative ordinance, pointing to Calvary and Christ. This simple view of the subject, however, has not suited the genius of Rome. To magnify her priesthood, (for this is the object,) she has converted it into something

---

* Text Book, 163. † Idem. ‡ Chap. xxxviii.
§ Dens, chap. xxxix. ‖ Dens, chap. xli.

very different, and given to her priests a power in this ordinance, which is actually higher, so far as we know, than that possessed by God himself; certainly, a power so absurd that he never employed it. This power is, the conversion of the whole substance of the bread into the literal body of Christ, and of the whole substance of the wine into the literal blood of Christ; the accidents, that is, the shape, colour, taste, &c., of the bread and wine remaining; not however inhering in their own substance, but in the substance of the body and blood of Christ!—"Whosoever shall deny," is the doctrine of Trent, " that in the most holy sacrament of the eucharist, there are truly, really, and substantially contained the body and blood of our Lord Jesus Christ, together with his soul and divinity, and consequently *Christ entire;* but shall affirm that he is present therein only in a sign or figure, or by his power, let him be accursed."—"Whosoever shall deny that Christ entire, (totum Christum,) is contained in the venerable sacrament, under each species (sub unaquaque specie,) and under every part of each species, (et sub singulis cujusque speciei partibus,) when they are separated, (separatione facta,) let him be accursed."* This is plain; it was designed to be plain. The whole Christ, the Son of God, the Saviour of men, of whom it is said, " let all the angels of God worship him;" this glorious personage is actually converted by the words of a Roman priest, into the form and appearance of bread and wine ! " Credat Judæus Apella, non ego." Nor does the priest himself really believe it; for if poison be introduced into the wine, he will refuse to drink it.†

The first effect of this monstrous dogma, is what is called the adoration of the host, that is, the worship of the consecrated and transubstantiated bread and wine : " Whosoever shall affirm, that Christ the only begotten Son of God is not to be adored in the holy Eucharist with the external signs of that worship

---

* De sacro-sancto eucharistiæ Sacramento.
† Dens' Theol. xxxix.

which is due to God, (cultu latriæ) and, therefore, that the Eucharist is not to be honoured with extraordinary festive celebration, nor solemnly carried about in processions, nor publicly presented to the people for their adoration, (populo proponendum ut adoretur,) and that those who worship the same are idolaters; let him be accursed."* Here, a God is not only made out of bread and wine, but actually received and worshipped as such!

Nor is this all—the wheaten and vinous Christ is next converted into a sacrifice, and offered by the blaspheming priest, as an atonement for the sins of the living and the dead! "Whoever shall affirm, that a true and proper sacrifice (verum et proprium sacrificium) is not offered to God in the mass; or, that the offering is nothing else than giving Christ to us to eat; let him be accursed."—"Whosoever shall affirm, that the sacrifice of the mass is only a service of praise and thanksgiving, or a bare commemoration of the sacrifice made on the cross, and not a propitiatory offering; (non autem propitiatorium) or, that it only benefits him who receives it, and ought not to be offered for the living and the dead, (pro vivis et defunctis,) for sins, punishments, satisfactions, and other necessities, (pro peccatis, pœnis, satisfactionibus, et aliis necessitatibus,) let him be accursed."† On the same subject, Dens teaches that, "The sacrifice on the cross is altogether the same as to substance with the sacrifice of the mass; because the priest in both instances is the same! and the victim, Christ the Lord is the same!" Again he says, "Next to Christ, every priest legitimately ordained, is the true and proper minister of the sacrifice, because they only can perform this sacrifice, who have received supernatural power for this purpose." Again he says: "The value of the mass is infinite:" and again, "The mass is infallibly efficacious." "It is proper," he says, "to receive pay for the celebration of the mass." "Baptized heretics, he continues, are entirely excluded from

* Decrees of Trent, ibidem. † De sacrificio missæ.

all the direct benefits of the sacrifice of the mass." Still, however, "It is certain that the sacrifice of the mass, is infallibly of advantage to souls in purgatory, for the remission of the punishments remaining from guilt, at least as to a part."

Thus is the simple and sublime ordinance of the Holy Supper, converted from a purely commemorative ordinance, from being the means of cherishing the believer's faith in Christ, into a ceremony of superstition, absurdity and idolatry. Well might Christ say of such, "Ye blind guides, which strain at a gnat and swallow a camel." Matt. xxiii. 24.

4. Upon all the changes which Rome has introduced into the church and kingdom of God, it is not necessary to dwell. Suffice it to say, that every doctrine, every ordinance, every institution, every mode of worship, every thing, has undergone, in one form or another, some change in passing through the hands of omnipotent Rome. The church has become a temporal kingdom, the ministry not only a priesthood, but a set of earthly princes; the Bible, not a revelation from God to man, but a revelation from the priest to man; baptism, not an obligation to Christ, but an obligation to the church; confession to man, has taken the place of confession to God; obedience is no longer the evidence of faith, but the meritorious cause of salvation. Purgatory has been invented to terrify the credulous; and contributions and fasts, instead of being left voluntary to individual believers, are matters of ecclesiastical law, and of positive requirement. A system of tyranny has been erected on the ruins of freedom; and error and superstition have risen up in the place of truth and simplicity. If Peter or Paul were sent back from the world of glory, to contemplate the church of Rome; and if they were told, that the Roman church was held as the model of the system, which they originally advocated, these holy men would scarcely recognize a principle or a thing in all Romanism, identical with the church and the Christianity which they left in the world. Yea, Paul would see his

"man of sin," in all the perfection of maturity, in the awful spectacle presented before him, and misnamed *The Church*. Thus has Rome, lifting her hand higher than that of the Almighty, and speaking with a voice more terrific than that of the Holy One, dared to pull down what God has erected, and to erect what God has forbidden. In all this, however, she demonstrates her true character, proves herself to be Antichrist, and awakens in the bosom of the true believer the hope, that her destruction is advancing, and that "according as she hath glorified herself, so much torment and sorrow" will an avenging God give her.

CHAPTER VIII.

ANTICHRIST A PERSECUTOR.

Another mark of Antichrist, furnished in the Scriptures, is his persecuting spirit. "I beheld," says Daniel, "and the same horn made war with the saints, and prevailed against them." Dan. vii. 21. The same is expressed by John—"And it was given unto him to make war with the saints and to overcome them." Rev. xiii. 7. But John is yet more explicit: "And I saw the woman drunken with the blood of the saints; and with the blood of the martyrs of Jesus." Rev. xvii. 6. Again, "In her was found the blood of prophets, and of saints, and of all that were slain upon the earth." Rev. xviii. 24.

Persecution refers to those civil and temporal punishments which are inflicted upon men for opinion's sake. That such punishments were employed among the ancient Israelites, especially in relation to idolatry, is certain. Deut. xiii. xvii. and xviii. Was it designed by Christ, that they should also be used in the propagation of the Christian faith? Certainly not.

1. He has prescribed a different punishment for the rejecters of his gospel. "He that believeth not shall be damned." Mark xvi. 16. Eternal perdition is here denounced upon all who receive not Christ, after they shall have heard his gospel. Nor is this sentence to be executed by the minister; but simply proclaimed by him. Now if this is the punishment to be denounced against the rejecters of Christ's gospel, the substitution of temporal or civil penalties is both inappropriate and unlawful. Error is better removed

by argument, and fear excited by the threatened vengeance of the Lord.

2. Christ instituted no union between church and state. For the most part, persecution has been the offspring of the union here alluded to. Ecclesiastical censure has been enforced by the civil magistrate. The doctrine of Jesus, however, on this subject is, "My kingdom is not of this world; if my kingdom were of this world, then would my servants fight; but now is my kingdom not from hence." Here all connexion between church and state is expressly denied; and consequently persecution, as growing out of that connexion.

3. The practice, too, both of Christ and his Apostles, utterly condemns all such methods of promoting the truth. When twelve legions of angels were ready at the call of Christ to execute vengeance upon his crucifiers, he invoked not their assistance. Matt. xxvi. 53. And when John and James desired permission to call down fire from heaven upon a certain Samaritan village, the only response their Master gave them was, in the language of rebuke, "Ye know not what manner of spirit ye are of; for the Son of Man is not come to destroy men's lives, but to save them." Luke ix. 55. The Apostle Paul also asserts, "The weapons of our warfare are not carnal, but mighty through God." 1 Cor. x. 4. The rule, too, which he prescribes to Timothy, in all such cases, is of similar import. "The servant of the Lord must not strive, but be gentle unto all men, apt to teach, patient, in meekness instructing those that oppose themselves; if God, peradventure, will give them repentance to the acknowledging of the truth." 2 Tim. ii. 24, 25. It is true, that daring offenders were excluded from the communion of the church; and being so excluded, they were said to be "delivered unto Satan," 1 Tim. i. 20; or, "delivered unto Satan for the destruction of the flesh;" 1 Cor. v. 5; but the church proceeded no farther. Exclusion from her communion was her *ultima pœna;* the rest she left in the hands of God. It is true, that in that age of miracles, the sentence of the Apostles

THE ANTICHRIST. 233

was sometimes followed by divine and miraculous interposition, as in the cases of Ananias and Sapphira; but there were no physical punishments inflicted either by the church or the civil power. No such case can be found. If, then, Christ and his Apostles are to govern the Christian church, persecution, especially persecution followed by civil and executive punishments, so far from being agreeable to Christianity, is in direct violation both of its letter and spirit. Hence, during the first three centuries no such persecution existed in the Christian church. Christians then were persecuted, but did not persecute.

No sooner, however, was the unnatural alliance formed of church and state, than persecution began. "The administration of the church was divided," says Mosheim, "by Constantine himself, into an external and internal inspection. The latter was committed to bishops and councils; the former the emperor assumed to himself."* Here the evil began. Church power being placed in the hands, or rather assumed by the hands of a civil officer, was exercised as all other civil prerogatives; and the emperor soon began to punish heretics as he would rebels and insurgents. "Two monstrous errors," says Mosheim, "were almost universally adopted in this century; first, that it was an act of virtue to deceive and lie, when by that means the interests of the church might be promoted; and second, that errors in religion, when maintained and adhered to, after proper admonition, were punishable with civil penalties and corporal tortures."† These are truly a monstrous pair of twins; and 'if such was the first offspring of the connexion between church and state, is it wonderful, that bloodier and more dreadful things have resulted from this unnatural alliance?

The Donatists were the first to realize the effects of this civil administration of church affairs. The Numidians, and Donatus at their head, opposed the consecration of Cœcilianus as bishop of Carthage. For

---

* Century iv.   † Cent. iv., chap. iii.

this they were opposed by the rest of the church, and ultimately by Constantine. And so far did the latter carry his opposition, that he not only deprived the Donatists of their churches, and sent their leaders into banishment, but actually put many of them to death! Here we have the lamentable example of a Christian prince, yea, the first Christian prince, putting his own Christian subjects to death for matters of conscience and religion! Nor did matters assume a quiet aspect until the battle of Bagnia, under the reign of Constans, gave victory, the victory of the sword, to the imperial troops.

In the year 357, when the contest about Arianism was raging throughout the Roman empire, this same civil power in the administration of church affairs, interfered with the liberty of conscience in the Roman pontiff himself. Liberius was compelled by Constantius to embrace the Arian heresy.* Here, 'then, we see an instance in which the civil ruler makes the creed of one of the predecessors of those illustrious popes, who afterwards made emperors hold their stirrups, and bow in their presence. So generally did the sentiment prevail in this and the following century, that religious errors were to be removed by the authority of the state, that even Augustine coolly and deliberately advocates it. The following is his language: "If you suppose we ought to be moved because so many thousands die in this way, how much consolation do you suppose we ought to have, because far and incomparably more thousands are freed from such great madness of the Donatist party, where not only the error of the nefarious division, but even madness itself was the law."†

The same principle which began to produce such pernicious effects in the Roman empire, diffused itself also among those northern nations which subverted that empire. The kings of the Vandals," says Mosheim, "particularly Genseric, and Huneric his son, pulled down the churches of those Christians who ac-

* Mosheim, i. 329. † Contra Gaudentium, Ep. i.

knowledged the divinity of Christ, sent their bishops into exile, and maimed and tormented in various ways such as were nobly firm and inflexible in the profession of their faith. They, however, declared that in using these severe and violent methods, they were authorized by the example of the emperors, who had enacted laws of the same rigorous nature against the Donatists, the Arians and other sects, who differed in opinion from the Christians of Constantinople."*
Charlemagne, too, in the eighth century, did not hesitate to wage a most determined war against the Saxons, principally with the design of converting them to Christianity.

Such where some of the early fruits of the pernicious principle, introduced under the reign of Constantine. Religion and the sword, the bishop and the sovereign, went hand in hand; and when piety could not attract, or argument convince, power was made to determine the controversy. No wonder that slavery was the result; and that Europe for centuries was made to exhibit the humiliating spectacle of enslaved millions, under the tyrannical rule of domineering and despotic ecclesiastics.

It was left, however, for Rome, the Babylon of the middle ages, and the seeds of whose existence had been sowing for centuries—it was left for Rome to finish the tragedy, and to show to the world the cruelty of man to man, when bigotry rules in his bosom, and charity has forsaken his heart, and the sword stands ready at his bidding. Other powers may have slain the saints, but Rome alone "has been drunk with their blood." It is this awful spectacle that we now proceed to unveil.

It may not be improper here to remark, that persecution, so far from being a mere accident upon the Romish system, is the direct result of the system itself. If Jesus Christ is "Lord of lords," and the Pope is his vicegerent on earth; if the spiritual power is either superior to the temporal, or in necessary

---

* Century v., chap. v.

union with it; if the Pope is the infallible interpreter of the word of God, and all men are bound to adopt his interpretations; if submission and not liberty is the duty of Christians; and if there is no salvation but in the Romish church—if these premises are admitted, then is persecution not only a result of Romanism, but a necessary result: it is the duty of the church to persecute; it would be unkind and disloyal to act otherwise.

It is sometimes alleged, that other Christian bodies besides Romanists, have persecuted. This is true. But these persecutions, few in number, and feeble for the most part in their effects, have been excrescences upon such Christian bodies. They have been their deformities, not their glories—their injury, not their advancement. The fundamental principles of Protestant Christianity are, that the Bible is the only infallible rule of faith, and that in examining the Scriptures and forming his conclusions, every man must be left to his own conscience. True, any particular body of men who substantially agree in these conclusions, may adopt the same symbol of faith, and may, if they deem it necessary, refuse communion with others, whom they may consider as putting an interpretation upon the word of God, radically erroneous and essentially different from their own. But here, save as to argument and moral influence, the matter ends; the former having no more right to force the latter to their conclusions, than the latter have to force the former to theirs. This leads of course to a separation between the two bodies; not, however, to a religious war, where the sword is made the umpire of Christian faith. It produces, if you please, sects, not however crusades. It distributes the Christian Church into social combinations, formed upon the voluntary principle; it does not, however, drench Christian soil with Christian blood.

That this system, admitting as it does, of so many external varieties, is better, far better than the opposite one, no thinking man can deny. It places not only religion, but human nature itself upon the right basis. The acceptance of the gospel here, is what it always must be to be real, voluntary; and no one man, or set of men, are here allowed to lord it over others. We proceed, however, to consider the development of the contrary system—the system of oneness and of absolutism.

It will not be amiss to notice here the war of the Holy Crusades, as involving the general principle of persecution. In the latter part of the eleventh century, the Turks had taken possession of Jerusalem, and subjected Christian pilgrims to various oppressions. To repel these bitter enemies to Christians, Peter, a native of Amiens in France, and usually called the Hermit, aroused all Europe to engage in a holy war. Pope Urban the Second gave the scheme his most earnest support; the Council of Clermont decreed it. These crusades, therefore, had their origin in the church. Indeed, the Pope granted indulgences and dispensations to those who would engage in this enterprise. Of these crusades there were seven. Millions of lives were lost by them; the resources of nations were exhausted, and the greatest evils followed in their train. To justify them upon Christian principles is impossible. When Peter drew his sword in defence of his Master, the reply of that master was, "Put up again thy sword into his place; for all they that take the sword shall perish with the sword." Matt. xxvi. 52. If then, it was not lawful to defend Christ himself with the sword, it certainly was not lawful to defend his sepulchre with the sword.

To understand however, in what spirit these miscalled *holy* wars were carried on, let us notice the conduct of the crusaders, upon the first conquest of Jerusalem. "On a Friday," says Gibbon, "at three in the afternoon, the day and hour of the passion, Godfrey of Bouillon, stood victorious on the walls of Jerusalem. A bloody sacrifice was offered by these mistaken votaries to the God of the Christians: resistance might provoke, but neither age nor sex could mollify their implacable rage; they indulged themselves three days in a promiscuous massacre. After seventy thousand Moslems had been put to the sword, and the harmless Jews had been burnt in their synagogues, they could still reserve a multitude of captives whom interest or lassitude persuaded them to spare. Of these savage heroes of the cross, Tancred alone betrayed some sentiments of compassion. The holy sepulchre was now free; and the bloody victors prepared to accomplish their vow. Bareheaded and barefoot, with contrite hearts, and an humble posture, they ascended the hill of Calvary, amidst the loud anthems of the clergy; kissed the stone which had covered the Saviour of the world, and bedewed with tears of joy and penitence the monument of their redemption."*

Can any one imagine, that the Apostles Paul and Peter would have promoted, as Pope Urban did, an enterprise of this kind? Can any one suppose, that Timothy, or Titus, or Luke, would have preached as the Hermit did, a war of such exterminating vengeance against the enemies of Christianity? Can any one conceive, that the primitive church would have mixed in a scene of blood like this, with anthems and praises? Is it even possible to suppose that the Prince of peace, the author and founder of the Christian system, could sanction such conduct in his professed disciples? By no means; darkness is not more unlike light, than such bloody wars are unlike the gospel of the Son of God.

This spirit of persecution, however, in the papal church, did not confine itself to Turks and Moslems, and to the rescue merely of the holy sepulchre. Professing Christians were also made to feel its severity.

In the middle ages, there lived in the south of France, a people distinguished for their civilization, refinement and elegant language. The Catholic priesthood in this country was at the time exceedingly corrupt and ignorant. So much was this the case, that no situation in life was considered meaner than that of a priest. No wonder then, that a purer faith should

* Rome, chap. lviii.

be acceptable to the inhabitants of Languedoc, Provence, and Catalonia. This faith was preached among them, by a people usually called Albigenses. These Albigenses, who derived their name from Albigeois, a district in France, of which the town Albi was the capital, were a set of dissentients from the Church of Rome. "They considered," says Shoberl, "the Scriptures as the only source of faith and religion, without regard to the authority of the Fathers and of tradition. They held the entire faith according to the doctrines of the Apostles' creed. They rejected all the external rites of the dominant church, excepting baptism and the Lord's supper—as temples, vestures, images, crosses, the worship of holy relics, and the rest of the sacraments. They rejected purgatory, and masses and prayers for the dead. They admitted no indulgences, or confessions of sin, with any of their consequences. They denied the corporeal presence of Christ in the sacrament. They held that monasticism was a putrid carcase, and vows the invention of men, and that the marriage of the clergy was lawful and necessary. Finally, they declared the Roman Church to be the whore of Babylon, refused obedience to the Pope and the bishops, and denied that the former had any authority over other churches, or the power of either the civil or the ecclesiastical sword."*

As to their lives, the Albigenses were above reproach. Even their enemies admitted, that "they observed irreproachable chastity, that in their zeal for truth, they never on any occasion resorted to a lie; and that such was their charity, that they were always ready to sacrifice themselves for others."† When their Catholic neighbours were exhorted by the missionaries of Pope Innocent, to expel and exterminate them, their reply was, "We cannot, we have been brought up with them; we have relations among them; and we see what virtuous lives they lead."

It was to this class of heretics, that Pope Innocent III. turned his sacerdotal attention. At first he sent

* Persecutions of Popery, p. 20.   † Ibidem.

missionaries among them. Finding this measure too tardy and ineffectual, he next published a bull, requiring their princes and sovereigns to persecute them. These princes and sovereigns being rather tardy in executing such a bloody edict upon their own subjects, the Pope next excommunicates the princes, releases their subjects from allegiance to them, and even proceeded so far as to call for a general crusade against both princes and people. To induce other European powers and Christians to enter upon so bloody an enterprise, he publishes plenary indulgences to all soldiers and others, who would engage in this war, and offers to the princes of other countries, the vanquished territories of these heretical princes. Such offers coming from such a source, were not likely to be despised. Consequently, in the early part of the thirteenth century, a general crusade was raised against the Count of Thoulouse, the Viscount of Beziers, Alby and Carcassonne, and the other princes, who had not, in every iota, complied with the bull of Pope Innocent. The Abbot of Citeaux, who was the Pope's Legate, was placed at the head of the crusade. The number of these crusaders is variously estimated from 50,000 to 500,000. They were actuated with the greatest fanaticism; and spread ruin and slaughter wherever they went.

Raymond VI., the Count of Thoulouse, who had previously patronized the Albigenses, upon the approach of this vast multitude, attempted by concessions and penances to obtain the forgiveness of the church. He was required to surrender seven of his strongest castles, to abide the decision of his judges as to the charges preferred against him, and to be scourged upon his naked back around the altar of St. Gilles, with a rope around his neck. Roger, Viscount of Beziers, resolved to defend his territories against the fanatical hordes of the invaders. Beziers, one of his strongest fortresses, was first taken. The terrified inhabitants took refuge in the churches. These however proved but poor refuges to the fury of the crusaders. When the knights consulted the

Legate, as to the proper mode of distinguishing between the heretics and catholics, his reply was, "kill them all, the Lord will know his own." This sentence was rigidly executed; men, women, children, heretics and catholics, all being mixed in one general slaughter. In the church of the Magdalen seven thousand corpses were found; in the cathedral a greater number. "When the crusaders had slaughtered all, to the very last living creature, in Beziers," says Shoberl, "and had plundered the houses of every thing worth carrying away, they set fire to all the quarters at once; the city was but one vast conflagration; not an edifice remained standing, not a human being was left alive."*

When Carcassonne was captured, although the inhabitants generally escaped through a subterranean passage, yet four hundred persons were burnt alive, and fifty were hung upon gibbets. The same fate awaited the inhabitants of Lauraguais and Menerbais. When Brom was taken, Monfort "selected more than a hundred of the wretched inhabitants, and having torn out their eyes, and cut off their noses, sent them under the guidance of a one-eyed man to the castle of Cabaret, to intimate to the garrison of that fortress the fate which awaited them."† At the capture of Menerbe, one hundred and forty persons were burnt alive; at that of Lavaur eighty were hanged on the gallows; and when Cassero was taken, sixty more were committed to the flames.

Such was the general character of this eight years' war against these unoffending disciples of Jesus. Princes were humbled, their cities were burnt, their fortresses destroyed, their subjects butchered, and their country wasted, to eradicate from the earth, doctrines which Apostles preached, and which the primitive church held with the strongest faith. "No calculation," says the same writer, "can ascertain with any precision, the waste of property, and the destruction of human life, which were the conse-

* Persecutions of Popery, p. 20. † Idem.

quences of the crusade against the Albigenses." Nor let it be forgotten, that this crusade was summoned by the Pope, was conducted by his Legate, and was afterwards approved in the council of Lateran by an Assembly of Catholic divines.

In allusion to this crusade against the Albigenses, Daunau, himself a Catholic, remarks: "We do not intend to exculpate the Albigenses from all error. But to exterminate thousands of good men, because they have committed a self-delusion, and to dethrone him who governed them, because he did not persecute them enough, is rigour to excess, and reveals the character and manifests the power of Innocent III."* Hallam also remarks concerning this religious war—"It was prosecuted with every atrocious barbarity which superstition, the mother of crimes, could inspire. Languedoc, a country, for that age, flourishing and civilized, was laid waste by these desolaters, her cities burnt, her inhabitants swept away by fire and sword. And this was to punish a fanaticism ten thousand times more innocent than their own."† Such was one of the first efforts of Rome to fill herself with the blood of the saints.

The holy wars against the Waldenses will next claim our attention. Some writers suppose that the Waldenses took their name and origin from Peter Waldo, a wealthy merchant of Lyons. Others, however, place their origin in a much more remote antiquity. The opinion of Beza was, that Peter of Lyons derived his name Waldo, or Valdo, from the Waldenses. "According to other writers," says Hallam, "the original Waldenses were a race of uncorrupted shepherds, who, in the valleys of the Alps, had shaken off, or perhaps never learned, the system of superstition on which the Catholic church depended for its ascendency."‡ Shoberl traces their origin to Claude, Bishop of Turin, who, when image-worship was introduced, in the beginning of the eighth century, made a bold

---

* Court of Rome, p. 129.   † Middle Ages, chap. i. part i.
‡ Middle Ages, chap. ix., part ii.

THE ANTICHRIST. 243

stand against both this and several other corruptions of the Romish church. Here, amid the valleys of Piedmont, had these truly primitive and Christian people lived for centuries, separated by their locality from the rest of the world, and unobserved by even the eye of popish jealousy.

The character of the Waldenses and their doctrines may be learned from the following quotations. " All they aimed at," says Mosheim, " was, to reduce the form of ecclesiastical government, and the lives and manners both of the clergy and people, to that amiable simplicity, and that primitive sanctity, which characterized the apostolic ages, and which appear so strongly recommended in the precepts and injunctions of the divine Author of our holy religion."* " These pious and innocent sectaries," says Hallam, " of whom the very monkish historians speak well, appear to have nearly resembled the modern Moravians. They had ministers of their own appointment, and denied the lawfulness of oaths and of capital punishment. In other respects their opinions were not far removed from those usually called Protestant."† Reinerus Sacco, an Italian Inquisitor, writes thus of them: " While all other sects disgust the public by their gross blasphemies against God, this, on the other hand, has a great appearance of piety. For those who belong to it, live justly among men, have a sound doctrine in all points respecting God, and believe in all the articles of the Apostles' creed: but they blaspheme the Romish church."‡ Cassini, a Franciscan, thus speaks of them: " The errors of the Vaudois consist in their denial that the Romish is the holy mother church, and in their refusal to obey her traditions. In other points they recognize the church of Christ; and for my part, I cannot deny that they have always been members of his church."§ When Pope Innocent VIII. had urged Louis XII., king of France, to extirpate this sect from his kingdom, the monarch sent two commissioners,

* Ecclesiastical Hist., Cent. xiii. ‡ Shoberl, p. 60.
† Middle Ages, ix. ii. § Ibidem.

one of them a Dominican, and the royal confessor, to inquire into their character and views. These commissioners deposed upon oath, that "having visited the parishes and churches of the Vaudois, we find no images, no trace of the service of the mass, nor any paraphernalia, used in the ceremonies observed by Catholics. But having also made a strict inquiry into their manner of living, we cannot discover the least shadow of the crimes imputed to them. On the contrary, it appears that they piously observe the Sabbath, baptize their children after the manner of the primitive church, and are thoroughly instructed in the doctrine of the Apostles' creed and in the law of God."*

Notwithstanding, however, the purity of the doctrines and lives of the Waldenses, they erred in the vital point, they denied the supremacy of Rome, and rejected her numerous superstitions. This was enough, this alone, to render them obnoxious to papal wrath.

Besides some previous oppressions and slaughters to which this people were subject, in 1487, Innocent VIII. published a bull against them, "denouncing them as heretics, calling upon all the authorities, spiritual and temporal, to join in their extermination, threatening with extreme vengeance such as should refuse to take part in the crusade, promising remission of sins to those who engaged in it, and dissolving all contracts made with the offenders. Even the inquisitors and monks were exhorted to take arms against them, to crush them like poisonous adders, and to make all possible efforts for their holy extermination. This bull also granted to each true believer a right to seize the property of the victims without form or process."† The result of this bull was, that the Vaudois were overrun and butchered for several months by a body of eighteen thousand troops, and a vast host of undisciplined attendants.

In 1540 an edict was published in France against a portion of the Waldenses to the following purport:

* Shoberl, p. 60. † Ibidem.

THE ANTICHRIST.

"That every dissentient from the holy mother church should acknowledge his errors, and obtain reconciliation within a stated period, under the severest penalties in case of disobedience; and because Merindal was considered as the principal seat of the heresy, that devoted town was ordered to be razed to the ground; all the caverns, hiding-places, cellars, and vaults, in the vicinity of the town, were to be carefully examined and destroyed; the woods were to be cut down, the gardens and orchards laid waste, and none who had ever possessed a house or property in the town, should ever occupy it again, either in his own person or in that of any of his name or family, in order that the memory of the excommunicated sect, might be utterly wiped away from the province, and the place be made a desert."*

In what manner this decree was executed, is related by Anquetil, a Catholic writer:—" Twenty-two towns or villages were burned or pillaged with an inhumanity of which the history of the most barbarous nations scarcely affords an example. The wretched inhabitants, surprised in the night, and hunted from rock to rock by the light of the flames which consumed their habitations, frequently escaped one snare only to fall into another. The pitiful cries of the aged, the women, and the children, instead of softening the hearts of the soldiers, maddened with rage like their leaders, only served to guide them in pursuit of the fugitives. Voluntary surrender did not exempt the men from slaughter, nor the women from brutal outrages at which nature revolts. It was forbidden under pain of death to afford them harbour or succour. At Cabrières, more than seven hundred men were butchered in cold blood; and the women, who had remained in their houses, were shut up in a barn containing a great quantity of straw, which was set on fire, and those who endeavoured to escape by the windows were driven back with swords and pikes."

In 1655, Charles Emanuel, Duke of Savoy, issued

* Shoberl.

what is called "the bloody ordinance of Gastaldo." This ordinance decreed, "that such of the Vaudois as would not embrace the Catholic faith, or sell their possessions to those who professed it, must within a few days quit their native valleys." To enforce this decree, the Marquis of Pianezza entered the valleys with an army of fifteen thousand men. One of the commanders in that expedition gives the following as a specimen of its general character:—"I was witness," says he, "to many great violences and cruelties exercised by the banditti and soldiers of Piedmont, upon all of every age, sex and condition, whom I myself saw massacred, dismembered, and ravished, with many horrid circumstances of barbarity." Such was the cruelty of this holy war, that all Protestant Europe was excited by it. The following are extracts of a letter written by the immortal Milton, then secretary to Cromwell, to the Duke of Savoy, remonstrating with him for such barbarities. "His serene Highness, the Protector, has been informed that part of these most miserable people have been cruelly massacred by your forces, part driven out by violence, and so without house or shelter, poor and destitute of all relief, to wander up and down with their wives and children, in craggy and uninhabitable places, and mountains covered with snow. Oh the fired houses which are yet smoking, the torn limbs and ground defiled with blood! Some men decrepit with age and bed-rid, have been burned in their beds. Some infants have been dashed against the rocks; others have had their throats cut, whose brains have, with more than Cyclopean cruelty, been boiled and eaten by the murderers. If all the tyrants of all times and ages were alive again, certainly they would be ashamed, when they should find that they had contrived nothing in comparison with these things, that might be reputed barbarous and inhuman."

Such has been the character of this unnatural war, which Popery has been waging for centuries upon these inoffensive and feeble disciples of the Saviour. But for the interference of Protestant states, the very name of the Waldenses had been long since blotted out from the face of the earth. And even to the present time are they persecuted and oppressed by the same unrelenting foe; their privileges being curtailed, and their territory rendered smaller and smaller by the constant aggressions of their enemies.

Let us now turn to the persecutions waged by Popery upon the French Protestants, or Huguenots. D'Aubigné not only affirms, that the Reformation in France was independent, in a measure, of that in Germany and Switzerland, but also that it was antecedent to both. "The Reformation was not, therefore, in France, an importation from strangers; it took its birth on the French territory. Its seed germinated in Paris; its earliest shoots were struck in the university itself, that ranked second in power in Romanized Christendom. God deposited the first principles of the work in the kindly hearts of some inhabitants of Picardy and Dauphiny, before it had begun in any other country of the globe."* The means by which the gospel made its early progress in the French kingdom were principally these three: the translation of the Scriptures into French by Olivetan, the uncle of Calvin; the conversion of the Psalms into metre by a popular poet; and the earnest and constant preaching of the reformed pastors. "The holy word of God," says Quick, "is duly, truly, and powerfully preached in churches and fields, in ships and houses, in vaults and cellars, in all places where the gospel ministers can have admission and conveniency, and with singular success. Multitudes are convinced and converted, established and edified. The Popish churches are drained, the Protestant temples are filled. The priests complain that their altars are neglected, their masses are now indeed solitary. Dagon cannot stand before God's ark." These reformers also made great use of singing, employing it not only in their churches, but also in family worship, and even at their tables.

Such a state of things was not likely to exist long

---

* History of the Reformation, Book xii.

without opposition from the priesthood. Hence, of all Protestant churches, that in France has been chiefly drenched in blood. "No where," says D'Aubigné, "did the reformed religion so often have its dwelling in dungeons, or bear so marked a resemblance to the Christianity of the first ages, in faith and love, and in the number of its martyrs. If elsewhere it might point to more thrones and council-chambers, here it could appeal to more scaffolds and hill-side meetings."*

The reason why the French church has suffered more than others, is to be found in the degree to which the reformed opinions spread in France. These opinions were not extensive enough to be universal, nor were they limited enough to be inconsiderable. In England, Scotland, Germany, and some other kingdoms, the Reformation became the dominant religion. In Spain, Italy, Portugal, and some other states, it was too feeble to endanger many lives. But France occupied a middle ground. Though whole provinces became Protestant, yet the kingdom was Catholic; and though many of the princes and nobility were numbered among the reformed, yet the government was popish. This state of things placed the French church in a situation peculiarly critical, and caused her to suffer far more than sister churches of more favoured countries.

The term Huguenot, usually applied to these French Protestants, is supposed to have been derived from the circumstance, that under their persecutions many of these godly people used to meet at night for religious worship in private places, near the town of Hugon, in Tours. From these few, the whole class were called, by way of derison, Huguenots.

Persecution to blood, commenced against the Huguenots, as early as the year 1524, and it lasted, in one form or another, till 1815. Napoleon granted them toleration and equal privileges with the Catholics. But, upon the restoration of the Bourbons, popular

* History of the Reformation.

phrensy rose so high in the province of Gard, that several hundred Protestants lost their lives. Thus, for a period of two hundred and ninety-one years, has France dyed herself in the blood of some of her best and most loyal subjects, simply because they rejected the religion of the Pope. Indeed, even to the present time, there is a species of persecution kept up against the religion of Protestants in that country.

Previously to the year 1559, when a French General Assembly was organized, there had been one hundred martyrdoms among the French Calvinists. After this event matters became much worse. Troops were sent among them, and not less than forty towns, where Protestantism prevailed, were subject to their ravages. The Protestants were burned or killed in other ways, by the hundred, five hundred, and in one instance twelve hundred are said to have suffered at one time. It was at this period that the Huguenots fled to arms. They resolved to defend their religion and their rights by the sword. This movement, be it remembered, was not ecclesiastical, but civil. Protestants composed a considerable portion of the French population. They had rights as well as others. Many of them were of the nobility and the aristocracy of the country. When, therefore, the French government, instead of defending those rights, sought to invade and overthrow them, was it not the duty of the Protestants to defend them? How could men see their property confiscated, their wives and daughters insulted, and themselves murdered, and not resist? Self-defence is always lawful; and not even the religion of Jesus was designed to annihilate its impulses. And when a lawful self-defence was impossible, it was the duty of French citizens to protect themselves by the means that Providence had put into their hands. Petitions to the king and parliament were of no avail; the courts gave them no protection; their fellow citizens were seeking their lives and property. What could they do? Resistance was the only alternative—and they did resist. In many battles, too, they were victorious. This course brought the government to pause.

Peace was made with the Huguenots, and they were allowed certain rights and privileges. The fatal doctrine, however, that leagues and promises with heretics, are not binding, caused such treaties to be several times violated and renewed. Three civil wars preceded the massacre of St. Bartholomew's. At length, Charles and the Catholic party, instigated by Catharine de Medicis, the queen-mother, plotted the secret destruction of those who had been found too strong upon the field of battle. Margaret, the sister of Charles, was to be married to the young King of Navarre, who was one of the Protestant leaders. For a time the Protestants were loaded with favours and caresses. To the marriage all their principal men were invited. During the week after that event, they were diverted by various entertainments and shows. The marriage took place on Sabbath, the 17th August, 1572; the massacre was decreed to take place on the following Sabbath, being St. Bartholomew's day. An attempt was first made to assassinate Coligni, the leader of the Protestant party. He was wounded, but not killed. While this illustrious man lay in bed of his wounds, and while the Protestants were all asleep, the bell of St. Germain, the appointed signal, was rung. The house-doors of the Protestants had all been marked during the night, with a white cross. Upon the sounding of the bell, the streets were all illuminated with lights from the windows of the Catholics, and the soldiers and citizens rushed forth, sword in hand, to destroy the Protestants. The scene which followed is indescribable. Men, women, children, the noble, the vulgar, were massacred as fast as found. Some were murdered in their beds, some in their parlours, some in their doors, some in the streets, and some on the tops of their houses. Multitudes were drowned or killed in crossing the Seine. "The rising sun," says Shoberl, "never beheld a scene of more thrilling horror than Paris presented on the morning of Sunday, the 24th of August, 1572. Blood stained the doors of houses, the interior of the apartments, the walls of the churches, the streets, the public gardens. At every step corses, mangled fragments of human flesh, lamentations and cries of anguish, the last groans of agony, the spoils of the vanquished, traces of the passages of the conquerors, exhibited all the appearances of a town taken by storm." This terrible scene continued the greater part of the week following. It is estimated that ten thousand Protestants, including the flower of the party, perished on this occasion. The greatest possible barbarity was exhibited in this dreadful massacre. The body of the admiral, who was killed with the rest, was treated with the greatest indignity. Its members were cut off, and the mangled trunk drawn through the streets for three days, amid the mockery and insults of the populace, after which it was suspended from a gallows. The murderers also placed themselves upon piles of the murdered, and auctioned off to their afflicted relatives the bodies of husbands, brothers, and sons!

Nor was it alone at Paris that the massacre occurred. The command of Charles was sent to every part of the kingdom, to destroy in a similar manner and at the same time, all the Protestants. " At Meaux, Orleans, Troyes, Lyons, Bourges, Rouen, Toulouse, and many other places, says a historian, "the cruelty of the Parisians was emulated, and thirty thousand persons were murdered in cold blood."*

The question now arises, what part had the Church, or rather the Pope, in these transactions? The proper answer is, every part. Charles was a Catholic, his court were Catholic, and the massacre was designed to defend Catholic principles. But more than this is true. In a letter addressed to Catharine, just after the battle of Jarnac, Pius V. "assures her, that the assistance of God will not be wanting, if she pursues the enemies of the Catholic religion, until they are all massacred, for it is only by the entire extermination of the heretics, that the Catholic worship can be restored." It also appears, from what M. Daunau affirms, that the Pope furnished money for the des-

* Grimshaw.

truction of these heretics. His language is, "Catharine de Medicis boasted of the devotion of her son Charles to the holy church; and she asked money, a great deal of money, because the war against heresy could not be waged without money."* In a letter to Charles in 1570, and just after the battle of Montcontour, the Pope urges upon the king the entire destruction of all dissenters from the Catholic faith. "The fruits," says he, "which your victory ought to produce, are, the extermination of those infamous heretics, our common enemies. If your majesty wishes to restore the ancient splendour, power and dignity of France, you must strive most especially to make all who are subject to your dominion, profess the Catholic faith alone." Such were the exhortations of Pope Pius V., to the immediate instruments of this massacre, just two years before it occurred. This Pope, however, died a few months before the event occurred for which he had been preparing the minds of Catharine and Charles. How the consummation of the matter affected Gregory XIII., his successor, may be learned from the following facts. When he heard of the massacre, he exclaimed—"good news, good news, all the Lutherans are massacred except the Vendomets (King of Navarre and Prince of Condé,) whom the king has spared for his sister's sake." The same night the event was celebrated by bonfires and the firing of cannon in the Castle of St. Angelo. "Gregory also ordered a jubilee and a solemn procession, which he accompanied himself, to thank God for the glorious success."† "History speaks of a painting," says Daunau, "which attests the formal approbation which the Pontiff gave to the assassins of Coligni, containing the following inscription: 'Pontifex Colignii necem probat.'"‡ "To this day (1790)" says Brizard, "the French, who visit Italy, behold not without indignation, this picture, which though half effaced, still portrays but too faithfully our calamities and the

* Court of Rome, p. 209.
† Shoberl.
‡ Court of Rome, p. 210.

excesses of Rome. Nor was this all; medals were struck at Rome having on one side an image of the Pope; on the other, the destroying angel, holding a cross in one hand, and slaughtering the Huguenots by a sword with the other; bearing also the inscription, Hugonotorum strages.

This whole work then of slaughter and death is to be ascribed to the Papacy, to the Roman Pontiff and his colleagues. Roman principles, Roman craft, Roman hate, and Roman instruments, produced this whole scene of wo and desolation. The cry of all this blood is against Rome, against Rome chiefly. And it is a cry, which will in time, be heard; for this city not only has in her the blood of saints and of all that were slain upon earth; but we are expressly told, that, in the day of wrath, that blood will be found.

The massacre of St. Barthlomew's, although it destroyed, according to different estimates, from forty to one hundred thousand Protestants, yet did not annihilate the party. Many Catholics, too, shocked with the wickedness of the government and the Pope, united with them. Henry III., the brother of Charles, formed an alliance with them against the Catholic party, called the Holy League. The successor of Henry III., was Henry IV., the King of Navarre, who had been educated a Protestant. Although Henry became a professed Catholic from political motives, yet, he did not forget the interests of his Protestant subjects. It was this sovereign, who published in their behalf, the famous Edict of Nantes. According to this edict, which was published in 1594, the government allowed to the Reformed all the favours in which they had been indulged by former princes, and added, a free admission to all employments of trust, profit and honour; also an establishment of chambers of justice in which the members of the two religions were equal in number; and permission to educate their children in any of the universities without restraint. Under the influence of this edict, which continued in force for ninety-one years, the Protestants enjoyed considerable prosperity. Urged however, by his Catholic subjects, and especially by the Jesuits, Louis XIV., revoked this wise and Christian Edict, on the 8th October, 1685. The removal of this protection exposed the Protestants again to all the evils, losses, insults and persecutions of the Catholic priesthood. Their churches were demolished, their preachers were banished, and their children were taken from them at an early age to be educated as Catholics. It was at this time, that from five hundred to eight hundred thousand Huguenots emigrated from France to other countries, where they could enjoy the free exercise of their religion. Even this relief, however, was soon taken from them, emigration being forbidden upon pain of death. The sufferings of the Protestants at this time are inconceivable.

Bishop Burnet, who was at that time travelling in France, gives the following account of this persecution. Writing from Nimmegen he says—" I have a strong inclination to say somewhat concerning the persecution which I saw in its rage and utmost fury, and of which I could give you many instances, that are so much beyond all the common measures of barbarity and cruelty, that I confess they ought not to be believed, unless I could give more positive proofs of them than are fitted now to be brought forth. In short, I do not think that in any age, there ever was such a violation of all that is sacred, either with relation to God or man. Men and women of all ages who would not yield, were not only stript of all they had, but kept long from sleep, drawn about from place to place, and hunted out of their retirements. The women were carried into nunneries, in many of which they were almost starved, whipped and barbarously treated. I went over a great part of France, from Marseilles to Montpelier, and from thence to Lyons, and so to Geneva. In all the towns through which I passed, I heard the most dismal account of things possible. To complete the cruelty, orders were given that such of the new converts as did not at their death receive the sacrament, should be denied burial, and that their bodies should be left, where other dead carcasses were cast out to be devoured by wolves and dogs. The applauses that the whole clergy give to this way of proceeding, the many panegyrics that are already writ upon it, and the sermons, that are all flights of flattery upon this subject, are such evident demonstrations of their sense of this matter, that what is now on foot may well be termed the acts of the whole clergy of France, who have yet been esteemed the most moderate part of the Roman communion."

The above was written but eighteen months after the revocation of the Edict of Nantes. But matters became much worse. The following is the account of Quick, the statistical historian of the French church, and whose work was published in London in 1692. " Afterwards," says he, " they fell upon the persons of the Protestants, and there was no wickedness, though ever so horrid, which they did not put in practice, that they might force them to change their religion. Amidst a thousand hideous cries and blasphemies, they hung up men and women by the hair or feet to the roofs of the chambers, or hooks of chimneys, and smoked them with wisps of wet hay till they were no longer able to bear it; and when they had taken them down, if they would not sign an abjuration of their pretended heresies, they then trussed them up again immediately. Some they threw into great fires, kindled on purpose, and would not take them out till they were half roasted. They tied ropes under their arms, and plunged them into deep wells, from whence they would not draw them till they had promised to change their religion. They bound them as criminals are when put to the rack, and in that posture, putting a funnel into their mouths, they poured wine down their throats, till its fumes had deprived them of their reason, and they had in that condition made them consent to become Catholics. Some they stripped stark naked, and after they had offered them a thousand indignities, they stuck them with pins from head to foot; they cut them with penknives, tore them by the noses with red hot pincers, and dragged them about the rooms till they promised to become Roman Catholics, or that the doleful cries of these poor tormented creatures, calling upon God for mercy, constrained them to let them go. They beat them with staves, and dragged them all bruised to the Popish churches, where their enforced presence is reputed for an abjuration. They kept them waking seven or eight days together, relieving one another by turns, that they might not get a wink of sleep or rest. In case they began to nod they threw buckets of water in their faces, or holding kettles over their heads, they beat on them with such a continual noise, that those poor wretches lost their senses. If they found any sick who kept their beds, men or women, they were so cruel, as to beat up an alarm with twelve drums about their heads for a whole week together, without intermission, till they had promised to change. In some places they tied fathers and husbands to the bed-posts, and ravished their wives and daughters before their eyes. And in another place rapes were publicly and generally permitted for many hours together. From others they plucked off the nails from their hands and toes. They burnt the feet of others. They blew up men and women with bellows till they were ready to burst in pieces. If these horrid usages could not prevail upon them to violate their consciences, and abandon their religion, they did then imprison them in close and noisome dungeons, in which they exercised all manner of inhumanities upon them. They demolished their houses, desolated their lands, cut down their woods, seized upon their wives and children and shut them up in monasteries. When the soldiers had devoured all the goods of a house, then the farmers and tenants of these poor, persecuted wretches, must supply them with new fuels for their lusts, and bring in more substance to them. If any endeavoured to flee away, they were pursued and hunted in the fields and woods, and shot at as so many wild beasts."

The numbers who perished in this persecution will not be known till that day when the "books shall be

THE ANTICHRIST. 257

opened. Multitudes perished by torture, multitudes in the galleys and in dungeons, and multitudes by the sword.

For the accomplishment of this work of inhumanity and blood, Pope Innocent XI. thus addresses Louis XIV. " The Catholic church shall most assuredly record in her sacred annals a work of such devotion towards her, and celebrate your name with never dying praises; but above all, you may most assuredly promise to yourself, an ample remuneration from the Divine goodness for this most excellent undertaking, and may rest assured, that we shall never cease to pour forth our most earnest prayers to that Divine goodness for this intent and purpose."*

We have thus noticed popish persecutions in but one of the many European kingdoms. What if we could give the exact statistics of this persecution in all the rest? What if Germany, if the Netherlands, if Spain, if Italy, if Portugal, if Switzerland, if Scotland, if Ireland, if England, should all exhibit their bloody books? Surely, we might say with John, " the world itself could not contain the books that would be written." These books, however, would not contain the history of the benevolent deeds of Christ, but accounts of the malignity and blood-thirstiness of Antichrist.

Mede has calculated from good authorities, "that in the war with the Albigenses and Waldenses there perished of these people, in France alone, 1,000,000. From the first institution of the Jesuits to the year 1580, a little more than thirty years, 900,000 orthodox Christians were slain. In the Netherlands alone, the Duke of Alva boasted, that within a few years he had despatched to the amount of 36,000 souls, and those all by the hand of the common executioner. In the space of scarce thirty years, the Inquisition destroyed by various kinds of torture, 150,000 Christians." Gibbon states it as a fact, though a melancholy one, that Papal Rome has shed immensely more Christian

* Lorimer's Protestant Church of France, p. 242.

blood, than Pagan Rome had ever done. He gives but one illustration; that, however, a fearful one. "In the Netherlands alone," says he, "more than 100,000 of the subjects of Charles V., are said to have suffered by the hands of the executioner."*

Nor let it be said, that much of this bloodshed is to be ascribed to European princes and magistrates. With equal justice might the Jew affirm, that Jesus of Nazareth was condemned by Pilate, and executed by Roman soldiers. God, however, has charged the blood of his Son upon the Jews, by whose malignity and devisings Christ was crucified. Much more then, are the torrents of blood shed in Europe to be ascribed to the Papacy, to the Catholic church. These princes and magistrates were Catholic subjects, and they only executed the mind and will of the church. They were instigated by priests, yea, by the Pope himself. They were often complained of as being too tardy and too merciful; yea, some of them were involved in ruin, along with their heretical subjects, for their forbearance. Those of them too, who were most ferocious, who effected most brutally the work of ruin, received from Catholic dignitaries, and even from the Pope, the greatest amount of commendation. Thus Monfort, Catharine de Medicis, Charles IX., (whose remorse before death caused the blood to ooze from the pores of his body!) Louis XIV., &c., were congratulated by the Gregories, and Innocents of their times, as faithful and zealous sons of the church, and as worthy the peculiar favour of heaven. This alliance, however, or rather identity, between the Papacy and policy of Europe in persecuting the saints, is matter of express and repeated prophecies. "These have one mind," says John, "and shall give their power and strength unto the beast." Again, "For God has put it into their hearts, to fulfil his will, and to agree and give their kingdom unto the beast, until the words of God shall be fulfilled." Rev. xvii.

Whether, then, the Papacy be, or be not the subject

---

* Rome, chap. xvi.

of the prophecies alluded to in the first part of this chapter, let each one judge for himself. Was the power predicted, "to make war with the saints and overcome them?" This Rome has done. Was it to "be drunken with the blood of the saints and with the blood of the martyrs of Jesus?" No other kingdom nor power has drunken so deeply of this blood, as Papal Rome. Was the blood of all that were slain upon the earth to be found in the subject of these prophecies? Rome has been, either directly the originator, or indirectly the associate, of nearly all the wars which have desolated Europe for a thousand years past. Thus, as streams may be traced to the fountain, and rays of light to the sun, so may these prophecies be traced to the Papacy, and applied only to it. This is the "beast that made war with the saints,"—this "the woman in scarlet, drunk with their blood,"—this is ANTICHRIST.

CHAPTER IX.

ANTICHRIST THE POSSESSOR OF GREAT RICHES.

Another scriptural mark of Antichrist is, the possession of great riches. "And the woman was arrayed in purple and scarlet colour, and decked with gold and precious stones and pearls, having a golden cup in her hand full of abominations and filthiness of her fornications." Rev. xvii. 4. Again in chapter xviii., verses 16, 17, John represents her merchants as exclaiming, upon her destruction, "Alas, alas, that great city, that was clothed in fine linen, and purple, and scarlet, and decked with gold and precious stones, and pearls! for, in one hour, so great riches is come to nought."

Bloomfield and Stuart apply the symbols in these chapters to pagan Rome; so, also, does the commentator on the Doway Bible. "By Babylon," says this Roman Catholic interpreter, "is meant, either the city of the devil in general; or, if this place be to be understood of any particular city, pagan Rome, which then, and for three hundred years persecuted the church, and was the principal seat both of empire and idolatry." Even this popish annotator, however, suggests another meaning: "The beast which supports Babylon," says he, "may signify the power of the devil, which was and is not, being much limited by the coming of Christ, but shall again exert itself under Antichrist." This is certainly preferable to the following: "The beast means the Roman emperors, specially Nero, of whom the report spread throughout the empire is, that he will revive, after being apparently slain, and will come as it were from the abyss, or hades."* This is certainly jejune and far-fetched

---

* Stuart.

THE ANTICHRIST. 261

enough! and I am sorry to say, that many of the interpretations of this learned expositor, are of a similar character.

That papal Rome is chiefly intended in each of these chapters, is almost absolutely certain. The whole prophecy is strikingly applicable to papal Rome, while but little of it can have any application to pagan Rome. The prophecy ends with a particular description of the entire destruction of the city spoken of: "The voice of harpers, and musicians, and of pipers and trumpeters, was to be heard no more at all in her; the light of the candle was to shine no more at all in her; and the voice of the bridegroom and of the bride was to be heard no more at all in her." But the city of Rome has never to this day, been thus entirely destroyed. Similar prophecies are used in the Old Testament in reference to Nineveh, Babylon, Tyre, and other cities. But such prophecies have been literally fulfilled. Where is Babylon? where is Nineveh? Their very sites can scarcely be found. But Rome still has music, and dancing, and the light of the candle, and the voice of the bride! These prophecies, then, have not all of them been fulfilled. But, if ever fulfilled, they must be in papal, and not in pagan Rome.

If, then, papal Rome be here meant, she is described as exceedingly rich. And that this part of the prophecy is as applicable to the Papacy, and has been as literally fulfilled as any other, we shall presently show.

That the ministers of religion should be supported by those for whom they minister, is a dictate of common justice. If religion be without any foundation in truth, if indeed there be "no God," then should the whole system be abolished as unnecessary and pernicious. If, however, there is a God, and if it is the duty of all men to worship and serve him, then ought the principles of religion to be taught, and its teachers, like all other citizens, should derive their support from the business to which they are devoted. Hence, among all nations, provisions have been made, either

23*

by the state or by independent societies, for the support of the ministers of religion.

This principle was incorporated into the Jewish law, and has also been sanctioned by Christ and his Apostles. "Even so," says Paul, "hath the Lord ordained, that they which preach the gospel should live of the gospel." 1 Cor. ix. 14. The Catholic priesthood, however, have turned the Christian ministry into the means of acquiring wealth. Originally, its object was to instruct and save men; support was only incidental to it. It was so among the Israelites; it was particularly so among the Apostles and ministers of Christ. Who has ever heard, that Peter or Paul, Timothy or Luke, was enriched by preaching the gospel? The first Christians "took joyfully the spoiling of their goods, knowing that they had in heaven a better and an enduring substance." Heb. x. 34. In those days, a profession of Christianity subjected men to the loss of their goods, and its official publication was attended with poverty, persecution, and even death. "At first," says Neander, "it is highly probable, that those who undertook the church offices in various congregations, continued their former calling, and maintained themselves and their families by it afterwards, as they had done before. But when the members of the churches became more numerous, and the duties of the church officers were increased, it was often no longer possible for them to provide at the same time for their own support. From the church fund, which was formed by the voluntary contributions of every member of the church, at every Sunday service, or, as in the north African church, on the first Sunday of every month, a part was used for the pay of the spiritual order."* Such was the simple and moderate way in which the first ministers of the Christian religion gained their maintenance. Splendid endowments, large estates, vast incomes, were then not even thought of, as a compensation for ministerial labours. A support was all the spiritual

* Church Hist., part ii. sect. ii.

THE ANTICHRIST.

teacher asked; it was all that the congregation provided. In after times, however, matters were reversed, and, by the indefinite multiplication of the ceremonies of Christianity, the means of wealth to the clergy became proportionably increased: the people thus became poor, and the clergy rich.

This change in the original economy of the church, began in the third century, when the church was united to the state by Constantine. "The bishops," says Mosheim, "assumed in many places a princely authority. They appropriated to their evangelical function the splendid ensigns of temporal majesty. A throne, surrounded with ministers, exalted above their equals the servants of the meek and humble Jesus, and sumptuous garments dazzled the eyes of the multitude into an ignorant veneration for their arrogated authority."* "From the year 321," says Daunou, "Constantine permitted the churches to acquire landed property, and he allowed individuals to enrich them by legacies."† Here was the commencement of that wealth which afterwards drained the resources of nations, and was one principal means of both power and corruption in the Christian church.

Monastic establishments were also another source of wealth to the papal church. These institutions were originally designed as sacred retreats from the fashions and pomp of the world; they soon, however, degenerated into the abodes of vice and crime, and became the banking-houses of all Catholic Europe. The novice was required to surrender, not simply himself, but also his possessions to the care of the holy brethren. Great sums were appropriated to them by the wealthy, and even governments assisted in annexing to them rich domains of landed property. " Time," says Gibbon, " continually increased, and accidents could seldom diminish, the estates of the popular monasteries; and in the first century of their institution, the infidel Zosimus has maliciously observed, that for the benefit of the poor, the Christian monks had

---

* Century iii. † Court of Rome, p. 3.

reduced a great part of mankind to a state of beggary." And yet he adds in a note, "the wealth of the eastern monks (of whom the above remark was made) was far surpassed by the princely greatness of the Benedictines."*

State patronage, however, and monasteries, will by no means account for the vast wealth of the Roman Catholic communion. To ascertain this, we must descend into the deep caverns of superstition— we must follow all the windings of papal fraud and imposition—we must dig into her mines of relics—we must descend into purgatory, and look amid its fires; and, as if this were not enough, we must ascend up into heaven, and there, from amid the thrones of saints and intercessors, we must follow the golden streams that issue forth, and which, by means of priestcraft, are poured into the coffers of the Papacy; yes, heaven, earth and hell, are all laid under contributions by the inventions of this tyrannical religion, to sustain the power and increase the wealth of the hierarchy.

The following is the testimony of one who had for years been a Roman Catholic priest. "Look," says he, "at all the Roman institutions; from its chief tenets, the real presence of God in the eucharist, and the infallibility of the church, down to the holy water and the wax-taper, and there is not one of them which is not either a means of grasping money, or power, or of entrapping the female sex! Ask," continues he, "of popery, who instituted the belief of the real presence of God in the wafer? He will answer, Christ himself, when he said in the last supper—'hoc est corpus meum.' Popery knows well the falsity of this answer; but in accordance with this creed, it has established the mass, which produces immense sums of money to the whole priesthood. Why has popery established indulgences? In appearance, it is a means of atoning for one's sins; but in reality, it is to coin money from the sins of men. Why has popery instituted those thousand corporeal mortifications? In appearance, to show a

* Rome, chap. xxxvii.

great aversion to earthly pleasures; but in reality, to have an occasion for selling dispensations to many people, who have neither the courage nor desire to practice mortifications. Why has popery established those intimate relations between saints and men upon the earth, through relics, images, adorations, and a thousand other superstitions? In appearance, to help us in the great work of our salvation; but in reality, to place itself as an intermediate between saints and men, and to sell their intercession; to make money with all these practices and beliefs, and root more deeply its power in each mind."* Nor are facts like these supported by the testimony of a single priest—it is the testimony of all history. "Many of the peculiar and prominent characteristics in the faith and discipline of those ages," says Hallam, "appear to have been either introduced, or sedulously promoted, for the purposes of sordid fraud. To those purposes conspired the veneration for relics, the worship of images, the idolatry of saints and martyrs, the religious inviolability of sanctuaries, the consecration of cemeteries—but above all, the doctrine of purgatory, and masses for the relief of the dead. A creed thus continued, operating upon the minds of barbarians, lavish though rapacious, and devout though dissolute, naturally caused a torrent of opulence to pour in upon the church. Donations of lands were continually made to the bishops, and still, in more ample proportions, to the monastic foundations. Large private estates, or, as they were termed, patrimonies, not only within their dioceses, but sometimes in distant countries, sustained the dignity of the principal sees, and especially that of Rome. The French monarchs of the first dynasty, the Carlovingian family and their great chief, the Saxon line of emperors, the kings of England and Leon, set hardly any bounds to their liberality, as numerous charters still extant in diplomatic collections attest. Many churches possessed seven or eight thousand *mansi:* one with only two thousand, passed for only indif-

* Con. Cath. Priest, pages 5—7.

ferently rich. And, as if all these methods for accumulating what they could not legitimately enjoy, were insufficient, the monks prostituted their knowledge of writing to the purpose of forging charters in their own favour! If it had not been," says the same author, "for certain drawbacks, the clergy must, one would imagine, have almost acquired the exclusive property of the soil. They did enjoy nearly one half of England, and, I believe, a greater proportion in some countries of Europe." In a note he also states, that, "according to a calculation founded on a passage in Knyghton, the revenue of the English church in 1337, amounted to seven hundred and seventy thousand marks per annum;"* that is, according to the estimate of the same author, about fifty-three million nine hundred thousand dollars! Nor is this all: the Pope came in for his share of the spoils. Besides tythes, Peter-pence, &c., which he usually received from the English church and government, in his war with the Emperor Frederic, he laid a special tax upon the church of England. "The usurers of Cahors and Lombardy," says Hallam, "residing in London, took up the trade of agency for the Pope; and in a few years, he is said partly by levies of money, partly by the revenues of benefices, to have plundered the kingdom of nine hundred and fifty thousand marks; a sum, equivalent, I think, to not less than fifteen millions sterling at present."

But let us adduce other testimony. Hume, in his History of England, states, that "among their other inventions to obtain money, the clergy had inculcated the necessity of penance, as an atonement for sin; and having again introduced the practice of paying them large sums, as a commutation, or species of atonement for the remission of those penances, the sins of the people by these means had become a revenue to the priests; and the king computed, that by this invention alone, they levied more money upon his subjects, than flowed by all the funds and taxes

* Middle Ages, chap. vii.

THE ANTICHRIST. 267

into the royal exchequer."* The same author states, that during the reign of Edward III., A. D., 1253-55, Otho, the Pope's legate, "carried more money out of the kingdom than he left in it." About this time, the chief benefices in England were conferred upon Italians, most of whom were non-residents. A complaint was consequently entered by the king and nobility before the Pope, at a general council held at Lyons, "that the benefices of the Italian clergy in England, had been estimated, and were found to amount to sixty thousand marks a year, a sum which exceeded the annual revenue of the crown itself." Instead, however, of this complaint arresting the rapacity of the Pope, "Innocent exacted the revenues of all vacant benefices; the twentieth of all ecclesiastical revenues without exception, the third of such as exceeded a hundred marks a year, and the half of such as were possessed by non-residents. He claimed the goods of all intestate clergymen; he pretended a title to inherit all money gotten by usury; he levied benevolences upon the people; and when the king prohibited these exactions, he threatened to pronounce upon him the same censures, which he had emitted against the Emperor Frederic."†

During the reign of Henry IV., A. D., 1413, "the Commons," says the same author, "made a calculation of the ecclesiastical revenues, which, by their account, amounted to four hundred and eighty-five thousand marks a year, (about thirty-three millions nine hundred and fifty thousand dollars,) and contained eighteen thousand four hundred ploughs of land. They proposed to divide this property among fifteen new earls, one thousand five hundred knights, six thousand esquires, and a hundred hospitals; besides twenty thousand pounds a year which the king might take for his own use: and they insisted, that the clerical functions would be better performed than at present, by fifteen thousand parish priests, paid at the rate of seven marks a piece of yearly stipend."

* Henry II., A. D. 1163. † Henry III.

According to this estimate of the House of Commons, the Roman Catholic religion taxed the English public in the reign of Henry IV., about twenty-six millions six hundred thousand dollars of our money more than the support of the gospel in that kingdom required! This is also exclusive of the proceeds from the lands! Can any one imagine a greater oppression? Can any one conceive of a wider departure from the simple and unpretending religion of Jesus? And to make the picture still more dark, all this went to a priesthood, who, for the greater part, led vicious and dissolute lives.

The fiscal condition of the Catholic church in England during the reign of Henry VIII., and in the year 1538, when the monasteries and other religious institutions were suppressed, may be learned from a work in the British Museum, published in 1717. This work is termed, "A summary of all the religious houses in England and Wales, with their titles and valuations at the time of their dissolution." The number of such houses "is stated to be one thousand and forty-one; the aggregate annual valuation of them at the same period was £273,106, reckoning only the rent of the manors and produce of the demesnes, and excluding fines, heriots, renewals, dividends, &c. This sum would be represented in 1717, a little less than two hundred years afterwards, as stated by the same authority, by £3,277,282, as a consequence of the decrease in the value of money. Assuming that the decrease has been the same in the last century, it would now be represented by about £20,000,000; or $96,000,000!

"The proportion of the land of the country, held by the church at that time, and of which the monks were lords, is stated at fourteen parts in twenty. In 1815, the annual assessed value of the real property of England and Wales, as stated in parliamentary records was £51,874,490. Fourteen twentieths of this sum, being the ancient proportion of the church revenues, would be about £34,500,000, or, $166,987,168! a sum, three fourths as large as the present annual revenue of the government of Great Britain, from all its sources and for all its purposes. Besides, too, this amazing absorption of the public wealth by the regular orders of the priesthood, there were four orders of mendicant monks, who not only lived on the residue of the property of the country, but abstracted large sums for their pious purposes. It is also stated by the same authority, that the Grand Duke of Tuscany—which is a district of Italy one hundred and fifty miles by one hundred— once ascertained and published, that the Church of Rome absorbed seventeen parts in twenty of the revenue of the land within his jurisdiction!!*

Here then, is the state of things, at the time of the Reformation. Was ever an event more needed than that Reformation? Here we see the professed ministers of Christ, who himself had not where to lay his head, not only lording it over princes in power and authority, but actually undermining their thrones and all national prosperity, by an accumulation of wealth truly fearful.

But it is alleged, that Popery has changed, that it is not now so exorbitant. Let us see. In France, says the same author, under the old regime in 1789, the annual revenues of the church were 405,000,000 francs; or, £16,200,000; or, $77,760,000. Under the present system it is but $6,182,400, and divided among Catholics and Protestants acccording to their numbers. That is, when the Catholic church in France had full sway, and only as late as 1787, that church levied upon the country, 71,577,600 dollars, beyond the sum which is appropriated at present for the support of religion in France.

The state of things is no better in Spain. The sum which the church property of Spain would yield, after providing for the decent maintenance of the clergy, was calculated by the Cortes of 1822, when joined to certain royal domains, lying useless to the state, to amount to £92,00,000; or, $441,600,000!! The present entire annual revenue of the Spanish

* Colton's Four Years, ii. 113.

church, is £10,514,000; that of the state as lately reported by Count de Toreno, is about £5,000,000;"* that is, the Spanish church absorbs twice the income of the kingdom of Spain!

The question naturally rises here, what becomes of so much money? The proper answer, no doubt is, that it requires all this capital to forge the bolts and bars, and to weld the chains, by which 200,000,000 of people are kept subject to a system of priestcraft and superstition, the most monstrous and terrific that has ever existed upon the earth. There is probably not a country on the globe, where the power of such capital is not felt. See at present, even in these United States, what European and priestly-gotten wealth is accomplishing! See the splendid cathedrals, the noble churches, the costly buildings, which these hidden streams of money are starting up among us!

Besides this general use of such funds, it requires vast resources to support Popery. Superstition is always an expensive system. Truth is simple; and requires but small means. Error, however, is complex and involved, and demands the glitter of much gold and silver to sustain it. The number of ecclesiastics in Spain as estimated within a few years past, is 160,043. Besides these, there are lay-assistants to the amount of 20,346; making a total to be provided for of 206,002. When the population of Spain is divided by this sum, it will give one ecclesiastic or lay-assistant, to about every sixty-seven persons. Now, how is it possible for sixty-seven persons, large and small, either to take up the whole time of a religious teacher, or to render him a support? Add to this the princely mode of living among bishops, archbishops, cardinals, and popes, and we shall soon see, that the popish system is and must be, not only the most tyrannical system on the globe, but also, the most expensive.

But let us go to Rome itself. See there the successor of St. Peter occupying the throne of the Cæsars—not only the king and sovereign of the States of the

* Colton's Four Years, p. 115.

Church, but the emperor over far and distant nations. Look at the Vatican, look at St. Peter's! What wealth, what immense wealth exhibits itself around the very seat of him, who styles himself, the vicegerent of Christ on earth! Nor is this all; all kinds of superstitions are practised in Rome for the sake of getting money. "I thought," says, Dr. Sturtevant, writing from Rome, "when I last wrote to you, that I had some faint glimpse of the deceits and delusions practised on the followers of popery. I could see depths, frightful and immense, of treasures of gold and silver, which papal imposition had extorted from the ignorant and superstitious, to pamper and uphold the dominion of the prince of darkness; but I had not fathomed the greatest reservoir of all, I mean indulgences. No measures also are untried, that crafty policy suggests, to solicit contributions for the relief of suffering souls in purgatory. Agents bearing lanterns with a painted glass, representing naked persons enveloped in flames, parade the streets and enter houses with tales that alarm, and appeals that excite the compassion of these holy souls. So great is the dread of purgatory, that besides the satisfactions they make in their lifetime, many deluded souls leave large legacies to the church to procure masses daily, weekly, monthly, and yearly, as far as their money will go. Many would rather starve their surviving families, than neglect the souls of the departed. This doctrine is a mine as profitable to the church as the Indies to Spain."* All this takes place under the eye, and by the authority of the Pope; yea, he himself is the chief tradesman in such things. The same writer speaks of the Pope himself, as at one time clothed "in robes of white and silver;" at another as decked "in scarlet and gold." The crowns and mitres of the bishops and cardinals who attended his Holiness, were also "glittering with jewels and set with precious stones." Surely, we have here almost the exact counterpart of what John predicts—"And the woman was arrayed in purple

---

* Letters from Rome.

and scarlet colour, and decked with gold and precious stones and pearls." And if we consider the vast treasures of the Roman Catholic priesthood in all countries, and the wonderful resources of Roman Catholic institutions, the exclamation " so great riches!" used by the inspired writer, will not be found inappropriate.

Thus have we ascertained another coincidence between Antichrist and the Papacy. Antichrist was to revel in wealth, and glitter in jewelry and pearls. He was to possess the riches of the nations. Rome has enjoyed all these for centuries. Seated as a queen, this idolatrous church has decorated herself for the espousals of all the kings and princes of Europe, and of the world. She has had no mean lovers; for the great and the noble, conquerors and sovereigns, have all bent at her feet and reveled in her smiles. But this very glory in which she arrays herself, these meretricious ornaments in which she displays herself before the nations, only proclaim with the tongue of living thunder, that she is not the spouse of Christ; and that the day of her doom is approaching, when "the voice of the bride will no longer at all be heard in her; and when the light of a candle shall no longer at all shine in her." Hasten it, O Lord, in its time, and let all the powers of Antichrist fall before thy victorious truth!

CHAPTER X.

ANTICHRIST THE POSSESSOR OF GREAT POWER.

A LARGE number of scriptural predictions concerning Antichrist, refer to the extent and greatness of his dominion. Daniel asserts that "his look was more stout than his fellows:" that is, that the evil power spoken of, should be an object of greater notoriety, than the other ten kingdoms, with which it was to be associated. The saints of the Most High were also to be "given into his hand," for a period of twelve hundred and sixty years; and even then, were to be delivered from his hand only by some remarkable interpositions of God himself. Dan. vii.

The Apostle Paul describes the same wicked king, as "opposing and exalting himself above all that is called God, or that is worshipped," 2 Thess. ii. 4: that is, as elevating himself to the very pinnacle of power both in church and state. The Apostle John, however, is more explicit in his description. In reference to this same evil king, or Antichrist, represented as a beast rising out of the sea, he says: "And the dragon gave him his power, and his seat and great authority." The dragon here referred to, is pagan Imperial Rome. Antichrist, therefore, occupying the very metropolis of the old Roman Empire, was to possess both its authority and power. But this is not all; "power was given him," says John, "over all kingdoms, and tongues and nations." Since the previous description represented the power of Antichrist, as co-extensive with that of the Roman Empire, it is probable, that the "kindreds, and tongues and nations," here spoken of, were such as were previously

24*

subject to Roman authority. But the direct power of Antichrist was to be as absolute as his dominion was extensive. "And he causeth all, both small and great, rich and poor, free and bond, to receive a mark in their right hand or in their foreheads; and that no man might buy or sell, save he that had the mark, or the name of the beast, or the number of his name." All the offices and privileges of society, were to be interdicted to all, be they sovereigns or subjects, high or low, who should not yield implicit obedience to this tyrannizing power. The means, too, by which this evil king was to exercise such dominion is also foretold. "The ten horns which thou sawest are ten kings; these have one mind, and shall give their power and strength to the beast." Rev. xiii. xvii. Antichrist is himself but "a little horn,"—his regal power is small; but, by means of the ten greater horns, or kingdoms, which with himself arose out of the ruins of old Rome, he exercises an absolute sovereignty over the earth. Such are some of the many predictions concerning the power and dominion of Antichrist. Nor can one well avoid exclaiming while reading such prophecies, Surely John must be the historian and not the prophet, of modern Europe! But the infatuation of the human mind, when under the influence of error, is amazing. The Jews, even while crucifying the true Messiah, were looking for a messiah to come; and Papists, while exhibiting in their own system, and especially in their head, all the full-drawn features of the scriptural Antichrist, are yet speaking of Antichrist as something future.

We are now prepared to meet the Papist on his own ground. He boasts of antiquity, of universality, of authority, and of unity. All these in a certain sense we grant him. But, then, these very things are the evidences of the antichristian character of his whole system. They are the marks of "the beast," they are the boastings of the "little horn;" they are the exaltations of "the man of sin;" they are the divinely inspired criteria, by which the people of God are to know and avoid Antichrist.

That Jesus Christ did not lodge either supreme spiritual, or supreme temporal power, in the hands of any one man, must appear evident to every candid reader of the New Testament. It is true, that during the lifetime of our Lord, and for some time afterwards, Peter, because more bold and fervid, and because he was older probably than the other Apostles, acted a more conspicuous part than his brethren. Equally true, however, it is, that the Apostle Paul, because yet bolder and more daring than even Peter, and possibly more endued from heaven, is represented in the later periods of the inspired history, as taking the lead of all the Apostles in the Christian ministry. But neither of these Apostles is spoken of as being the head over the other. Nor were they, or either of them, promoted in the apostolic office, above their fellow Apostles. As witnesses of the life, character, doctrines, death and resurrection of their common Master, the Apostles were all on an exact equality. As publishers of his gospel to mankind, they had all received, not a similar, but the same commission. As sharers in the influences and gifts of the Holy Spirit, they had all partaken of one common baptism. And as planters of churches, and overseers, of the flock of Christ, they were all equally interested, equally esteemed. No disparity is there among them, except in gifts and natural endowments, except in grace and its manifold operations. In office they were one, in honour one, in love one. They were one family, one brotherhood, one Apostolate.

Much less did Jesus entrust to the hands of any one, or even all of his Apostles, supreme temporal authority. He taught them, that " his kingdom was not of this world," and " to render unto Cæsar the things that were Cæsar's." The Apostles, too, following the instructions of their Master, enjoined it upon their disciples, "to be subject to the higher powers," assuring them, that "the powers that be are ordained of God," and were therefore entitled to obedience and respect from all Christians. Rom. xiii. " Whoever has read the gospel," says a Catholic writer, "knows, that Jesus Christ founded no temporal government, no political sovereignty. St. Peter and his colleagues were sent, not to govern, but to teach; and the authority with which they were invested, consisted only in the light and benefits which they had to diffuse. Every one knows, he continues, that before Constantine, the Christian churches were only particular associations, too often proscribed, and always strangers to the political system. The popes (bishops) in those times of persecution, and of fervour, certainly did not aspire to the government of provinces. It was enough for them to have the power of being virtuous with impunity. They obtained on earth no crown, but that of martyrdom."*

Such was the state of original Christianity. No supreme spiritual, or supreme temporal power, was placed in the hands of any one man. The Apostles, as such, were on a perfect equality. The same equality was maintained among the ministers who succeeded them. The churches were separate associations, each possessing its own local officers, and each independent of the rest. Nor was Christianity united to the state; it was enough, that it was tolerated by the civil authority.

It is a singular phenomenon, however, in the history of the world, that the system of religion which Jesus taught, of which he was himself the pattern, and which he left to mankind as a rich legacy—that a religion so pure, so unostentatious, so separated from the insignia of power, that such a religion should have been so perverted in the hands of wicked men, as to become the greatest engine of power, the world has ever known; that its very doctrines, and promises, and revelations, its officers and organization, its rewards and its hopes—that all these, so full of grace, so redolent of heaven, should be formed into a great system of terror, in which the powers of three worlds are made to rest in fearful suspense upon the conscien-

*Daunou, p. 1—3.

ces of mankind! This transformation, we say, is wonderful, is wonderful indeed. And yet it is a transformation which has actually taken place; yea, upon which the eyes of men for more than ten centuries have been quietly gazing.

The power of the Papacy is three-fold, indicated, as some say, by the triple crown, which the Pope wears as the badge of his dominion. The first of these is regal, or that which he wields over the "states of the church." The second is pontifical; or that which he exercises as supreme head of the church. The third is imperial, or that which he would exercise over the nations of the earth.

It is not intended to dwell upon the first of these powers. According to most historians, the Pope became a temporal prince in the year 754, by a grant from Pepin, king of France. This temporal dominion, the Pope has possessed ever since. In itself it may be considered a small matter; the prince of a petty state, is not likely to exert any great influence any way, upon the history and destiny of nations. Even this fact, however, has in it a remarkable fulfilment of prophecy. "I considered the horns," says Daniel, "and behold there came up among them another little horn; before whom there were three of the first horns plucked up by the roots." This prediction accurately describes the Papacy as a temporal sovereignty. It came up among, or as some say, behind, or according to others after, the first ten horns upon the Roman beast. The Pope as a temporal prince, is located on the very apex, if we may so say, of the head of the beast. He is the central power. He came up too, later than the rest; the ten Gothic kingdoms, having been previously formed. He also arose imperceptibly into this condition. Even to this day is it debated, precisely when the Pope became a temporal prince. The fact then, that the chief pontiff of Christendom is the sovereign also of a petty kingdom, though in itself unimportant, yet is essential to the scriptural evidence, that the Papacy is Antichrist. It is one of those personal and smaller matters, which as strongly as any thing else, indicate the fulfilment of a particular prophecy.

It is, however, the possession by the Papacy of the supreme spiritual, and the supreme temporal power, which must chiefly engage our attention. We are to survey the Pope, not as a petty Italian prince, but as the chief pontiff and the august emperor of Christendom. It is in the occupancy and exercise of these two offices, that the Papacy has disturbed, or rather moulded, all the political and religious systems of Europe ; and it is in its assumption of these fearful powers, that its antichristian character is most discernible.

The spiritual government at Rome may be divided into four periods—the congregational and presbyterial, the episcopal, the patriarchal, and the papal.

The original church government at Rome was congregational and presbyterial. The supreme power was in the church, or body of believers; the officers of the church were presbyters and deacons. The Epistle to the Romans is addressed by Paul "to all that be in Rome, beloved of God, called to be saints." Rom. i. 7. Again the Epistle of Clement to the Corinthians is from "the church of God which is at Rome."*
If then, Paul wrote not to one man, or to a body of men, but to the church generally; and if Clement wrote not in his own name, but in the name of the church at Rome, it is evident, that at that time, the supreme spiritual power at Rome, was in the Roman church; that is, in the body of believers in that city.

The church at Rome, however, was organized as other apostolic churches, with bishops, or elders, and deacons. First, there is no good reason, why this church should be organized differently, and we know that other churches were so constituted. Phil i. 1. Acts xx. 1 Tim. iii. Secondly; we have the testimony of Clement that this was the case. "The Apostles thus preaching," says he, "through countries and cities, they appointed the first fruits of their conversions to be bishops and ministers (elders and dea-

* Epis. Clem.

cons) over such as should afterwards believe, having first proved them by the Spirit." This however was done by the vote of the brotherhood. "Wherefore," continues Clement, "we cannot think that those can justly be thrown out of their ministry, who were either appointed by them, (the Apostles) or afterwards chosen by other eminent men, with the consent of the whole church. But we see how you (the Corinthians) have put out some from the ministry, which by their innocence they had adorned."* The original ecclesiastical government then at Rome, as in all the early churches, was congregational and presbyterial; that is, the power was in the people, but was ordinarily exercised by presbyters or elders.

The next form of this government was episcopal. It is evident, that between the close of the first century and the beginning of the fourth, most, if not all, of the early churches assumed the episcopal form. Some one of the congregational presbytery had been made permanent moderator, or sole head over the rest. As proof of this, let the following testimony of Jerome be considered: we quote from Bishop Hopkins's "Church of Rome in her primitive purity." "With the ancients," says this learned father, "presbyters and bishops were the same; but, by degrees, in order that the plants of dissension might be rooted up, the care of government was committed to one. Therefore, as the presbyters know themselves, by the custom of the church, to be subject to him who may be set over them, so should the bishops know, that they are superior to the presbyters, more by custom, than by the truth of our Lord's disposition; (magis consuetudine quam dispositionis dominicæ veritate) and that they ought to govern the church in common:" (et in commune debere ecclesiam regere.)†

The fourth form of the spiritual government at Rome, was patriarchal. Constantine, wishing to adapt the ecclesiastical to the civil polity, introduced a new arrangement in ecclesiastical government. This gave rise to the appointment, throughout the Roman em-

* Epist. to Cor.   † Page 305.

pire, of bishops, archbishops, metropolitans, exarchs, and patriarchs. Under this new economy, Antioch, Alexandria, Rome, and afterwards Constantinople, became each the seat of a patriarch. Between these patriarchs, there arose of course some rivalry. The Roman patriarch, however, was generally superior, chiefly because he lived at the capital of the empire. When, however, ancient Byzantium, under the new name of Constantinople, became also the seat of civil authority, the two patriarchates of the two capitals of the empire, soon overshadowed those of Alexandria and Antioch. Rome, then, had but one rival, the patriarch of the eastern empire. As that patriarch was powerfully supported by the eastern court, it was far more difficult to gain ascendency over him, than it had been over other rivals. Power between these two ecclesiastical potentates was well nigh balanced for several centuries. At length, however, in the ninth century, a rupture took place between them, which divided Christendom into the eastern or Greek, and the western or Latin church.

Besides the rivalry here alluded to, the Roman patriarch had other obstructions to his absolute headship over even the western church. These obstructions were found in the rights of metropolitans, and other subordinate presiding church officers. Each bishop and archbishop had his prerogatives: each state claimed for the church established in it, certain privileges. All these must be removed before the Roman bishop could become the absolute autocrat of the Latin church. "Their first encroachment of this kind," says Hallam, "was in the province of Illyricum, which they annexed in a manner to their own patriarchate, by not permitting any bishops to be consecrated without their consent. This was before the end of the fourth century. Their subsequent advances, however, were very gradual. About the middle of the sixth century, we find them confirming the elections of the archbishops of Milan. They came by degrees to exercise, though not always successfully, and seldom without opposition, an appellant jurisdiction over the causes of bishops, deposed or censured in provincial synods. Valentinian III., influenced by Leo the Great, one of the most ambitious of pontiffs, went a great deal farther, and established almost an absolute judicial supremacy in the Holy See. 'We decree this,' says the emperor, 'by a perpetual sanction, that it is lawful for French bishops, as well as for those of other provinces, in violation of an ancient custom, to attempt nothing, without the authority of that venerable man, the Pope of the eternal city; but, let whatever the Apostolic Seat has sanctioned, or may have sanctioned, be to them all for law.'"* This occurred in the year 455; and although there was resistance to this imperial decree, yet it shows what the designs both of the Emperor and the Pope were.

Gregory I. greatly increased the power of the Roman See. "He dwelt," says Hallam, "more than his predecessors, upon the power of the keys, as exclusively, or at least principally, committed to St. Peter. In a letter to the Spanish churches, he uses the following language—"a sede apostolica, quæ omnium ecclesiarum caput est"—"from the apostolic seat, which is the head of all the churches." This was at the close of the fifth century.

The celebrated edict of Phocas, in 606, constituting the Roman bishop the head of the church, is well known. In that decree it is asserted, that "the name of *universal* becomes only the Roman church, as that which is the head of all the churches, and is appropriate to none but the Roman pontiff."†

It is strange to observe here, that the very supremacy which emperors and popes were pressing upon metropolitans and other bishops, those bishops were themselves inviting. In a synod of French and German bishops held at Frankfort, in 742, it was decreed, that as a token of their subjection to the See of Rome, all metropolitans should receive from the hands of the Pope, the pallium, as a badge of office—"metropoli-

* Middle Ages, chap. vii. † Baronius.

tanos pallia ab illa sede quærere, et per omnia præcepta S. Petri canonice sequi."

It was in the latter part of this century, that one Isidore Mercator, or Peccator, who was either a sycophant of the Pope, or the rival, possibly, of some metropolitan or other church dignitary, issued the Decretals of the early popes or bishops of Rome. These Decretals were a summary of the pretended decrees which Anaclet, Clement, Euaristus, and other popes, to the time of St. Sylvester, had passed. They were all fabrications of the grossest kind. In them, however, the greatest possible amount of power was conceded to the popes of Rome. "Every bishop was amenable only to the immediate tribunal of the Pope. Every accused person might appeal directly to the chief pontiff. New sees were not to be erected, nor bishops translated from one see to another, without the sanction of the Pope." "They also forbid the holding of any council, even a provincial council, without the permission of the Pope."* "Upon these spurious decretals," says Hallam, "was built the great fabric of papal supremacy, over the different national churches; a fabric which has stood after its foundations crumbled beneath it." It is evident, however, that the churches of Europe must have been previously prepared for the yoke, or such gross fabrications never could have been made the means of enforcing such bondage.

But one more step was needed to complete the spiritual ascendency of the Roman hierarch; he needed agents, amenable only to himself, and who should go or come according to his will. These he found in several monastic orders, whom he freed from all subjection to metropolitans and bishops, but held in entire subserviency to himself as sole head of the church. These were his most faithful and devoted allies; and as many of them had great power over the people, and even over kings, the authority of the Roman prelate became supreme throughout Christendom.

* Daunou, 27.

Thus did the little church planted in apostolic days beside the throne of the Cæsars, struggling itself through centuries for a bare existence, watered by the tears and cemented by the blood of martyrs—thus did this little church, prostrate at first before the imperial throne, climbing up afterwards around that throne, and subsequently occupying the seat of that throne, thus did it become mistress of Christendom, and its pastor, monarch of the world! How little did the first band of Christian disciples at Rome, meeting, it may be, in a garret, or a retired chamber, how little did they anticipate a result like this! How little did they desire it! Their form of government was entirely different. With them, power, (if it deserved the name) was in the hands of the brotherhood. The church as composed of individual members, was supreme. Their discipline was exercised by faithful presbyters; men chosen by themselves, and under whose teachings and control, they enjoyed both liberty and order. With them, there was no pomp, no show. No St. Peter's excited the wonder of travellers; no Vatican received their humble pastors. The crown was on no head, the sword in the hand of none. Nor did they boast of supremacy over their brethren; they were satisfied to be themselves Christians. Such was the Roman church in her infancy; such in her purest, and really apostolic days. With this church, we claim fraternity; and although Rome to us is no more a veneration, than Ephesus or Antioch, or any other of the early churches; yet, amid all the rubbish of the Papacy, and the solemn mockeries of Antichrist, yea, beneath, it may be, the very chair of St. Peter, there is dust, forgotten dust, that we do esteem. It is the dust of those tried and worthy men, who planted the Roman church; who were living examples of Christian doctrine and practice in that church; who studied the Scriptures daily, and met each night for prayer; who despised tyranny, but rejoiced in the freedom of the gospel; who lived in love and fellowship with Christ; such men, we repeat it, we love; their principles we love; their names we venerate. But, with Rome as she now is, with Rome as she has been for more than a thousand years, we can have no sympathy, no fellowship, no common interest. Our prayer is, that she may be overthrown, and that her arm of iron may be removed from oppressed Christianity.

We are now to consider the imperial, or supreme political power of the Papacy. This power was the result chiefly of the spiritual headship of the Papacy over Christendom. Had the popes been but the temporal lords of their own small territory, or but the metropolitans of a particular district, their authority would have been limited. As temporal princes, they could have claimed obedience only from their own subjects; and as the occupants of an episcopal see their supervision could have extended over none but the churches of their own diocese. But when the Pope was constituted supreme pontiff, especially when he was considered as the Vicar of Christ upon earth, and his decisions regarded as final and infallible, a supremacy over thrones and kings was the inevitable result. Politics and religion cannot be kept entirely separate. There are many points at which the state must touch the church, and there are many moral questions which must relate to princes and cabinets. Even were the church and state entirely distinct in their general administrations, one infallible and supreme head of the church, would be at least liable to interfere with the free and regular exercise of the civil government. In cases, however, where church and state are united, the interference is inevitable, and must be frequent. Now in Europe, from the days of Constantine, there was the closest union between religion and politics. Long before the downfall of the Roman Empire, this system was adopted. And when that empire sunk, and the modern kingdoms of Europe arose on its ruins, neither prince nor bishop thought of a separation between these two systems. A national, or rather an imperial religion, every where existed. The consequence of this was, that while popes and bishops were in a certain sense, held as the subjects of kings and princes, the latter were also considered spiritually as the subjects of the former. Possibly, some might imagine, that such mutual subjection might be maintained without detriment to the peace of society. Such, however, the history of Europe has proved, is not likely to be the case. Especially is it not likely to succeed on such a magnificent scale, as was attempted in Catholic Europe. There are too many national interests and prejudices, too many kings and bishops, too many passions and motives to ambition, for a scheme like this to exist without agitation, without tyranny and rebellion. Hence, the history of Europe throughout the papal supremacy, exhibits not the smoothness of a lake unruffled by the passing breeze, but the turbidness of a sea, dashed and tossed by conflicting winds. Papal unity in these times was but one perpetual struggle; and papal harmony, but the symphony of uninterrupted discords. The result, however, of such struggles and agitations, at least for centuries, was the gradual but complete ascendency of papal power over the sovereigns of Europe.

Nor was the high political power of the Pope, the result alone of his pontifical station; that station itself was made the abode of certain divine attributes. The popular idea was, that God and St. Peter were ecclesiastically one. The Pope, personally, might be but a man; he might have faults, yea great faults; yet, as Pope, he was God's representative, Christ's vicar; he could not err; and his will was supreme in heaven, as well as on earth. His anathema was held in the utmost dread; and his interdict subjected even the greatest princes to the deepest humiliations. At his command all the services of religion were arrested; marriages, masses, and even burials were prevented. Subjects were freed from their allegiance to their lawful sovereigns, and even the assassination of the prince was considered a virtue.

Among the proximate causes which advanced the power of the Pope, Daunou, mentions the following. "The political revolutions which followed the

dethronement of Augustulus, the accession of Pepin to the throne of France, and of Charlemagne to the Empire; the weakness of Louis-le-Debonnaire, the division of his states among his children, the imprudence of some of the kings who invoked the thunders of the Holy See against each other; the fabrication of the Decretals, the propagation of a canonical jurisprudence, quite contrary to the ancient laws of the church; the rivalries between the two houses of Germany, the projects of independence conceived by several of the Italian cities, the crusades, the inquisition, and the innumerable multitude of monastic establishments; these," says this Catholic authority, "are the causes which brought on, established, aggrandized, and so long sustained the temporal power of the Popes, and facilitated the abuse of their spiritual functions."*
Thus did the state of things both without and within the church, the agitations of the political system, and the doctrines of the religious, unite in the elevation of the Papal See above the capitals of Europe. Nor should we omit in this catalogue of causes, the ambition of the Roman Pontiffs themselves. Gregory VII., Innocent III., Julius II., and Boniface VIII., were as ambitious of power, as an Alexander, a Cæsar, or a Napoleon. Their desire was, not simply supremacy in the church, or even in Europe, but supremacy throughout the world.

The gradual development of this wonderful system of power, will now be considered. From the days of Constantine, Christian bishops, and especially Roman bishops, exerted more or less influence upon the policy of the country. "Even under the Roman Emperors," says Hallam, "they had found their way into palaces; they were sometimes ministers, more often secret counsellors, always necessary but formidable allies, whose support was to be conciliated, and interference respected."†

After the fall of the throne of the Cæsars, the civil obedience of the bishop of Rome became, after a

---

* Court of Rome, 253. † Middle Ages, chap. vii.

THE ANTICHRIST.

short interval, subject to the eastern Emperor, and to the Exarch of Ravenna, as his lieutenant. The veneration, however, of the new Gothic kingdoms for their spiritual head, and the ancient habit of the west in rallying around a western political centre, together with some difference of doctrine between Rome and Constantinople, well nigh counterbalanced the authority of the successors of Constantine; and while they exalted the Pope, made his subjection to a distant sovereign, rather tacit, than efficient. Hence, the readiness of the Papal See to constitute a western emperor in the person of Charlemagne; and hence the haughty language it sometimes employed toward the eastern court. The following is an extract of a letter to Leo III., from Gregory II., whom Gibbon styles, "the founder of the papal monarchy," and whom also Catholic writers are in the habit of representing as a model of patience and loyalty. "You now accuse," says Gregory, "the Catholics of idolatry; and by the accusation you betray your own impiety and ignorance. To this ignorance we are compelled to adopt the grossness of our style and arguments. The first elements of holy letters are sufficient for your confusion; and were you to enter a grammar school, and avow yourself the enemy of our worship, the simple and pious children would be provoked to cast their hornbooks at your head. You assault us, O tyrant, with a carnal and military hand; unarmed and naked, we can only implore Christ, the Prince of the heavenly host, that he will send unto you a devil, for the destruction of your body and the salvation of your soul. Abandon your rash and fatal enterprise, reflect, tremble, repent. If you persist, we are innocent of the blood that will be spilt in the contest; may it fall on your own head."[*] Such was the language of Gregory II. to the greatest emperor of Christendom, and also his own lawful sovereign. Gregory III. his immediate successor, went still further, and excommunicated the whole sect of the Iconoclasts, and Leo among them.[†]

[*] Rome, xlix.   [†] Daunou, p. 13.

The authority of the popes over the new kingdoms was of a more decisive character. The first remarkable interference of this authority in political matters occurred in France. Pepin, the son of the celebrated Charles Martel, was exercising the authority, but durst not usurp the name, of king. This name belonged to Childeric, a regular descendant from Clovis, who had established the French monarchy. The case was referred to Pope Zacharias. He decided that Childeric, the lawful sovereign, should be shorn and placed in a convent; and that Pepin should assume both the name and the insignia of royalty. True, the decision in this case was but that of a supreme judge, giving his opinion in a question of doubt and perplexity. But what right had a Christian pastor to decide who should reign over a political kingdom? If the reference was a matter of policy on the part of Pepin, and of conscience on the part of the French, it was also one of power in the hands of the Pope. His sentence was authoritative, and it was final. Hence Eginhard, the biographer of Charlemagne, says that Pepin was made king—"jussu et auctoritate Pontificis Romani"—"by the command and authority of the Roman Pontifex." This occurred about the middle of the eighth century.

Fifty years after the important decision above alluded to, that is, on Christmas day, A. D. 800, Pope Leo III. crowned Charlemagne, the son of Pepin, Emperor of the West. Daunou affirms that this was done, not by the Pope, alone, but by "an assembly of the clergy, of the nobility, and of the people of Rome."* Anastasius, however, affirms, that Charles was made emperor — "Dei nutu atque B. Petri clavigeri regni cœlorum"—"by the will of God and of the blessed Peter, the keys-bearer of the kingdom of heaven." "On Christmas day," says Grimshaw, "when the monarch was attending mass in St. Peter's church, at Rome, the supreme Pontiff advanced, and placed upon his head an imperial crown; and having con-

---

* Court of Rome, 24.

ducted him to an imperial throne, declared, that he should thenceforth be styled Emperor and Augustus."*

As the chair of St. Peter had virtually made both a king for France, and an emperor for the west, the subsequent subjection of these thrones to the dictation of the Pope, would seem to be a matter of course. The son and successor of the late emperor, was the first to experience evils of this kind. Louis I., surnamed Le Debonnaire, divided his kingdom among his three sons, Lothaire, Pepin, and Louis. The birth of a fourth son, by a second marriage, Charles the Bald, was the means of associating the three first against their father and the last. In these royal controversies, not only the prelates of France, but the Pope also took a prominent part. Gregory IV. allied himself to the three rebellious sons. He entered France in person, and without the permission of Louis. He caused the army of Louis to desert him, and became thus the means and instigation of the dethronement of the son of Charlemagne. It was at this time, that in a letter to the bishops, he uses the following insolent language: — "Know ye that my chair is above the throne of Louis." " It would be painful" says Daunou, " to trace the details of the well known humiliations of Louis I. How Hebo, his creature, and other bishops condemned him to a public penance; how upon his knees before these prelates he recited publicly a confession of his crimes, among which he enumerates the march of his troops during the carnival, and the convocation of a parliament on holy Thursday; how, dragged from cloister to cloister, to Compeigne, to Soissons, to Aix-la-Chapelle, to Paris, to St. Denis, he seemed destined there to terminate his days." Such was the son of Charlemagne in the hands of the ecclesiastics, who had aspired to control the throne of France and of the empire.

Louis II. was equally subservient to the power of the Pope. "He went on foot before the pontiff, served

* Hist. France, 31.

him as an esquire, and led his horse by the bridle!" Charles the Bald, in a submissive letter to the clergy, affirmed, that "the bishops are the throne where God sits to render his decrees!" The power of the Pope, however, was far superior at this time to that of either bishops or kings. An experiment was made of that power. Lothaire, king of Lorraine, and great grandson of Charlemagne, had repudiated his wife, Theutberge. This repudiation had occurred after a lawful examination before a council of bishops. The Pope, however, Nicholas I., thought proper to annul the whole proceedings. He ordered the king to take back the wife from whom he was lawfully divorced; threatened him with excommunication if he refused; sent a legate to compel compliance with his mandate; and even proceeded so far as to depose two of the bishops, who sat in one of the councils by which the divorce was granted. Lothaire was forced into obedience, although ably defended by his brother, the Emperor Louis. Thus did the arbitrary will of the new sovereign of the Seven Hills, control at once, emperors and kings, councils and bishops! This occurred about the year 863.

Under the Pontificate of John VIII., Charles the Bald was made emperor, when his brother, the king of Germany had superior claims to that office. The language used by the pontiff on the occasion, is significant: "We have judged him worthy of the imperial sceptre—we have elevated him to the dignity and power of the empire—we have decorated him with the title of Augustus."* In a council at Troyes, in France, over which this same pope presided, besides various excommunications against persons of distinction, it was decreed, "that bishops shall be treated with respect by the secular powers, and that none shall be so bold as to sit in their presence, unless they shall be directed to do so."

Such were the perpetual collisions between the civil and ecclesiastical powers in France, during the

* Court of Rome, 47.

Carlovingian race of kings. The officers of the church, instead of being subject to civil rulers, arrogated to themselves a vigilant supervision over those rulers. Crowns were conferred by popes; and thrones made vacant by their simple volition. No doubt, the contests between the descendants of Charlemagne had a powerful tendency to promote the frequent exercise and gradual ascendency of ecclesiastical power. There were many other causes, however, conspiring to the same result. The general ignorance that prevailed, the gross superstitions that were practised, the erroneous notions entertained of the office and prerogatives of church-officers—especially the almost divine homage paid to the Pope—all these tended to lower the civil and exalt the ecclesiastical authority. The Papacy had not as yet, however, reached its full grown stature. Other centuries were required for this.

Before we trace its fuller developments, however, through these centuries, it will be proper to notice an event which powerfully accelerated its advancement. This event was the fabrication of two documents, the objects of which were to elevate the power of the Pope to the highest possible pitch. The Decretals and the Donation of Constantine were both invented, it is thought, in the eighth century. The former, which we have already noticed, was designed to establish the absolute supremacy of the Pope in the church, the latter to give him supreme control in the state. The following is a quotation from the latter document. It employs the language of Constantine the Great. "We ascribe to the See of St. Peter, all dignity—all power—all imperial power. Besides, we give to Sylvester and his successors our palace of Lateran—we give him our crown, our mitre, our diadem, and all our imperial vestments—we remit to him the imperial dignity. We give, as a pure gift, to the holy pontiff, the city of Rome, and all the western cities of Italy, as well as the western cities of other countries. In order to give place to him, we yield our dominion over all these provinces, by removing the seat of our empire to Byzantium, considering that it is not right that a terrestrial emperor should presume the least power, where God has established the head of religion."* This document is admitted, by all Catholic writers at the present time, to be a mere forgery; and yet, so ignorant were men in the middle ages, and so blinded by papal authority, that it was universally received as authentic. "This donation," says Daunou, "obtained belief so long, that in 1478, Christians were burnt at Strasburg for having dared to doubt its authenticity!" It is easy to see what an exaltation of papal power, what a stretch of papal ambition, would naturally arise from a popular and general belief like this.

In the tenth century, we have another most painful instance of the deep humiliations to which the throne of France was again subjected by the Pope of Rome. Hugh Capet had supplanted the Carlovingian line of kings, and established the Caputian—that which continues to the present time. His son and successor, Robert, had married Bertha, his cousin of the fourth degree, to whose son also, by a previous husband, he had stood as god-father. The validity of this marriage, although authorized by seven bishops, was denied by the Pope. As the king was unwilling to put away his wife, he incurred from the holy see the sentence of excommunication, and his kingdom was laid under an interdict. "It was the first time," says Daunou, "that the church of France saw herself under an interdict, or received the injunction to suspend the celebration of divine offices—the administration of the sacraments to adults—the religious burial of the dead." Such was the effect of this sentence of excommunication, that the king of France was deserted by all his attendants and domestics, save two servants, who are said, on the authority of a cardinal,† to have cast to the dogs what provisions were left from the royal table, and also to have purified by fire every vessel the excommunicated monarch touched! Humbled by such rigorous treatment, Robert was compelled to

* Court of Rome, 4.   † Peter Damière.

yield, and Gregory V. had the satisfaction to see both bishops and king subservient to his pontifical mandate.

Thus were matters preparing for a universal Theocracy. The full conception of that theocracy, and its partial completion, was the work of the celebrated Hildebrand. "The idea," says Daunou, "of a universal theocracy, had taken in his ardent and severe mind, the character of a passion. His whole life was consecrated to this enterprise."*

To accomplish this vast scheme, Hildebrand attempted, first, to make the church independent of the state, and next to extend the power of the church gradually, but universally over the state. To render the church less dependent upon civil authority, he virtually abolished the right of lay-investiture, required every bishop to come to Rome for consecration, and established a new mode of electing the Pope. The power of nominating a successor in the chair of St. Peter was at this time in the emperors of Germany. According to the decree however, of Nicholas II., of which Hildebrand was the real author, "the cardinal bishops were to choose the supreme Pontiff, with the concurrence, first of the cardinal priests and deacons, and afterward of the (Roman) laity. Thus elected, the new Pope was to be presented to Henry, and to such of his successors, as should personally obtain that privilege."† To render his authority yet more efficient, Gregory had a special legate or representative, clothed with extraordinary powers, in each country of Europe. These legates collected taxes, intimidated bishops, and kept even kings in awe. They were ready at any moment, either to report misconduct to Rome, or to fulminate from their own seats, in the name of the Pope, the anathemas of the Holy See.

* Court of Rome, 77.
† Hallam.—Under Alexander III., the laity were excluded, and the consent of the sovereign not required in the election of a Pope. Two thirds of the college of cardinals decided the choice. This is the present mode of electing the Pope.

There are twenty-seven maxims, ascribed to Gregory VII., from which the character of his administration may fairly be inferred. The following are a few of them:—"That the Pope has the right to depose all princes, to dispose of all crowns, to reform all laws. That he can never err, that he alone can nominate bishops, convoke councils, preside at them, dissolve them: that princes must kiss his feet, that by him subjects are absolved from their oath of allegiance; in a word, that there is but one name or power in the world, viz., the Pope."

Nor did Gregory simply write maxims. His acts corresponded with his creed. "It would be necessary," says Daunou, "to enumerate all the princes who reigned during the time of this Pope, in order to furnish the list of those, who were smitten, or menaced by him with excommunication. Sardinia and Dalmatia, he considered only as fiefs, dependent on the tiara. To Demetrius of Russia, he wrote: "We have given your crown to your son." Nicephorus Botiniates, the Greek emperor, he commanded to abdicate his throne. Boleslas, king of Poland, he declared fallen, adding that Poland should no longer be a kingdom. Solomon, king of Hungary, he bid go to the Hungarian old men and learn, that their country belonged to the Roman Church. To the Spanish princes he wrote, that St. Peter was their lord paramount, having the right to the revenues of all their little states. Robert Guiscard he punished by anathemas. From the Duke of Bohemia, he exacted the tribute of a hundred marks of silver. Philip I. of France he denounced as a tyrant, plunged in crime and infamy; and upon William the Conqueror, he enjoined it as a duty, to render homage for his kingdom, to the Apostolic See. The greatest trophy, however, of the ambition of Gregory, was the Emperor Henry IV. Contrary to the new doctrines of Papacy, Henry had made some investitures; this was a capital offence. Gregory despatches two legates to Germany, to summon the emperor to appear at Rome, to answer in person to the Pope, for the crimes alleged against him. The emperor refused. This refusal led to a rupture between the two potentates, in which Henry was excommunicated by the Pope in the following words:—" On the part of God Omnipotent, and by my plenary authority, I forbid Henry, the son of Henry, to govern the Teutonic kingdom, and Italy. I absolve all Christians from the oaths which they have made to him, or which they shall make to him. It is forbidden to every person to render him any service as to a king." The humiliations of Henry, consequent upon this sentence of excommunication, are thus described by Hallam. " Gregory was at Canossa, a fortress near Reggio, belonging to his faithful adherent, the Countess Matilda. It was in a winter of unusual severity. The emperor was admitted, without his guards, into an outer court of the castle, and three successive days remained from morning till evening, in a woollen shirt, and with naked feet, while Gregory, shut up with the countess, refused to admit him to his presence. On the fourth day he obtained absolution, but only upon condition of appearing on a certain day, to learn the Pope's decision, whether or no he should be restored to his kingdom, until which time he promised not to assume the ensigns of royalty."*

Such was the height of power, to which the Papal See had advanced, towards the close of the eleventh century. Gregory VII. however, only drew the outlines of a dominion, which his successors, and especially Innocent III., were to establish and complete. We have already noticed how the Donation of Constantine and the Decretals of Isidore tended to augment papal power. We must now notice another instrument of the same kind. This instrument is "the Digest of Gratian." This Digest consists of a compilation of various canons for the regulation of ecclesiastical polity. It was divided into three parts, the first treating of ecclesiastical persons, the second of judgments, and the third of sacred things. Its popularity and influence were wonderful. " It was ex-

* Middle Ages.

plained," says Daunou, "in the schools, cited in the tribunals, and invoked in treaties. It had almost become the public law of Europe, when the return of light dissipated, by slow degrees, the gross imposture." The character and design of this celebrated Digest may be learned from the following. "By it," continues the same author, "the clergy were held not to be amenable to answer in the secular tribunals: the civil powers were subjected to ecclesiastical supremacy: the state of persons, and the acts which determine it, were regulated, validated, or annulled, by the canons and the clergy; the papal power was enfranchised from all restrictions; the sanction of all laws of the church was ascribed to the Holy See, that See itself being independent of the laws published and confirmed by itself." Such was the jurisprudence, by which papal authority was carried to its summit, throughout Europe, a jurisprudence, whose origin was fraud, whose popularity was based upon ignorance and superstition, by which all civil rights were trampled in the dust; and whose sole object was, the independent establishment of one vast papal monarchy. This new system of law was first published by a Benedictine monk, in the year 1152. Pope Eugene III. gave it at once his pontifical sanction, and thus constituted it the law of the church; and virtually the law of Europe.

We are now about to stand upon the summit of papal ascendency. For nearly nine hundred years, that is, from Constantine the Great, to Pope Innocent III., the bishop of Rome had regularly been rising in influence and power. For about six hundred years, that is, from the grant of Pepin to the same pontificate, had this bishop not only been a temporal prince, but had been gradually establishing his authority over the thrones and crowns of all other temporal princes. At that period, when other kingdoms have usually begun to wane, and to feel the decrepitude of age, the papal power was only in its strength, exhibiting a healthfulness which indicated the absence of decay, and wielding an influence at once absolute and formidable to the kings of the earth. "The noonday of papal dominion," says Hallam, "extends from the pontificate of Innocent III. inclusively, to that of Boniface VIII.; or in other words, through the thirteenth century. Rome inspired during this age all the terror of her ancient name. She was once more the mistress of the world, and kings were her vassals."

The empire of Innocent III. and of the popes of the thirteenth century, was as great, if not greater, than that of the old Romans under Trajan and Adrian. By the conquest of Constantinople, the east had been brought into subjection to the Pope. Nations farther north than ever acknowledged an emperor or a consul, bowed to the chair of St. Peter; while westward, the broad Atlantic only was the boundary of the Pope's dominion. Africa was in possession of the infidels, but even here, the crusaders took several of their strong holds.

But the dominion of the popes was as powerful as it was extensive. Innocent established himself in Italy more firmly than his predecessors. "He abolished the consulate, and arrogating to himself imperial rights, he invested the prefect with his powers. He installed public officers, and received the oaths of the senators. Out of Rome also, Orbitello, Viterbia, Ombria, Romagna and the Marche d'Ancona, acknowledged Innocent III. as their sovereign. Reigning thus from sea to sea, he conceived the hope of conquering Ravenna, of getting fully the inheritance of Matilda, and of getting more in subjection to him the two Sicilies."*

The authority of Innocent, however, extended beyond Italy. "In one year" says Daunou, "Innocent III. gave three crowns, that of Wallachia, of Bohemia and of Arragon. He also conferred that of Armenia."

The power of this pontiff, however, was more felt in abasing than in giving crowns. The three most powerful sovereigns during the pontificate of Innocent, were Otho IV. emperor of Germany, Philip Augustus,

* Court of Rome, 125.

king of France, and John, king of England. Otho he excommunicated; Philip he not only excommunicated, but laid his kingdom under an interdict; and John he brought to the deepest possible humiliation. The crime of John was his opposition to an appointment, which the Pope had made, of an archbishop of Canterbury. The pontiff first laid an interdict upon the kingdom of John; he next excommunicated the monarch, delivering him over to the wrath of God; he then deposed him, as no more fit to occupy the throne of England. And as if this were not enough, he even ventured to cede to his rival Philip, the entire dominion of the English monarch.

The Pope however, had in England one of his "legates." Pandolph undertook to effect a reconciliation between the pontiff and the king. He advised John to receive from the Pope as a pure gratuity and in the most humble manner, the kingdom from which he had been deposed. The following is the account which Daunou gives of this affair. "John upon his knees before Pandolph, put his hands between those of this priest, and pronounced, in the presence of the bishops and lords of his kingdom, the following words: 'I, John, by the grace of God, king of England, and lord of Ireland, for the expiation of my sins, of my free will, and with the advice of my barons, give to the Roman church, to the Pope Innocent and his successors, the kingdom of England and the kingdom of Ireland, with all the rights attached to the one and to the other. I will hold them hereafter of the Holy See, of whom I will be a faithful vassal, faithful to God and to the Church of Rome, to the sovereign Pontiff, my lord, and to his successors lawfully elected. I bind myself to pay every year a rent of a thousand marks of silver (about sixty three thousand dollars,) that is to say, seven hundred for England and three hundred for Ireland.'"* The money was immediately paid. The legate having kept the sceptre and crown of the monarch five days, returned them as a pure

---

* Court of Rome, 123.

THE ANTICHRIST. 299

gift. He then left England, and entering France, forbade Philip to wage war upon England, as now a fief of the papal autocrat.

But Innocent went further. As if the powers of excommunication and interdict, were not adequate to his purposes, he employed two other modes of executing his will. These were, crusades and the inquisition. The crusades had hitherto been employed only against Mohammedans. Innocent turned them against Christians. The Greek church was the first to experience the dreadful effects of this mode of conversion. Constantinople was taken, its palace rifled of its treasures, French emperors appointed, while Innocent congratulated himself by saying—" God, wishing to console the church by the union of the schismatics, has caused the empire to pass from the proud, superstitious, and disobedient Greeks, to the humble and submissive Latins."

The Albigenses were the next class of Christians to experience the vengeance of a crusade. Innocent ravaged their country, transferred the territory of Raymond, their protector, to Monfort, and reduced to desolation and ruin, these once flourishing provinces. Nor was this all. Whatever Christian prince now began to prove refractory, was threatened, not simply with excommunication and an interdict, but with a crusade. Thus did this Pope ingeniously turn toward the household of faith, that tremendous power, which had hitherto been directed only against the infidels of Asia.

But there was another instrument wielded, indeed originated, by this sagacious pontiff—the Inquisition. The object of this barbarous tribunal, was not simply to ascertain heresy, but to eradicate it from the conscience and heart. For accomplishing this work, the Apostles had depended upon truth accompanied by the Spirit of God. Not so Pope Innocent and his illustrious successors. They resorted to torture, and to torture of the most dreadful character. The suspected person was confined to a most loathsome dungeon, from which the light was excluded. He was subjected to the most rigorous treatment. He was frequently brought before his spiritual judges, and every effort was made to force him to the confession of his heresy. If obstinate, he was tied, suspended by a pulley and suddenly dropped down, often to the dislocation of his bones, or the fracture of his limbs. He was compelled to drink great quantities of water, until unnaturally distended, when an iron bar was placed across his stomach and pressed by great weights. Or, if this kind of torture did not answer, he was gradually roasted before slow fires. These tortures were varied, according to circumstances, and they were also protracted more or less according to the perseverance or timidity of the subject. In all cases however, they were horrible and excruciating to the last degree. Multitudes perished under them, and multitudes who endured them, were only transferred from this dreadful court, to meet a yet more terrible death.

Innocent was the author of this institution. "The friars Raynier, and Guy, and the arch-deacon Peter of Castelnau, are the first inquisitors," says Daunou, "known in history. Innocent enjoined it upon princes and people to obey them; upon princes to proceed against the heretics denounced by these missionaries; upon the people to arm themselves against princes who were indocile, or had too little zeal."* The first inquisitorial commission was sent by Innocent into Languedoc, to extirpate the heresy of the Albigenses. Proving useful here, it was subsequently introduced into all the countries of Italy, except Naples; into the kingdoms also of Spain and Portugal, and attempts were made to erect it in all the other kingdoms of Europe.

Such was the pontificate of Innocent III., the haughtiest, and probably the most successful of the popes. "A pope," said he, "a vicar of Christ, is superior to man, if he is inferior to God. He is the light of day; the civil authority is but the fading star of night."

* Court of Rome, 130.

THE ANTICHRIST. 301

We cannot here pursue a minute history of the popes, or point out the almost innumerable instances in which they domineered over the princes of the earth. We refer the reader on this subject to the standard histories on modern Europe, and to authors who have made it their business to delineate the usurpations and blasphemies of this proud and insatiable power. Let us, however, notice some of the doctrines taught by those famous instruments called papal bulls.

In a bull of Boniface VIII., against Philip IV., is the following language. "God has established me over the empires to pluck up, to destroy, to ruin, to dissipate, to edify, to plant." In another, called Unam Sanctam, Boniface thus expresses himself: "The temporal sword ought to be employed by kings and warriors for the church, according to the order and permission of the Pope. The temporal power is subjected to the spiritual power, which institutes it, and judges it, and which God alone can judge. To resist the spiritual power, then, is to resist God, unless we admit the two principles of the Manicheans."[*] Pope Pius V., in the bull in which he excommunicated Queen Elizabeth, expresses himself thus: "He that reigneth on high hath constituted one (the Pope) prince over all nations, and all kingdoms, that he might pluck up, destroy, dissipate, ruinate, plant, and build."[†] Sixtus V. also, in the bull in which he excommunicated the King of Navarre, and the Prince of Condé, asserts, that "the authority given to St. Peter and his successors, excels all the powers of earthly kings and princes."[‡]

Such have been the gradual development, and the ultimate height, of the papal empire. Presiding at first, but as a Christian pastor, over a small congregation, the Roman bishop rose by degrees, and under a great change of circumstances, became the supreme political, as well as the supreme spiritual, head of Christendom. Indeed, much more than this is true;

[*] Court of Rome, 149.   [†] Barrow, 19.   [‡] Ibid. 18.

as vicar of Christ, as the sole and supreme representative of the Eternal, the Pope has arrogated to himself honours and prerogatives not less than divine. Were this system carried out, the world would be subject to one man, and that one man would become the universal object, not only of civil and ecclesiastical, but also of religious homage. Every throne on earth would be extinguished but that of the Pope; every capital would be destroyed but that of the Pope; every system of religion would be annihilated but that of the Pope. It is impossible that a system of this kind should always exist. Man could not bear, God would not suffer, its perpetual continuance. Such a system is monstrous, is unnatural, is contrary to every political, social, moral, and religious interest of mankind. It withers the heart, it paralyzes society, it degrades man, it insults God. Hence, about the beginning of the fourteenth century, causes began to work, whose tendency was the gradual, but ultimate overthrow of this whole system. These causes began in politics, began in education, began in religion, began in everything. Public sentiment, that had long favoured the Papacy, had come to its flood, and an ebb of human opinion began, adverse to the whole system of spiritual despotism. These causes, with great and powerful auxiliaries, are still at work; and although there have been obstructions in their way, still are they destined to operate till the entire papal fabric shall only be among the legends of the past. Cold, and long, and dreary, it is true, has been the winter, through which the church and society have passed. But the spring has dawned, the summer is approaching, the warming sunbeams are falling, the earth is relaxing, the fields are smiling, and no power of man can prevent the rich harvest of blessings, that God is about to bestow on a ransomed and love-lit world. True, the papist would still carry us back to his dreary Decembers—to his dark and gloomy winters; he would still surround us with snow, and frost, and death. But no, the voice of God has gone forth; the Spirit of the Eternal is moving on the hearts of men, and retrogression is impossible. Onward is the watchword, and onward all things will go; the Papacy to destruction, the church and society to liberty, salvation.

But let us now apply to our subject the facts we have here contemplated. The book of God foretells, that after the apostolic days, somewhere in the approaching future, a great power should arise, arrogating to itself divine honours, "exalting itself above all that is called God, or that is worshipped;" possessing "great authority," having "power over all kindreds, and tongues and nations; and causing all, both small and great, to receive a mark in their right hands or in their foreheads; and that no man might buy or sell, save he that had the mark." This power was also to have its seat at Rome; it was to be a nominally Christian power, for it was "to depart from the faith." It was to be in itself a small power, "a little horn," but to derive its strength from the kingdoms around it; "these kingdoms having one mind to give their power and strength to the beast." Such are the predictions; but where shall we find the facts? We cannot find them in imperial Rome; for this power was to arise upon the ruins of the empire, and it was to continue in existence twelve hundred and sixty years, which the Roman empire did not. We cannot find them in any one, or even in all the kingdoms of Europe; we cannot find them among the Lutherans or the Calvinists. Hence Romanists, dissatisfied with all applications of these prophecies to the past, refer them to the future. They speak of Antichrist as yet to come. But, then, they forsake the prophecy; for it is certain that Antichrist was directly to succeed the downfall of the Roman empire. Where, then, is Antichrist? Let facts speak; let Europe, which has been down-trodden so long by papal power, testify. Let prostrated crowns, and abased monarchs, bear witness. Let the blood of martyrdom be heard—all these declare, that if there can be an Antichrist, the papal autocrat is he.

CHAPTER XI.

ANTICHRIST DISTINGUISHED FOR CRAFT AND PRETENDED MIRACLES.

In the "little horn" upon the head of the fourth beast in Daniel's vision, were "eyes like the eyes of man." This peculiarity was seen by the prophet in none of the other ten horns. These eyes were the symbols of knowledge and sagacity. And as the "little horn" indicated not a good, but a wicked power, they were designed to express the cunning and craft, which such wicked power would employ, in persecuting the saints and in opposing God. The Apostle Paul gives us the idea more literally. He describes the man of sin as coming " with all deceivableness of unrighteousness" (εν πασῃ απατῃ της αδικιας), and as " speaking lies in hypocrisy, (εν ὑποκρισει ψευδολογων.)

That these passages refer to Antichrist, even Romanists themselves admit. "The little horn," says the Commentator on the Doway Bible, "is commonly understood of Antichrist." The same authority says, "The man of sin agrees to the wicked and great Antichrist, who will come before the end of the world." The difference between this commentator and ourselves is, that, while he considers Antichrist as yet to come, we affirm, that he is even now in the world."

If then, these passages refer to Antichrist, they teach, that cunning and craft are to be among his chief characteristics. That these traits are more notorious in the papal church, than in any other establishment ever known among mankind, needs scarcely to be affirmed. The evidences of their existence have filled its history for more than a thousand years.

The first instance we notice of the craft of this church is, in its mode of interpreting the holy Scriptures. That the Scriptures are to be interpreted like all other books, is evident. Although the truth in them is inspired, that is, delivered from heaven, yet the language is human. The very object of this volume is, to make known to man, in his own modes of speech, the will of God for his direction and salvation. The Papacy, however, considers this book of such difficult interpretation, that, withholding it from the people generally, it only furnishes such portions as its forced, though *infallible* interpretations, have so far glossed, that the original meaning is entirely concealed.

We shall notice only two of the unnumbered perversions of this kind. In Matt. xvi. 18, Christ addresses Peter in the following language : " And I say unto thee, that thou art Peter, and upon this rock I will build my church, and the gates of hell shall not prevail against it." This text has been used by Catholic writers as the very foundation of their papal system. " It is proved," says Dens, " that Peter received supremacy from Christ above the other Apostles from Matt. xvi. 18, where the supremacy is promised, and John xxi. where it is conferred."* The passage referred to in John is the following : " Then said Jesus unto them again, Peace be unto you; as my Father hath sent me, even so send I you. Whosesoever sins ye remit, they are remitted unto them, and whosesoever sins ye retain, they are retained unto them." This latter passage, in which Christ addresses the apostles in a body, and in which he conferred upon them, if any thing, equal authority, is said to teach Peter's supremacy above his brethren. Surely, if this was the time, when Peter had conferred upon him the supremacy previously promised, he never received it at all. And as the text quoted to prove that Peter received the supremacy has failed, so, no doubt, will the text said to contain the promise of supremacy, also fail.

1. This supremacy is not contained in the words of this text. There is evidently a wide distinction be-

* Theol. xxiii.

tween the word Peter (Πετρος) and the two words, "this rock" (ταυτη τη πετρα) used in this verse. They are not the same, either in our English version, or in the original Greek.* The nearest that these words can approximate to identity, is in the following version of the text—'Thou art a stone, and upon this rock I will build my church.' Now it is certain, that if Christ had intended to say, that his church should be built upon a stone, he would have used the same word in both parts of the sentence. But he affirms that his church shall be built, not upon a stone, but upon a particular rock. Nor is this all—the word *Peter* here is evidently used as a proper name, and not as a collective noun. If then Christ had intended to affirm, that he would build his church upon the apostle, he would have used the following mode of address: 'Thou art Peter, and upon thee will I build my church.' Where that apostle is meant in the next verse, this is the mode of expression: "I will give to thee the keys, &c." Besides the fact, too, that these words are really different in themselves, the sense of the passage requires, that they should be different. Suppose them identical; then Christ is made to say, that his church shall be built on Peter. Now, besides the positive falsehood, if not blasphemy, of such a declaration, there is absurdity in the very idea. How can a church, or government of any kind, be built upon a man? Romulus, though the first king, was not the foundation of the Roman government. Nor are the kings of England or France the foundation of the respective monarchies in those countries. The foundation of a government is its constitutional laws; the foundation of a church is its fundamental doctrines. It is absurd to speak of any man as the foundation of either church or state; a man may be a founder, or a builder, or a ruler, but never a foundation. But admit this absurdity; place Peter as the foundation of the church; then we deny that he can be its ruler. There certainly is some difference between the foundation of

* See Appendix, Note F.

THE ANTICHRIST. 307

a house, and its master. If Peter therefore be at the foundation, he cannot also be at the head of the church. The very ground therefore, which these critics take, defeats their object, and renders Peter's primacy, as contained in this text, impossible.

2. Nor does the context show that the primacy of Peter is contained in these words. The following verse has been quoted with this intention: "And I will give unto thee the keys of the kingdom of heaven." Now, there certainly must be a wide difference between occupying the foundation of a house, and carrying its keys. The two offices cannot be performed by the same person;* if Peter therefore be the foundation, he cannot be the keys-carrier, and if he be the keys-carrier, he cannot be the foundation. To suppose therefore, that our Lord intended to convey the same idea, by two such different and opposite figures, is to suppose him ignorant of the meaning of language. Nor can such supremacy be inferred from the preceding verses. Christ had asked the question—"Who do men say, that I, the Son of man, am?" The reply of the apostles was, "some, John the Baptist, some, Elias, and others Jeremias, or one of the prophets." He then asked the apostles themselves, as to their belief in the matter,—"But who say ye that I am?" Peter, more promptly than the rest, exclaimed: "Thou art the Christ, the Son of the living God."—" Blessed art thou, Simon Bar-jona;" says Jesus, "for flesh and blood hath not revealed it (viz. that I am the Christ, the Son of the living God) unto thee, but my Father, which is in heaven. And I say unto thee, thou art Peter, (that is, by this confession, thou well deservest the name I have given thee) and upon this rock (the truth which thou hast confessed, that I am the Christ) I will build my church, and the gates of hell shall not prevail against it." Such is evidently the meaning of the passage. Hence at the conclusion of the conversation, Jesus charged his disciples, that "they should tell no man that he was Jesus, the Christ." This was

---

* See Appendix, Note G.

the truth after which the Saviour was inquiring; it was the truth which Peter confessed; it was the truth which Christ affirmed had been revealed to him by his Father; it was the truth which he wished, for the present, to be kept secret;—and it is the truth upon which the Christian church, both was to be, and is founded.

Roman Catholic writers tell us, that Christ used the Syriac word, *Cephas*, which has no variety of gender. Admit it. They still have to prove, that by the use of the word *Cephas* in the second instance, Christ did not mean a rock, but the apostle of that name. Matthew, however, must have understood the Syriac. He was also inspired in writing the Greek. Why, then, does he render the second Cephas by *petra*, and not by *petron?* If he believed his Master meant the same thing, in the twofold use of the term *Cephas*, why did he use, in the second instance, a word which always signifies a rock, but never the apostle Peter? This supposition makes even this inspired writer to err, worse than a mere tyro in the use of language. Thus, it is impossible, upon any rational mode of criticism, to wrest out of this passage the primacy of the apostle Peter. It is not there, nor the promise of it.

3. Nor can such primacy be educed from this passage through the analogy of Christian doctrine. Were the primacy of Peter of the importance ascribed to it by Papists, then might we expect to find it so interwoven with Christian doctrine in the Holy Scriptures, as to leave no doubt of its reality. We find it, however, not even hinted at in the doctrinal portions of the New Testament. "Other foundation," says Paul, "can no man lay than that is laid, which is Jesus Christ." 1 Cor. iii. 11. In the book of Revelation, too, where John speaks of the twelve foundations of the holy city, he does not represent the name of Peter as the only one written on those foundations; but "the names of the twelve apostles of the Lamb." Rev. xxi. 14. The apostle Paul also represents converted gentiles, as being built, not upon Peter, but "upon the foundation of the apostles and prophets, Jesus Christ himself

being the chief corner-stone." Eph. ii. 20. Let it be observed here, too, that neither John nor Paul represents the apostles, or the apostles and prophets, as the foundation either of the church or holy city. John speaks of the names of the apostles only as being written on the twelve foundations. And Paul draws, in 1 Cor. iii., a very broad distinction between the foundation, which an apostle lays, and an apostle himself. The primacy of Peter, then, is no such article of Christian faith, that one must infer it from Matt. xvi. 18, because, by a great perversion of language, it may be inferred from that passage.

4. Nor can the primacy of Peter be inferred from this passage, from any thing afterwards recorded, either in the life of this apostle, or in the history of the early church. What sovereignty did Peter exercise, either at Jerusalem, at Antioch, or any where else? Was he a very Pope, and were the other apostles but cardinals around him? Every one knows the entire falsehood of such a supposition. The apostle Paul declares, that "he was not a whit behind the very chiefest of the apostles." 2 Cor. xi. 5. And in enumerating church officers, he places at the head of the list, not Peter, but the "apostles" jointly. "And God hath set some in the church, first apostles." 1 Cor. xii. 28.

Thus have we shown, from the words themselves, from the context, from the analogy of Scripture doctrine, and from subsequent facts, that the primacy of Peter is neither contained nor promised in this text. Yet, Papists deduce from it the three following conclusions:—that Peter was constituted head of the church, that this supremacy was set up at Rome, and that it has been left in that city as a legacy to all succeeding—I know not whether to say—apostles, bishops, or popes!

The other passage of Scripture which Papists have forced into their service, is that contained in Matt. xxvi. 26-28. "And as they were eating, Jesus took bread and blessed it, and brake it, and gave it to the disciples, and said, Take, eat; this is my body. And he took the cup and gave thanks, and gave it to them saying, Drink ye all of it; for this is my blood of the new testament, which is shed for many for the remission of sins." To most readers this passage is perfectly simple and of easy comprehension. No one but a Papist would ever imagine, that by the expressions, *this is my body*, (τουτο εστι το σωμα μου)—*this is my blood*, (τουτο γαρ εστι το αιμα μου)—that Christ meant his literal body and blood. The body of Christ was then before the very eyes of the disciples unbroken; his blood was in his veins unshed. It must, therefore, have been perfectly manifest to the apostles that their Master was speaking figuratively, and not literally. But, upon this simple language, have Romanists founded the monstrous doctrine of *transubstantiation!* The following is a decree of the Council of Trent: "Whosoever shall deny that in the sacrament of the most holy eucharist are contained truly, really, and substantially the body and blood, together with the soul and divinity of our Lord Jesus Christ, and therefore the entire Christ, but shall say that he is in it only as in a sign, or figure, or virtue; let him be accursed."* Here, not only are the words of Christ literalized, which they were not intended to be, but they are transcended. The most rigid interpretation that can be adopted, would only require that the bread should be the body, and the wine the blood of Christ. But even this literalism did not satisfy Rome. She must have also the "soul" and "divinity" of our Lord—yea, the "*entire Christ.*" Nor is this all: the entire Christ, she teaches, is contained in each fragment of the bread, and in each drop of the wine. Nor is even this all; the bread and wine, thus converted into the entire Christ, even in their minutest particles, are offered to the people to be adored with the worship of *latria*, that which is paid to God only! Nor is even this all. The sacrifice of the mass is next offered, for the living and the dead. Here is certainly one of the most extraordinary bundles of absurdi-

---

* De sacro-sancto eucharistiæ Sacramento.

ties, which ever entered into the head of mortal. Bread and wine, converted by a priest, into something like a thousand Christs at a time! And as this is a daily service, performed in many places over the earth, and also in past generations, many millions of times, almost as many Christs have thus been formed, as there are particles of sand on the banks of the Tiber! How shocking to common sense is such a doctrine! And yet, this is the Papal mode of interpreting Scripture! No wonder that Papists prohibit the common reading of the word of God; for even the most superficial acquaintance with this holy volume, would be sufficient to overthrow their entire system.

The two texts of Scripture we have been considering, through the gross perversions of their meaning by Papists, have given rise to the *Pope* and the *Mass*, those tremendous agents of papal power and papal superstition. The same mode of interpretation is pursued, in deducing from the oracles of God, scriptural authority for all their various inventions and superstitions. Thus it is coolly affirmed, by Dens, that since the candlestick in the Jewish tabernacle had seven branches, therefore, there are seven sacraments; and that since Peter alone of all the apostles walked with Christ on the water, therefore, we may infer his primacy.

A second instance of the craft of the Papacy, may be found in its use of tradition as a divine rule of faith. One would imagine, that its convenient mode of interpreting Scripture would answer all its purposes. But no, the Bible, even when eclipsed and surrounded by papal interpretations, still emits too much light upon the consciences of these crafty men, to allow all their gross departures from its teachings. They need, therefore, another and a yet more flexible rule of faith. Hence, tradition is placed upon equal footing with Scripture in matters of faith and practice. But even tradition, and especially early tradition, is too inflexible for them. They must, therefore, invent some method to divest it of its power of reproof. What is that method? Peter Dens shall inform us: "Whatever the Catholic church holds, or decrees as such, is to be regarded as tradition."* This is perfectly legitimate; for if the church has the right to make tradition its rule of faith, instead of the Scriptures, it certainly must have the right also, to mould and fashion that tradition as it pleases. Here then is another abyss of papal fraud. This crafty power passes off to hundreds of thousands of men, its own fabricated traditions, as containing that will of God, which they are bound to obey! Here are the eyes of "the little horn,"—here "the man of sin," coming in "all deceivableness of unrighteousness."

But neither perverted Scripture, nor perverted tradition could give to this wicked power sufficient liberty. It had recourse, therefore, to positive and barefaced forgeries. The chief pillars of papal usurpations in the middle ages were the false Decretals, and the Donation of Constantine. These two instruments gave to the Pope unlimited power, in both church and state; and yet, they were both mere fabrications! "No one," says Hallam, "has pretended to deny for the last two centuries, that the imposture of the Decretals is too palpable for any but the most ignorant ages to credit."† "The falsity of the Donation," says Daunou, "according to Fleury, is more generally admitted, than that of the Decretals of Isidore; and if the Donation of Constantine should yet obtain any credit, it would be sufficient to transcribe it, in order to show it to be unworthy of belief."‡ Here, then, are two celebrated forgeries, known to be such by the papal hierarchy, and yet for centuries appealed to, for the support and extension of papal authority over the liberties both of church and state!

But the power of the Pope needs to be extended in another direction. It is not enough to annihilate the independence of thrones, and the freedom of the people of God; the infernal regions must be entered,

---

* Theol., ch. xviii. † Middle Ages, ch. vii.
‡ Court of Rome, 3.

and the fires of purgatory kindled. "Purgatory," according to Bellarmine, "is situated in the centre of the earth; it forms one of the four compartments into which the infernal regions are divided. In the first of these the damned are placed; the second is purgatory; in the third reside the spirits of infants who died without baptism; the fourth is *limbus*, the abode of the pious who departed this life before the birth of Christ, and were delivered by him when he descended into hell. The pains of purgatory are so horribly severe that no sufferings ever borne in this world can be compared with them. How long they continue is not known; but it is thought that the process of purification is very gradual, and that some will not be thoroughly cleansed till the day of judgment."

This is the doctrine which the Council of Trent enjoins, shall be "everywhere taught and preached" (doceri et ubique prædicari). But no such doctrine as this, is contained in the word of God. The blood of Christ, we are there assured, "cleanseth us from all sin." 1 John i. 7. The apostle Paul also teaches that "there is no condemnation to them that are in Christ Jesus." Rom. viii. 1. He also asserts that for such "to be absent from the body, is to be present with the Lord." 2 Cor. v. 8. A wonderful salvation would that of Christ be, indeed, if after souls had taken refuge in him as their Saviour, they must still be sent down to the infernal regions, to suffer in the fires of purgatory, the expiation of their offences! Such a doctrine is a reproach upon Christ, is contrary to the whole teaching of the Scriptures, is calculated to enslave even those who are pardoned, and is, moreover, subversive of the entire scheme of salvation by grace. There is no grace in it, as certainly there is no truth. Why then such an invention? Simply to increase the power and wealth of the Roman priesthood. These are the motives; and if these could cease to operate, the fires of purgatory would long since have been extinguished.

Look next at the long catalogue of sacred relics. The apostle Paul taught, that in his day, as now, "the fashion of this world passeth away." And Isaiah had affirmed even before Paul, that "all flesh is grass, and all the goodliness thereof as the flower of the field." Moses too had declared earlier still, "dust thou art and to dust thou shalt return." These physical laws, however, seem to have had no application to the bones of saints, the wood of the Saviour's cross, or even to his coat. All these, and ten thousand others like them, are carefully preserved by pious Roman Catholics, as mementos of ancient piety, and objects of religious homage! "They show at Rome," says a modern traveller, "the heads of St. Peter and St. Paul encased in silver busts and set with jewels; a lock of the virgin Mary's hair, a phial of her tears, and piece of her green petticoat; a robe of Jesus Christ sprinkled with his blood, some drops of his blood in a bottle, some of the water which flowed out of the wound in his side, some of the sponge, a large piece of the cross, all the nails used in the crucifixion; a piece of the stone of the sepulchre on which the angel sat; the identical porphyry pillar on which the cock perched when he crowed, after Peter denied Christ; the rods of Moses and Aaron, and two pieces of the wood of the real ark of the covenant."* Now can any one imagine, that Papists who have the least intelligence can possibly believe that these are *bonâ fide* relics! They know that they are not. Why then are they employed as objects of religious veneration? To delude the vulgar, to extort money from them, and to deepen the shades of that already too dark superstition, in which Catholic ecclesiastics are made to move, as supernatural beings! O Popery! Popery! Thou hast an awful doom before thee, when the Judge of all shall tear off thy mask, and reveal thy nakedness to an abhorring world!

These are only a few of the many "lies spoken in hypocrisy" by which this unnatural and wicked system is sustained. This whole papal fabric is based

* Cramp. 361.

in fraud, is pillared on falsehood, is defended by deceit, and propagated by hypocrisy.

We now proceed to consider the miracles performed by the Papacy, as proof of its antichristian character. The Apostle Paul represents Antichrist as coming "after the working of Satan, with all power, and signs and lying wonders."—(σημειοις, και τερασι ψευδους.)

It is a remarkable fact, that while all other sects and religious parties believe that miracles have long since ceased, the ends having been answered for which they were appointed, papists still pretend, that miracles are performed in their communion. Were such miracles real and not pretended, and were they, moreover, performed by holy men, and in the cause of truth, the Romish church would stand out before the world, as a divinely constituted body, and as having the indwelling of the Holy Ghost. But, if these miracles are base impostures, and if they are performed by wicked men in defence of error, then do they proclaim with the voice of thunder, that the Papacy is Antichrist, and that the Roman church is but marking herself with the signs of the beast.

That the Papacy sanctions modern miracles is certain. What is the doctrine of transubstantiation, but a standing recognition of miraculous power in the Romish priesthood? Can we imagine a greater miracle, than the formation of a " whole Christ," from a piece of bread? Neither Moses, nor Elijah, nor Peter, nor Jesus, performed so wonderful a miracle as this. Extreme unction is also attended with miraculous effect. " Whosoever shall affirm," says Trent, " that the sacred unction of the sick does not confer grace, nor forgive sins, nor relieve the sick, (*nec alleviare infirmos,*) but that its power has ceased, as if the gift of healing existed only in past ages; let him be accursed." Every saint, too, who is canonized at Rome, must have performed miracles, previously to his being admitted to such exalted honour. " Before a beatified person is canonized, the qualifications," says Buck, "of the candidate are strictly examined into, in some consistories held for that purpose; after which one of the consistorial advocates, in the presence of the Pope and cardinals, makes the panegyric of the person who is to be proclaimed a saint, and gives a particular detail of his life and miracles; which being done, the holy father decrees his canonization, and appoints the day." Such canonization, however, cannot take place until fifty years after the candidate's death; when, as one would think, it must be a pretty difficult task, either to establish or disprove the reality of his miracles.

As specimens of the miracles performed in the papal church, we give the following. "At Hales," says Hume, "in the county of Gloucester, there had been shown, during several ages, the blood of Christ brought from Jerusalem; and it is easy to imagine the veneration with which such a relic was regarded. A miraculous circumstance also attended this miraculous relic; the sacred blood was not visible to any one in mortal sin, even when set before him; and till he had performed good works, sufficient for his absolution, it would not deign to discover itself to him. At the dissolution of the monastery, the whole contrivance was detected. Two of the monks, who were let into the secret, had taken the blood of a duck, which they renewed every week: they put it into a phial, one side of which consisted of thin and transparent crystal, the other of thick and opaque. When any rich pilgrim arrived, they were sure to show him the dark side of the phial, till masses and offerings had expiated his offences; and then finding his money, or patience, or faith nearly exhausted, they made him happy by turning the phial."

This is a specimen of a *bonâ fide* Roman Catholic miracle! For several generations, had our English ancestors paid their homage at this celebrated monastery. They revered the very earth on which such a

* Hist. Eng., ch. xxxi.

holy building stood. They venerated the monks resident here, as men of peculiar sanctity, and as the intimate friends of the Deity. They especially worshipped the holy relic, and felt, whenever they saw the precious blood, that their sins were all forgiven. They left their offerings and gifts with a cheerful heart, and returned to their homes, not only to tell the glad story, but also to forward other pilgrims to the holy spot. And what does the whole turn out to be? The blood of a duck every week renewed! A base trick of designing and covetous monks! Surely, we must blush for humanity at a scene like this. All this is done, too, under the holy sanctions of religion, and as carrying palpable evidence to the heart of every beholder, of the truth of the gospel, and the authority of the papal church.

The same historian furnishes another example of the same kind of miracles. "A miraculous crucifix," says he, "had been kept at Boxley in Kent, and bore the appellation of 'the rood of grace.' The lips, and eyes, and head of the image, moved on the approach of its votaries. Hilsey, bishop of Rochester, broke the crucifix, at St. Paul's cross, and showed to the whole people, the springs and wheels by which it had been secretly moved."* Here was another papal wonder. Multitudes had worshipped this crucifix, as they would Christ himself. They had felt all the emotions of joy and astonishment while gazing upon it. They had enriched its keepers, and blessed their own consciences with the tokens of pardon and salvation. And what is this great wonder? The mere mechanism of Romish priests, to enforce superstition, to exalt themselves, and to enrich their fraternity. And yet these are the proofs incontrovertible—the miracles which papists boast as affording divine testimony to the purity and authority of their system! From the benefits of such miracles, may God ever deliver his church and people!

The two following miracles are taken from the

* Hist. of Eng., chap. xxxi.

Roman Breviary. "St. Francis Xavier turned a sufficient quantity of salt water into fresh, to save the lives of five hundred travellers, who were dying of thirst, enough being left to allow a large exportation to different parts of the world, where it performed astonishing cures! St. Raymond de Pennafort laid his cloak on the sea, and sailed thereon from Majorca to Barcelona, a distance of a hundred and sixty miles, in six hours!"*

These are but a few of the myriads of similar miracles which Popery tolerates, which Popery practises, and of which Popery boasts! That they are incredible, every one can at once perceive—that they are not only superstitious, but fraudulent, none can doubt. Why then their existence? Why, they were invented, ages past, to support the church and to make gain. They are a part of the transmitted commerce of mystical Babylon. But for such miracles, much of the trading capital of Rome would be left in the market. The business, therefore, must be kept up; and as long as there are devotees simple enough to credit such things, there will, of course, be found priests wicked enough to defend and practise them. And there is another reason:—Rome must fulfil her destiny; she must correspond to every prophecy concerning her; and one of these prophecies is, that she will practise, through the working of Satan, "signs and lying wonders."

Here, then, we have two additional marks of Antichrist most strangely meeting in the Papacy. Antichrist was to practise craft and deceit, above all other powers. For these things Rome has been unrivalled in the history of human governments. Antichrist was also to perform "lying wonders," and "signs;" he was to be notorious for false miracles. Such miracles are every where characteristic of the Romish communion. If, then, scriptural predictions are expected to have their fulfilment in corresponding facts, what set of facts can more clearly indicate the fulfilment of

* Cramp. 365.

prophecy, than these to which we have alluded? Strange, strange indeed, must it be, that all the prophecies concerning Antichrist, should point directly to Rome, and yet Antichrist not be at Rome! But these prophecies do not lie; nor can we well be mistaken in their application. They refer to the Papacy—they proclaim the Pope as Antichrist. The conclusion may be personal, it may appear invidious, but it is inevitable: the Pope is as truly Antichrist, as Jesus of Nazareth is the Christ.

CHAPTER XII.

ANTICHRIST A REPROBATE.

By reprobation, we mean that judgment of God whereby some men, on account of their sin, are given up to a course of presumptuous wickedness and to final destruction. Reprobation refers both to individuals, and to whole classes of men. Pharaoh was a reprobate; for this is what is meant by God's "hardening his heart." Exod. xiv. 4. Judas was also a reprobate; hence he is called by Christ, "the son of perdition." John xvii. 12. The Canaanites were reprobates; hence they were doomed by God to utter destruction. Deut. vii. The apostle Paul also represents the gentile world generally, as in a state of reprobation. Rom. i. He also speaks of the unbelieving Jews as in a similar condition. Rom. xi. Reprobation, however, as applied to the Jews and gentiles in these passages, refers not to races, but to generations of men. The gentile world was ultimately brought under the light of the gospel, and multitudes of them became the children of God. The Jews are also to be reclaimed; for blindness has happened to them only "in part;" that is, for a certain fixed period. The reprobation, however, of Antichrist is of a worse character. Like Pharaoh, like Judas, like the ancient Canaanites, his reprobation is unto perdition. Hence he is called "the son of perdition," 2 Thess. ii. 3; and is said to "go into perdition." Rev. xvii. 11. We are not to understand by this, that all the individuals attached to this Antichristian system will perish. By no means. As the apostle Paul said of his Jewish brethren, even so say we of Papists, that "there is a remnant among them according to the election of grace." Rom. xi. 5.

"The apostle," says Dr. Hill, "is not to be understood as meaning, by the strong expressions he has subjoined to this prophecy, that all who ever believed the errors of Popery are certainly damned. We believe that many worthy, pious men, by the prejudices of education and custom, have been so confirmed in doctrines, which we know to be erroneous, as to be unable to extricate themselves."* Still, however, the errors of Antichrist are so radically subversive of the gospel, the whole system is so extravagant and enormous, that the great body of its adherents are not only given up of God now, but will hereafter suffer his severe wrath. This is a matter of express and positive prediction—"and for this cause God shall send them strong delusion, that they should believe a lie; that they all may be damned, who believed not the truth, but had pleasure in unrighteousness." 2 Thess ii. 11, 12.

Reprobation, so far as it is accomplished in this life, relates to the mind, the heart, the will, the conscience and the actions of men. In his description of it in Rom. i., the Apostle represents God as giving men up to "a reprobate mind;" to "vile affections;" and to "do those things which are not convenient." In 1 Tim. iv. 2, he also includes in reprobation, "a seared conscience;" and in Rom. ix. 18, a hardened heart, or powerful self-will. These are apt, all of them, to follow each other in regular order. Where the mind is "reprobate," the affections will be "vile;" where the conscience is "seared," the will will be stubborn; and where all these exist, the actions will be wicked. What a catalogue of crimes arises from a fountain like this, any one may learn, by reading the latter part of the first chapter of the Epistle to the Romans.

The reprobation of Antichrist is contained in these words—"and for this cause, God shall send them strong delusion (ενεργειαν πλανης) that they should believe a lie." Macknight renders the passage thus: "And for this cause God will send to them the strong-

* Divinity, 716.

working of error to their believing a lie." Doddridge paraphrases it thus—"God will in righteous judgment give them up to a reprobate and insensible mind, and will send upon them the energy of deceit; he will suffer them to deceive others, till they are themselves deceived, so that they shall believe the lie they have so long taught." The expression is remarkably strong; and it teaches, that those who are involved in this judicial sentence of God, will be buried in an almost hopeless delusion.

We have already shown that the previous part of these predictions refers to the Papacy. Of course then this passage must have the same application. Nor will it be found upon examination, that other features in this system of evil have been better described by the apostle than that of its actual reprobation. God has sent upon the champions and abettors of this system "strong delusion," and there can be but little doubt, that they have been permitted to believe "a lie."

1. The first mark of reprobation is, a darkened or reprobate mind. The evidence which the apostle gives of the existence of such a state of mind, is idolatry. "Professing themselves to be wise, they changed the glory of the incorruptible God into an image made like to corruptible man." Now whatever plea Papists may employ for using in their acts of worship images of the saints, and even of Christ, there certainly can be no apology for representations of the "incorruptible God." But they do make and tolerate such images even of the Deity himself. "When the Deity is thus represented," says a decree of Trent, "it is not to be supposed that the same can be seen by our bodily eyes, or that a likeness of God can be given in colour or figure."* The catechism uses the following language:—"To represent the persons of the Holy Trinity by certain forms, under which, as we read in the Old and New Testaments, they deigned to appear, is not to be deemed contrary to religion or the law of

---

* Sessio xxv.

God."* Peter Dens also asks the following question: "Are images of God, and of the most Holy Trinity, proper?" The answer given is—"Yes: although this is not so certain as concerning the images of Christ and the saints; as this was determined at a later period."† Here then, are three respectable witnesses, yea, standard authorities, proving that the church of Rome does "change the glory of the incorruptible God into an image made like to corruptible man." Now, Paul declares, that such conduct is evidence of a darkened mind, and that it is a characteristic feature in God's judicial reprobation. As certain then, as that Rome sanctions this gross idolatry, is it that she is reprobate in mind.

2. Another mark of reprobation is vile affections. "Wherefore God also gave them up to uncleanness, through the lusts of their own hearts, to dishonour their own bodies." Probably no three causes have ever led to more fearful scenes of licentiousness, than monasticism, nunneries, and the celibacy of the Roman clergy. And if to these causes we add the virtual subversion of the law of God by the Papacy, and the facilities of absolution, and even of indulgences, we shall at least see a machinery at work, which under ordinary circumstances, would inevitably lead to fearful results; and if we are to credit history, and especially the testimonies of many, who have themselves been behind the curtains, our inferences will scarcely reach the realities that occur under this dreadful system of delusion. Those who may wish to know more on these subjects, we refer to Peter Dens, " De Pollutione," &c., to the narratives of Gavin, "the Confessions of a Catholic priest;" and other works of a like nature. They will here find specimens of "vile affections," strong enough certainly, to show that this feature of reprobation is not wanting in the papal system.

3. A third mark of reprobation is great perversity of will, an invincible adherence to error. This is the

* Catechism, p. 360. † Chap. xxxiii.

cardinal feature, in the reprobation, predicted of Antichrist. "And for this cause, God shall send them strong delusion, that they should believe a lie." Nor can there be found on earth, a people more fixedly set in their errors and superstitions, than papists. This is the boast of their church. And even, when contradicted by innumerable facts, they still repeat in triumph the adage, "Once a Catholic, always a Catholic." To any one who considers the papal system, and who reflects upon the mode of education employed by Romanists, such rigid adherence to their system can be readily accounted for: indeed, it is wonderful, that any of them are ever converted. They are born and raised behind walls of error heaven-high. How then are they to escape? This very boast however, of papists, is but another indelible feature of their judicial reprobation. If their system held them with a less grasp — if there were only a little liberty granted, there might be some hope. But "the strong delusion" is upon them; and God only can so far remove it, as to call some of his elect, even from these iron walls of Satan.

4. A fourth sign of reprobation is a seared conscience—"Having their conscience seared with a hot iron." Conscience has more or less restraint upon most men. It often makes even the daring transgressor quail beneath its just and retributive scourges. But human nature may proceed to that degree of wickedness, that even conscience will neither upbraid nor admonish. This is always the case under God's fearful sentence of judicial reprobation. A long course of sin, like iron, heated seven times, sears the sensibilities of this inward monitor, and destroys its power of vital action. No condition of the soul is worse than this; yet, this is the predicted state of conscience in Antichrist. And what conscience, pray, have the leading actors of the Papacy had, for centuries on centuries past? Can there be any conscience in men who openly set aside the revealed authority of Jehovah? Any conscience, where a mere man is made to exercise the prerogatives of the Son of God? Any

conscience, where the most barefaced idolatry is set up under the sanctions of Christianity? Any conscience, where every sort of fraud is used to obtain the money of poor deluded mortals? Any conscience, where men are deliberately seized, and tortured, and killed, in the name of Christ! Any conscience, where crimes of the blackest dye are perpetrated under covert of oaths, and vows, and the mask of religion? Surely, if ever conscience were "seared with a hot iron"—if it were ever destroyed, it must be in the breasts of such men.

5. A fifth mark of reprobation as given in the Scriptures, is depraved and wicked actions. The following is a list of those actions as furnished by the Apostle Paul. "Being filled with all unrighteousness, fornication, wickedness, covetousness, maliciousness; full of envy, murder, debate, deceit, malignity, whisperers, backbiters, haters of God, despiteful, proud, boasters, inventors of evil things, disobedient to parents; without understanding, covenant-breakers, without natural affection, implacable, unmerciful." How far the crimes, here specified by the Apostle, are to be found amid papal influences and institutions, let those judge who are best acquainted with this system of priestcraft and oppression. Some of these crimes are written upon the front of Popery in bold relief. Among these are the following—covetousness, malignity, murder, deceit, boasting, inventing of evil things, disobedience to parents, covenant-breaking, and unmercifulness. With these sins the history of the Papacy abounds.

Thus have we discovered in the Papacy, all the marks of God's judicial reprobation. The understanding has here been darkened, the heart given up to vile affections, the will has been rendered stubborn, the conscience has been seared, and the life filled with unrighteous deeds. But is this reprobation to be final? Is there to be no reformation, no return to right principles? The prophecies answer these questions in the negative. Antichrist is "the son of perdition"— the "Lord is to consume him with the spirit of his mouth, and to destroy him with the brightness of his coming." When too, we consider the actual state of Popery, we discover in it those fixed elements which at once render the hope of reformation fruitless, and ultimate destruction inevitable. Popery itself, as well as prophecy concerning it, declares, that it is to be destroyed, not reformed.

If Popery be ever reformed, such reformation must arise from one of three sources—it must either originate in the system itself, or it must arise from without that system, or it must come from heaven.

1. Such reformation cannot arise from within the system of Popery itself. The principles, the very frame-work of this system are such, that its reformation is utterly impossible. True, Papists may be more moral in one age than in another, they may be less superstitious in some countries than in others, and there may be made some external and unimportant changes in some of its ceremonies and customs; but a radical and thorough reformation, such as the word of God requires, never can be made in it, without the abandonment of the whole system. Take its fundamental doctrine, that the Pope is the vicar of Christ on earth. How can this article be changed, so as to agree with Scripture, without destroying the very fulcrum of the papal system? Take the doctrine of transubstantiation. How can this creed be reformed, but by denying the doctrine itself? Look at the doctrines of purgatory, of absolutions, of indulgences. What reformation can be made with respect to these, but to renounce them? Consider the whole system of saint and image worship. How can this be reformed? In no manner whatever. It can only be abandoned. What are we to say, too, of its traditions and seven sacraments? How are they to be reformed? They cannot be. What is here needed is a forsaking of the ground taken by Romanists. And so throughout. The position assumed by the church of Rome, ensures the destruction of that church, in one or the other of two ways. Either its advocates, as Luther and the Reformers, must forsake the establishment, and thus

let it perish, by desertion, or they must adhere to it, till God shall vindicate the rights of his own truth and name. Many, no doubt, will pursue the former method; but the body will perish with the system.

2. Nor can the Papacy be reformed from any thing without itself. Even in the freest countries on the globe, the Papacy is a consolidated and isolated system. Its arms of iron grasp all its own interests within itself, and it seeks seclusion from all others. Civil governments can have but little influence in changing its character. Older than all modern systems of civil polity, compactly framed together, claiming even superiority above the state, Popery receives upon its indurated exterior the influences of civil government, as the massy rock does the passing stream: such waves come, meet, are broken to pieces and fall backward, leaving the unmoved rock still cold and fixed on its original basis. Nor can Popery be reformed from the influence of Protestant churches. There is literally "a great gulf fixed" between it and them. It is not only forbidden to other ministers to enter a popish pulpit, but even their members are forbidden to enter the doors of other churches. Nor can Popery be reformed by the Bible;—that word is itself a prisoner within the iron walls of this dreadful system. Nor can Popery be reformed by the circulation of tracts and books;—all tracts and books, containing any thing contrary to its own system, are strictly forbidden in their Index Expurgatorius. When a pope can say, even in relation to the circulation of the Holy Scriptures—" Bible societies fill me with horror; they tend to overthrow the Christian religion; they are a pest which must be destroyed by all possible means:"* when even a pope can speak thus, and speak thus of the Bible, what hope can we have for Papists in the circulation of books? True, individuals may thus be converted; but the Papacy will remain unchanged. Nor can philosophy and science reform the Papacy; if so, the doctrine of transubstantiation had long ago been

---

* Letter of Pope Pius VII. to Guesen, Primate of Poland, dated 1816.

renounced as unphilosophical and absurd. Nor can the general intercourse of other Christians, and of citizens generally, reform the papal system. All this is counteracted by the confessional, whose province it is to guard the entrance-doors of heresy and change.

Thus is there no external source, from which influences may come, to reform this monstrous system of error and tyranny. A stone may now and then be removed from its place in this great temple of error; occasionally a pillar may fall; but the old building stands, sunk, like the pyramids of Egypt, in the sands of its own superstitions, venerable for age, a monument of oppression and of pride; the gray relic of the past, the wonder of the present, and the prophet of the future; there it stands, and will stand, till God shall shake the earth, and thus, by his power dash it to pieces.

3. Nor will the Papacy be reformed from heaven. The conversion of the gentiles to Christianity, took place, according to the previous decree and promise of God. Long before Peter preached to Cornelius, had the Spirit of God said concerning the Messiah, " I will give thee for a covenant of the people, for a light of the gentiles." Isa. xii. 6. And the ingathering of Israel to the same Messiah, which is yet to take place, is also included in the purposes of God. Rom. xi. But the decrees and purposes of God, concerning Antichrist, have no such promises of grace and mercy. Here the cloud is without a bow, the night without a star. " And a mighty angel took up a stone like a great mill-stone, and cast it into the sea, saying, Thus with violence shall that great city Babylon be thrown down, and shall be found no more at all." Rev. xviii. 21. Utter destruction is to be the end of this system, and of all who adhere to it. As Sodom and Gomorrha, the old world and the Canaanites, were all made so many examples of the righteous judgments of God, so will it be with Rome. Unreformed, and unreformable, she will go " into destruction," to meet the solemn doom from that righteous Judge, whose truth she has despised, whose name

THE ANTICHRIST. 329

and authority she has trampled under foot, and whose "glorious gospel" she has made but the theatre of her pride, her avarice, and her various abominations.

Here, then, is another mark of Antichrist, deeply branded upon the forehead of the Papacy. Antichrist was to be a reprobate, given up of God to a course of the most presumptuous wickedness, and doomed to ultimate destruction. The Papacy, we have seen, is reprobate, and its advocates are under " strong delusion;" they believe "a lie," and seem to be left of God to wander in the mazes of superstition and error, to that fearful doom which is before them. From that doom, with which the *body* is to meet, may God by his grace, avert the wandering feet of many a poor, benighted victim of this unnatural and unchristian system!

CHAPTER XIII.

THE DOWNFALL OF ANTICHRIST.

Prophecy never leaves the church in despair. Whatever evils it may foretell, it always represents them as in the hand of God, and as overruled by him to ultimate good. Hence, it predicts not only the rise and character of evil powers, but also their overthrow. This rule has special application to Antichrist. The holy prophets of old saw this power arise; they saw it arrogating to itself all dominion and rule; they saw it trampling upon the earth, and destroying the saints; they saw it arrayed in purple and enriched with jewels. But the Spirit carried their minds further, and revealed to them its utter destruction, and the subsequent triumph of the glorious kingdom of the Son of God. Indeed, the prophets, like ancient Israel, seem to have been travelling through a dreary wilderness, while wandering over the domains of the man of sin, only, that they might rest themselves, and teach the church to rest in that promised country—that Immanuel's land—which lay beyond those barren wastes. Their prophecies ultimately terminate in Christ, and are lost only in the blaze of his everlasting reign.

1. In predicting the downfall of Antichrist, the sacred prophets teach us, first, who is to be its author. This is the Lord Jesus Christ. "Whom," says Paul, "the Lord shall consume with the Spirit of his mouth, and shall destroy with the brightness of his coming." John also declares—" These (the beast and his allies) shall make war with the Lamb, and the Lamb shall overcome them: for he is Lord of lords and King of kings; and they that are with him, are called, and chosen, and faithful." Rev. xvii. 14. Daniel also re-

fers to the same thing, when he speaks of "one like the Son of man," receiving at the overthrow of the "little horn," dominion, and glory, and a kingdom, that all people, nations, and languages should serve him. Dan. vii. 14. The great adversary, then, of Antichrist is Christ himself. True, the Son of God, for wise purposes, has permitted Antichrist to usurp great authority; he has suffered him, for a long period, to trample upon his truth, and to persecute his church. But the day of vengeance will come at last, when he shall receive double for all his pride and wickedness, and when the insulted Redeemer will pour upon him the just retaliation of that wrath, with which he has been anathematizing the saints of the Most High.

2. While, however, the Lord Jesus Christ is to be the immediate author of the overthrow of Antichrist, still here, as elsewhere, he will employ various instruments for that purpose. The first of these instruments will be his own glorious gospel. "Whom the Lord shall consume with the spirit of his mouth"—(τω πνευματι του στοματος αυτου.) Macknight renders the passage thus—" Him the Lord will consume by the breath of his mouth;" and remarks, "so πνευμα should be translated in this passage, where the preaching of true doctrine, and its efficacy in destroying the man of sin, are predicted."

The errors of Popery arose, for the most part, in times of great ignorance. And as from their very nature they could not stand the light, it became the settled policy of Romish ecclesiastics, to exclude that light as much as possible from the minds of men. The conversion of the preacher into the priest, the saying of mass in the stead of proclaiming salvation, the invention of numerous and burdensome ceremonies, the introduction of saint and image worship, and especially the interdicts placed upon the reading of the Scriptures; all these were so many means invented by crafty men, to shut out the light of the gospel from the dupes of this dreadful delusion. Now, the remedy, and the only remedy for evils of this nature, is the general diffusion of the Holy Scriptures and their glorious doctrines, through all those countries where these delusions exist. This is the first step; and it is that which God usually employs first in the overturning of the kingdom of darkness. Previous to the overthrow of Judaism, as a system of error, an unusual amount of light was poured upon the national mind. John, Christ, the apostles, all laboured, and the most of them died in this work. A chosen number were thus called out, from the great body of the nation, in whom the succession of truth was to continue, and a fuller vindication was thus given to the providence of God, in the overthrow and dispersion of the rest. Christ could thus say, without the possibility of contradiction, "This is the condemnation, that light has come into the world, and men loved darkness rather than light because their deeds were evil."

It was, too, by this means primarily and chiefly, that the Reformation from Popery in the sixteenth century occurred. A few individuals, by the Spirit of God became experimentally acquainted with the truth of God's word. This truth they began to proclaim to others. This truth, by the translation of the Scriptures into the language of each nation, they placed in the hands of others. This truth, in every possible way, they defended and maintained; and for it many of them were carried to the stake, or perished in dungeons.

There can be but little doubt, therefore, that in the final overthrow of the Papacy, the word of God will precede all other agents. And is not this word going forth at the present time? Are not Bible Societies and their agents, missionaries and their assistants, publishing and scattering the word even within the dominions of the Pope? Is not this word, too, producing its effects? Like its Author, has it not already begun to "purge the papal floor, gathering the wheat into the garner, and preparing the chaff to be burnt with unquenchable fire?" Go forth, thou mighty instrument of the Lord, thou forerunner of his power, thou leveler of the nations; go forth, and accomplish thine own most glorious work!

THE ANTICHRIST. 333

It is evident, however, that the Lord Jesus will employ other, and more coercive instruments in the overthrow of Popery. The Romans were employed to disperse the Jews; Constantine was called forth to uproot paganism; Frederick, the Elector of Saxony, the Landgrave of Hesse, Henry VIII., and other European princes, were also employed to protect and extend the great Reformation. Thus is fulfilled the word of Isaiah, "kings shall be thy nursing fathers, and queens thy nursing mothers." Indeed, it would seem but a just retaliation, that as Antichrist has employed the civil powers to persecute and destroy the Church, so God, in his providence, should also use the same instruments to afflict and overturn his unrighteous administration.

We are, however, not left to conjecture on this subject. "But the judgment shall sit," says Daniel, "and they shall take away his dominion, to consume and destroy it unto the end." (vii. 26.) Gesenius understands by the word דינא (dhinaa), not judgment, but judges; "but the judges shall sit." The reference evidently is to those cabinets or councils, which European princes were to assemble in opposition to the pretensions of the Pope. Some such councils have already been held, and by means of them, several states originally papal, are now protestant, and seem destined so to remain. But others will yet be held, whose results will be still more decisive and overpowering to the dominions of the Man of Sin; for Daniel declares that his dominion will thus be "consumed and destroyed to the end."

If, however, any doubt should remain, as to the agency of European princes in the destruction of the Papacy, it will be enough to remove such doubt, to refer to the testimony of John:—"And the ten horns which thou sawest upon the beast, these shall hate the whore, and shall make her desolate and naked, and shall eat her flesh and burn her with fire." Rev. xvii. 16. The beast here alluded to, is papal, or rather political Europe; its horns the sovereigns of the several European states; and the whore, the Romish church, which by forsaking Christ and worshipping idols, has become like an adulterous woman, who has departed from her own husband to seek other lovers. These horns, says John, that is, these kings, shall hate the whore, that is the papal church, and shall make her desolate.

It is then among the decrees of heaven, that the princes of Europe are to be the agents whom God will employ in overturning and utterly destroying the papal power. A sort of friendship may be maintained between these princes and the Autocrat of Rome; toleration may for a time be given to papal doctrines, the armistice of centuries may continue a little longer. But when "the words of God are fulfilled," that is, when the prophetic period of twelve hundred and sixty years shall have expired, there will be a crisis, a tremendous crisis. Antichrist will then put on all the remainder of his strength; he will call to his aid those that are still devoted to his cause; he will use stratagem and deceit. But all in vain; for the battle will be the Lord's; and the triumph of Antichrist will be forever destroyed. It is supposed by many expositors, that it is this scene which is described in Rev. xiv. 19, 20: "And the angel thrust in his sickle into the earth, and gathered the vine of the earth, and cast it into the great wine-press of the wrath of God. And the wine-press was trodden without the city, and blood came out of the wine-press, even unto the horses' bridles, by the space of a thousand six hundred furlongs." When God overthrew the Jews, it so happened, that they were for the most part, within their capital. The destruction was thus more complete and sudden. So will it be with Antichrist, only a far more dreadful scene will follow. Driven probably, from post to post, the deluded advocates of this system, will, at last, plant themselves upon the strictly papal territory. Rome will be their head-quarters. That city, however, will not only be captured but burnt, while a scene of slaughter will follow, truly dreadful to behold. It was not easily, that the bigoted son of Abraham yielded to the Roman arm; and it certainly will not be easily, that the proud vicegerent of Christ, the successor of apostles, the head of the church, the sovereign of kings—it will not be easily, that he and his followers will resign their high pretensions. Resign them, however, they must and will—"for strong is the Lord God who will judge them."

3. The Scriptures also teach the manner in which Antichrist shall fall. He is to fall gradually, but utterly. "And they shall take away his dominion," says Daniel, "to consume, and to destroy it unto the end." The Vulgate renders the latter part of the passage thus, "ad delendum et ad perdendum usque in finem"— "for consuming and destroying it even to the end." The two cardinal ideas in the passage are, that the power of Antichrist is to be destroyed by successive blows, and that that destruction will be in the end complete. The destroying agents are to proceed from destruction to destruction, from uprooting his power at one post, to uprooting it at another, and they are to continue till the work shall have been finished. The apostle Paul also, in the passage already cited, expresses himself in a similar manner. "The word, αναλωσει, (consume)" says Chandler, "is used to denote a lingering, gradual destruction; being applied to the waste of time, the dissipation of an estate, and to the slow death of being eaten up of worms." "If St. John and St. Paul," says Benson, "have prophesied of the same corruptions, it should seem, that the head of the apostasy will be destroyed by some signal judgment, after its influence or dominion hath, in a gradual manner, been destroyed by the force of truth."* In the sixteenth chapter of the Apocalypse we have, in the pouring out of the seven vials, seven periods, or gradations, in this progressive destruction of Antishrist.

And how remarkably have these predictions, so far, accorded with the facts! The papal power was at its zenith in the thirteenth century. Every event

---

* Macknight.

almost that has occurred since that period, has tended to its gradual subversion. Among the causes of its decline, Daunou mentions the following. "The praiseworthy resistance of Louis IX., the firmness of Philip-le-Bel, the madness of Boniface VIII., the vices of the court of Avignon, the schism of the west, the pragmatic sanction of Charles VII., the revival of learning, the invention of printing, the nepotism of the popes of the fifteenth century, the bold attacks of Sixtus IV., the crimes of Alexander VI., the ascendency of Charles V., the progress of heresy* in Germany, in England, and other countries, the troubles of France under Henry II., the wise administration of Henry IV., the Edict of Nantes, the Four Articles of 1682, the dissensions which grew out of the formulary of Alexander VII., and of the bull, Unigenitus, of Clement XI.; finally, the senseless enterprises of such popes as Benedict XIII., Clement XIII., and some other pontiffs of the eighteenth century." The same author adds: "The papal power cannot survive such shame: its hour is come, and it remains to the popes only to become, as they were during the first seven centuries, humble pastors, edifying apostles. It is a dignity sufficiently honourable."† Remarks similar to these last, were made by Machiavelli as early as the sixteenth century. "We shall see," says he, in allusion to his history, "how the popes, first by their ecclesiastical censures, then by the union of temporal and spiritual power, and lastly by indulgences, contrived to excite the veneration and terror of mankind: we shall also see, how, by making an ill use of that terror and reverence, they have entirely lost the one, and lie at the discretion of the world for the other."‡ There can be but little doubt, that this celebrated historian has specified the primary cause of the overthrow of papal tyranny. That tyranny became itself so burdensome, that a change was demanded for the security, if not for the very existence of society.

In the latter part of the fourteenth century, Wick-

---

* Reformation.   † Court of Rome, 254.   ‡ Hist. Flor. p. 33.

liffe commenced his opposition to the Pope. In the early part of the fifteenth century, John Huss and Jerome of Prague were put to death for advocating his sentiments. A century after, Luther began his great work; and from that period till now, a uniform and constant resistance has been given by several nations of Europe to papal power. It is true, that some things have happened favourable to its temporary advancement. The organization of the society of Loyola may be specified as the principal one. But even this society, by its dangerous operation, by its pliable morality, by its very prevalence—yea, by its crimes, has only made Popery more odious in the eyes of mankind. Even the infidelity of France, the French revolution, and the wars of Napoleon, have all tended to the downfall of the Papacy. Thus have the moral and political movements in Europe, for five centuries past, proceeded *ad delendum et ad perdendum*, to the gradual overthrow of the papal power. And although matters have not as yet reached, *usque in finem*, to its entire subversion; yet that result cannot be very far distant.

4. The precise period of the final overthrow of Antichrist, is predicted in the Scriptures in such a manner, as to leave the calculations of even the best qualified persons in some doubt. There can be no question, but that in the Divine mind, the period is accurately fixed; but its revelation is partially obscure, as all such revelations usually are in the holy volume. If prophecy were perfectly plain in all its parts, it would rather be history than prophecy. If therefore our minds cannot know precisely "the times which the Father hath put in his own power," we should rejoice, that even an approximation to those times may be reached by us. In the mean time, we should patiently wait and hope for the coming of the Son of Man.

In Daniel vii. 25, it is said, the saints shall be given into the hand of the "little horn," until "a time and times and the dividing of time." In chap. xii. of the same prophecy, the wonders seen by Daniel, were to end at the expiration of "a time, times and an half, and when he shall have accomplished to scatter the power of the holy people, all these things shall be finished." John teaches us also, that "the holy city shall be trodden under foot by the gentiles forty and two months;" (Rev. xi. 2.,) that the two witnesses were to prophesy clothed in sackcloth, "a thousand two-hundred and three-score days," (verse 3); the woman also who fled into the wilderness, was to be nourished there, "a thousand two-hundred and three-score days," (xii. 6 ;) or for "a time, times and half a time," (verse 14.) The beast also was to continue "forty and two months," (xiii. 5.) Here are no less than seven times, in which the same number is used, and applied substantially to the same event. The period noted in these prophecies is 1260 prophetic days, that is 1260 years. Now, if we could only ascertain the precise point at which these 1260 years began, there would be no difficulty in ascertaining the date of their termination. Writers on prophecy, however, beginning at different periods, end also at different periods. On this subject we refer to the second chapter of this work. There we have ventured the opinion, that between the years 730 and 754—that is, between the overthrow of the Exarchate and the grant of Pepin, we are to date the rise of the Papacy, as a political power. Daunou fixes it in the year 800; he admits however, that before this, the Popes did exercise a power that was at least "efficient," if not "independent." Machiavelli dates the papal power from the subversion of the Exarchate; or at least, from the time that the Exarchate fell into the possession of the Popes. His language is—"No more Exarchs were sent from Constantinople to Ravenna, which was afterwards governed by the will of the Pope."* According to this calculation, the final overthrow of the papal power will take place in the latter part of the next century. The author however, does not insist upon these dates as correct. It may occur sooner, it

---

* His. Flor. 35.

will scarcely be delayed later. It is enough to know, that the work of gradual subversion is now in progress; and that the final catastrophe, will take place ere long. "Amen, even so, come Lord Jesus."

5. The result of the overthrow of Antichrist will be, the establishment upon earth of the glorious kingdom of Christ. "And the kingdom and dominion, and the greatness of the kingdom under the whole heaven, shall be given to the people of the saints of the Most High; whose kingdom is an everlasting kingdom, and all dominions shall serve and obey him." Dan. vii. 27. As the destruction of the Jewish temple and the dispersion of the Jewish nation, were to precede the universal spread of the gospel, and seemed necessary to its general reception, so the overturning of this nominally Christian, but really antichristian power, appears to be demanded in the providence of God, to the general enlightenment of the world. Nothing, too, especially in Europe, can possibly be conceived of, more favourable to the universal triumphs of truth, than such an event. Were the Pope displaced, were Romanism destroyed, were the worship of saints and relics discontinued, were priestcraft abolished, how rapid, how glorious would be the flight of the true gospel! How would the nations welcome it! How would a liberated world bask in its sun-beams! There can, too, be but little doubt, that the manner in which the Papacy will be overthrown, will give the nations a greater relish for pure doctrines. This power is yet to exhibit some dreadful deeds of oppression. Its iron yoke will yet gall more deeply, its prisons yet groan more dreadfully. And when too, God, in a way remarkably providential—in a way to be seen and known of all, shall so interpose, as to deliver mankind from these, the last struggles, the dying efforts of an old tyranny; how sweet upon the ear will fall the notes of gospel truth! How precious to the heart will be the influences of gospel grace! What countless multitudes will then crowd the temples of salvation, and what marshalling millions will then bend

before Him, who is "the Lord of lords, and King of kings."

Thus will the downfall of Popery be the signal for the universal triumph of pure Christianity. "The man of sin," will thus yield to the Man of grace, even Christ our Lord, and the long reign of wickedness be supplanted by the peaceable and righteous kingdom of the Son of God. Scattered Israel will, in the mean time, be regathered, and Jew and gentile, yea, a ransomed world, will rejoice in him, who is the "Alpha and the Omega, the First and the Last."

Thus have we attempted to prove, from its location at Rome, from the time of its rise, from the peculiarity of its character, from its apostasy, from its idolatry, from its blasphemy, from its innovations, from its persecutions, from its riches, from its power, from its craft and pretended miracles, from its reprobation, and even from its begun downfall, that the Papacy is the Antichrist predicted in the word of God. The very same kind of evidence, derived too from the same source, which proves that Jesus of Nazareth is the Christ, also demonstrates that the Papacy is the Antichrist. The two sets of testimonies stand or fall together. The prophecies that are fulfilled in Jesus are scarcely more numerous, as they are not more explicit, than those fulfilled in the Roman hierarchy. The light of heaven marks out the Roman High Priest as Antichrist; it converges there, and if it finds not there its object and completion, it is difficult, if not impossible to prove the actual fulfilment of any set of predictions whatever. We do not affirm that every individual pope either has been or will be lost. Much less would we affirm, that all who are attached to this dreadful system must perish. We leave individual men in the hands of a just and righteous Judge. He knows their hearts, and will reward them according to their works. It is possible, that even in Rome itself, there may be a "remnant according to the election of grace." The Spirit of God may pluck souls from perdition, even under the hands of Antichrist. Many too, no doubt there are many in

America, many in most papal countries, who are ignorant of the real nature of Popery. They see only its exterior; they have not examined its principles. The condition of such we sincerely pity; and we earnestly pray, that the God of grace may bring them to the light. It is, however, the papacy, the hierarchy, the priesthood of this system, that we designate as Antichrist—that we have proven from the Scriptures to be Antichrist. Just so far as this hierarchical influence extends, just to the degree to which its essential principles go, does Antichrist reign. May that influence be destroyed; may those principles perish; especially, may our free country be rescued from a system, whose dilapidated tyranny in the old world, is seeking its repairs in the new.

NOTES.

Note A.

Many critics suppose, that what is indicated in Daniel's vision, by the ten horns on the head of the fourth beast, is also signified by the ten toes on the feet of the image seen by Nebuchadnezzar. These ten toes were seen in the vision to be "part of iron and part of clay;" which was interpreted to mean, that the ten kingdoms, indicated by the ten toes, should be "part strong and part broken." Some of these ten kingdoms were to possess the Roman iron, but others were to be like "potter's clay." The following statements of Daunou, will cast some light upon this subject. "It was," says he, "in the eighth century, that we perceive the first symptoms of the temporal power of the Roman prelates. The different causes which were to terminate in this result, then began to be perceptible." Among these causes he specifies the weakness of many of the new governments. "In the mean time, the new thrones which had here and there been erected by some conquering barbarians, began already to totter under their successors, whose ignorance, often equal to that of their people, seemed to invite the enterprises of the clergy."* Here seems to be the clay alluded to in the vision. The firm principles of old Roman character, and the ignorance and impetuosity of the new invaders, constituted, when mixed together, a medley, "part strong and part weak," which was exceedingly favourable to the triumphs of clerical ambition.

Note B.

Romanists pretend to make a wide distinction between the homage they pay to God, and that they render to images, relics, saints, &c. They call the one *latria*, the other *doulia*. They have also invented an intermediate degree,

* Court of Rome, p. 10.

which they render to the Virgin, called *hyperdoulia*. These again are divided into absolute, respective, &c. It is evident, however, that such distinctions as these can better be recorded in a theological treatise than observed in daily practice. The heart is deceitful, is fickle. And when the worshipper bows to the cross or an image, or prays to a saint, it is not likely that the nicely distinguished ideas, contained under the words *doulia* and *latria*, can be very strongly apprehended by him. At any rate, such words, being also in a foreign language, must constitute a very thin veil between him and idolatry.

But the distinction here drawn between *doulia* and *latria*, is not tenable. The same Hebrew word (עבד) which means to serve or worship, is rendered both by *latreuo* and *douleuo*. And in the New Testament these words are both applied to the service or worship which is rendered to God. In Matt. vi. 24; Rom. vii. 6; Gal. iv. 8; 1 Thess. i. 9; are instances in which *douleuo* is employed to express the homage which is to be rendered to the supreme Being. The words are very nearly synonymous, both in their derivation and meaning. *Latreuo*, from which *latria* is derived, according to Wahl and others, has its root, *latris*, which means a hired-servant. *Douleuo*, from which *doulia* is derived, has *doulos*, a slave, as its root. If then, there be any difference between them, *douleuo* and *doulia* are certainly words of stronger import than *latreuo* and *latria*. Surely a system must be straitened for authority, when it establishes the worship of images upon a basis of this kind. This is the predicament of men, who violate, and teach others to violate, the express law of Jehovah—"Thou shalt not bow down thyself to them nor serve them."

NOTE C.

Professor Stuart in his late work on the Apocalypse, gives a very singular interpretation to this whole subject. According to him, "the beast that was and is not" refers to Nero; the woman in scarlet is pagan Rome; and the ten horns are ten dependent kings, the subjects of Nero's authority. He supposes the expression, "the beast that was and is not," to be an ingenious method employed by John to indicate Nero; and he gives a very learned Excursus to show,

how prevalent was the report, that after the death of this Emperor, he would revive again.

It is very probable, to say the least, and notwithstanding all that the learned Professor has advanced to the contrary, that the banishment of John took place under Domitian, and not under Nero. If so, of course there can be no prophetic allusion at all to the latter emperor in the visions of John. But, admitting that the Apocalypse was given under Nero, is it probable that a reigning emperor would constitute so important a figure in a prophecy evidently designed for future ages? As to the report about Nero's resurrection, is it not much more natural to suppose that a misunderstanding of the prophecy originated the report, than that the report suggested the prophecy? But there are other and stronger objections to this interpretation. Some no doubt will object to it, because it departs so widely from the interpretations given of this vision by English expositors for many centuries past. This, however, we will not urge. The learned professor in his very great zeal to make Nero the hero of these prophecies, makes not only the beast, but one of his heads also, to symbolize him! On verse 8th chap. xvii., he says, " Plainly here the reigning Emperor is characterized. The well known hariolation respecting Nero, that he would be assassinated and disappear for a while, and then make his appearance again to the confusion of all his enemies, solves the apparent enigma before us." Here he makes the beast, the symbol of Nero. The symbol, however, is changed in his commentary on verse 10th. "Five are fallen viz.: Julius Cæsar, Augustus, Tiberius, Caligula, Claudius; Nero is the sixth!" Here is certainly a strange confusion of prophetic imagery. The beast represents Nero, and yet his sixth head, also represents him!

Nor is the commentary any more satisfactory, where he explains the import of the ten horns. These he affirms are symbols of " ten contemporaneous kings, the dependents of Nero." When, however, he attempts to reconcile with this explanation what is said of the ten horns in verse 16, he appears to be greatly at a loss. "And the ten horns which thou sawest upon the beast, these shall hate the whore and shall make her desolate and naked, and shall eat her flesh, and burn her with fire." In commenting on this verse, the Professor, and possibly for good reasons, adopts the text of Scholtz and Griesbach. This text represents the horns and beast, as confederate against the woman. And the ten horns and the beast—*και θηριον*. The common text is, and the ten horns upon the beast—*επι θηριον*. The common text is that which has been followed by Wickliffe, Tyndale, and Cranmer; and which is also adopted by the versions of Geneva, Rheims and King James. We pass this by, however. That this prophecy foretells the utter destruction of Rome is conceded. "At all events," says he, " heathen and persecuting Rome is to be utterly destroyed." It is evident, however, that neither Nero nor his "contemporaneous kings," utterly destroyed Rome. How is the difficulty to be gotten over? First, an interpretation by Ewald is supposed to be satisfactory. This writer presumes that verse 16 refers " to the predicted return of Nero from the east, after his exile thither and his reunion with the confederate kings of that region, in order to invade Italy, and destroy its capital, where he was assassinated!" With this worse than mythological interpretation, however, the Professor is not altogether satisfied. He, therefore, gives one which he considers better. "The sentiment seems to be, that tyrants like Nero, and persecutors such as his confederates, would occasion wasting and desolation to Rome even like to that already inflicted by Nero, who had set Rome on fire and consumed a large portion of it!" Rome is to be utterly destroyed. The ten horns and the beast, that is, the confederated kings and Nero, were to be the authors of this destruction. When, however, we ascertain the facts, it is tyrants like Nero, and persecutors such as his confederates, who are to accomplish this destruction. Surely, after such an expenditure of learning and pains, one is at least disappointed in a result like this. But even this is not true. What tyrants or persecutors destroyed pagan Rome? If any, they must have been Constantine and Christian bishops! So that, this interpretation fails at every point.

There is another inconsistency into which this learned author falls. In his preface he tells us, that a right interpretation of the Apocalypse can never be given so long as this book is considered as an "epitome of civil and ecclesiastical history." But in his commentary on chapter vii. he says, " if we adopt the explanation made out by appeal to historical ground, then all is plain and easy." While thus the Professor condemns in others the explanation of these prophecies by an appeal to history, he still makes the same appeal himself, and considers it the only method of arriving at certainty.

Note D.

The following is a list of the commandments as used at the confessional.
"I. Thou shalt love God above all things.
II. Thou shalt not swear.
III. Thou shalt sanctify the holy days.
IV. Thou shalt honour thy father and mother.
V. Thou shalt not kill.
VI. Thou shalt not commit fornication.
VII. Thou shalt not steal.
VIII. Thou shalt not bear false witness, nor lie.
IX. Thou shalt not covet thy neighbour's wife.
X. Thou shalt not covet the things which are another's."*
The fact that the second commandment is left out in this list, would seem to indicate, that the Romish priesthood are self-conscious that the practices of the church are contrary to the express law of God.

Note E.

The following particulars are given by a traveller, as to the manner of spending a Sabbath in the city of Mexico. "At a corner of the great square are suspended huge placards, on which the nature of the day's amusements is depicted in every variety of colour. Here is a pictorial illustration of the most prominent attractions of the great theatre, which, in common with all the rest, is open twice on this day. A little further on is a full length figure of Figaro, which draws your attention to the fascinating allurements of the opera. The bull-fights next solicit your notice, announcing the most terrific particulars. Endless varieties of other exhibitions put forth their claims. A balloon ascension is advertised for the afternoon. One would suppose, too, that the old Roman gladiatorial shows were revived; for at one spectacle is a contest between a man and a bear. Cock-fights, dog-fights, and fandangoes are announced in every part of the city.

* Gavin.

Horse-racing, the circus, jugglers, posture-masters, tumblers, fire-eaters, concerts, fencing matches, pigeon shooting, gymnastic exercises, country excursions, balls graduated to every pocket, form but a fraction of the entertainments to which this day is devoted. The finale of the day is generally wound up by a splendid display of fire-works, and thus ends a Mexican Sabbath!" And yet the same writer speaks of a "crowded cathedral," and of "unaffected attitudes of devotion!" Jupiter or Mars might be worshipped in this way, but not the God of heaven.

Note F.

Schleusner defines the literal meaning of πετρος (*petros*), to be, "Lapidem qui e loco in locum moveri potest"—"a stone which can be moved from place to place." In this sense the word is not used in the New Testament. The only sense in which it is here employed is, as an appellative, or proper name. In this sense it is always and exclusively applied to the Apostle Peter.

The word πετρα (*petra*,) on the contrary, is in no case whatever used as a person's name. To suppose, therefore, that in Matt. xvi. 18, it refers to the apostle, is to give it an application which it never has, and of which, considering the gender, it is incapable. In Mark xv. 46, this word expresses the rock out of which Joseph's tomb had been hewn. In Luke viii. 6, it expresses the rock on which a part of the seed fell. In Matt. vii. 24, 25, it is used to denote the rock on which the wise man built his house. In Rom. ix. 33, and 1 Cor. x. 4, it is put for Christ himself. It is here, however, not used as a proper name, but as a figure, and applies more to the divinity than to the humanity of Christ. Schleusner says, it is used here "metaphoricé et modo plane singulari"—"metaphorically and in a sense evidently peculiar." Not a solitary instance can be found in which it refers to the apostle Peter, not one.

Note G.

This position may seem to be contradicted by comparing 1 Cor. iii. 11, with Rev. i. 18. This contradiction however is only apparent. In the first place, it is evident, that many things may be said of Christ, which could be applicable to no other being in the universe. He is divine, yet human—was dead, yet lives; exercises the highest prerogatives, yet has endured the greatest humiliations. Language therefore, which the Scriptures uniformly apply to him, they never apply to another. It is also evident, that the two texts under consideration, apply exclusively to Christ. The first refers chiefly to his atoning sacrifice for sin, the latter to his regal authority in heaven. When the Apostle too, says, "Other foundation ($\theta\epsilon\mu\epsilon\lambda\iota o\nu$) can no man lay than that is laid, which is Jesus Christ," he evidently refers to the doctrines and work of Christ, and not to Christ personally. It was by his preaching that he laid the foundation of Christianity at Corinth. That preaching however referred to facts and truths. It was therefore, these facts and truths, all of which related to Christ, that he calls "foundation already laid." Henry explains this language as applicable to "the doctrines of our Saviour and his mediation." Scott refers the phrase to "the person, mediatorial office, righteousness, atonement, intercession and grace of the Lord Jesus Christ." Bloomfield says, "The sense of Jesus Christ here is," as the best commentators have said, "the history of Jesus Christ, comprehending the doctrines and precepts, the promises and threatenings of the gospel."

These texts therefore present no objection to the general truth we have here laid down. It certainly is an incorrect mode of speaking, to affirm, that a man is the foundation of a society and yet its ruler. Nor do we recollect, either in common parlance, or in books, to have heard or read a solitary expression of this sort.

THE END.